STUDIES IN ECONOMIC HISTORY AND POLICY
THE UNITED STATES IN THE TWENTIETH CENTURY

The making of American industrial research

STUDIES IN ECONOMIC HISTORY AND POLICY
THE UNITED STATES IN THE TWENTIETH CENTURY

Edited by
Louis Galambos and Robert Gallman

Other books in the series:
Peter D. McClelland and Alan L. Magdovitz: *Crisis in the making: the political economy of New York State since 1945*
Hugh Rockoff: *Drastic measures: a history of wage and price controls in the United States*
William N. Parker: *Europe, America, and the wider world: essays on the economic history of Western capitalism*
Richard H. K. Vietor: *Energy policy in America since 1945: a study of business–government relations*
Christopher L. Tomlins: *The state and the unions: labor relations, law, and the organized labor movement in America, 1880-1960*

The Making of American Industrial Research

Science and Business at GE and Bell, 1876–1926

LEONARD S. REICH

Rutgers University

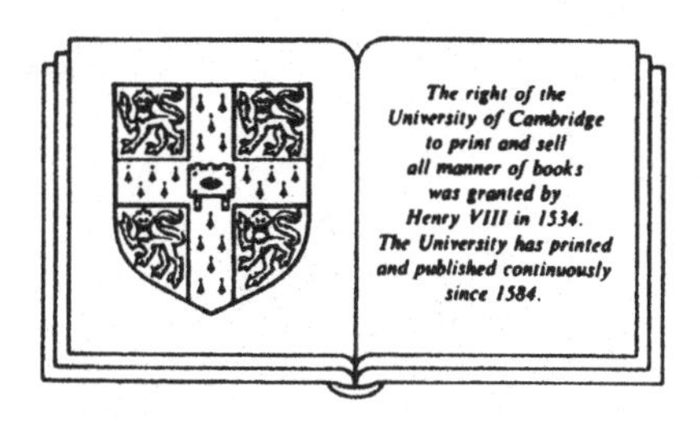
The right of the
University of Cambridge
to print and sell
all manner of books
was granted by
Henry VIII in 1534.
The University has printed
and published continuously
since 1584.

CAMBRIDGE UNIVERSITY PRESS

Cambridge

London New York New Rochelle

Melbourne Sydney

PUBLISHED BY THE PRESS SYNDICATE OF THE UNIVERSITY OF CAMBRIDGE
The Pitt Building, Trumpington Street, Cambridge, United Kingdom

CAMBRIDGE UNIVERSITY PRESS
The Edinburgh Building, Cambridge CB2 2RU, UK
40 West 20th Street, New York NY 10011–4211, USA
477 Williamstown Road, Port Melbourne, VIC 3207, Australia
Ruiz de Alarcón 13, 28014 Madrid, Spain
Dock House, The Waterfront, Cape Town 8001, South Africa

http://www.cambridge.org

First published 1985
Reprinted 1993
First paperback edition 2002

A catalogue record for this book is available from the British Library

ISBN 0 521 30529 2 hardback
ISBN 0 521 52237 4 paperback

For
M, C, T,
and
BJ

Contents

Illustrations

Editors' preface

Nothing is more important to the health of the American economy than making full use of this country's remarkable scientific and engineering resources. The federal and state governments have a substantial degree of responsibility for ensuring that new technical knowledge continues to be produced as it has in the past. But private businesses bear the primary responsibility for applying new ideas and for ensuring that our productive resources remain efficient and that our products remain competitive on world markets.

Research and development within our larger enterprises will have a great deal to do with those outcomes, but until recently we have known very little about the evolution of industrial research institutions. Scholars have told us very little about how they have actually functioned or about the results produced by different types of businesses and business policies. These are the subjects that Leonard Reich addresses in this newest volume of Studies in Economic History and Policy: The United States in the Twentieth Century. We are particularly pleased that Reich provides his readers with a comparative analysis of two of the pioneering industrial research laboratories in this country. As he shows, in General Electric and the American Telephone and Telegraph Company contrasting research styles produced sharply differing technological and business results. GE's broad, relatively unstructured approach helped the firm find new products and processes and chart a more innovative path of corporate growth. AT&T's more focused style of research concentrated enormous resources across a narrow innovative front and helped the firm achieve significant breakthroughs on well-defined problems.

In his studies of these two labs, Reich examines the firm's R&D effort in the larger context provided by the corporation and its relevant markets. His book is itself an exercise in innovation, blending the history of technology and business history in new ways that provide us with a substantially better understanding of the roles of science and technology in the modern corporate economy.

Louis Galambos
Professor of History
The Johns Hopkins University

Robert E. Gallman
Kenan Professor of Economics and History
The University of North Carolina

Preface

American industrial research is now in a period of resurgence. Faced with technological challenges from abroad, enjoying special tax benefits at home, and finding new commercial opportunities in such fields as molecular biology and microelectronics, American corporations have been putting their resources into research on an unprecedented scale. Graduates of advanced programs in science and engineering are being drawn into industry in increasing numbers, reversing a trend of the last twenty years, and many companies are undertaking research of the type usually carried out in universities. For the first time since the Second World War, American industry spent more on research than the federal government during the early 1980s. In its annual analysis of industrial research for 1983, *Business Week* noted a "deepening commitment to R&D," reflected in an inflation-adjusted spending increase of 6% over the previous year for the 800 companies surveyed, with total outlays of almost $40 billion.[1]

But is this money being spent wisely? Transforming scientific research into commercial technology is a very tricky business at best. Numerous studies have provided little evidence to support the assumption that research at the frontiers of science leads directly – or even indirectly – to advances in technology. Experience tells. For all the resources it devoted to research during the 1950s and 1960s, the federal government got very few usable results in return.

The question facing American managers is how to capture commercial benefits from the expanded research efforts their companies have decided to undertake. A considerable literature has developed over the last twenty years on the management of research, and it is clearly of great help. All of it stresses, in one way or another, the importance of tying corporate operations closely to the research-and-development process. Yet too short a tether can be as counterproductive as none at all. Striking a balance between science and business is difficult and requires continuing evaluation and adjustment. Companies must abandon short-term perspectives attuned to easily quantifiable results, especially those based on that corporate shibboleth, Return On Investment. ROI eschews the risks necessary for most long-term projects – the very ones that hold out promise of major advances and entree into new market areas. The remarks of one vice-president of corporate research indicate the scope of the problem: "We have been attempting to develop major new systems with ten-year technology, eight-year research programs, a four-year corporate plan, and one-year funding."[2] Such programs rarely work well. But which ones do?

There are no easy answers in the pages that follow – only lessons drawn from history. These are lessons about industrial growth and market control, about the development of scientific and technical communities with changing relationships to industry, and about the evolution of the industrial research process to make it fit the needs of two pioneering companies. In contemplating these lessons, we can begin to appreciate the complexities involved in a number of relationships: commercial science to technology; the labs to their companies; and the companies themselves to the economic environment in which they operated – an environment they then transformed through research. It is my hope that this study will be of interest not only to historians and other scholars, but to managers and industrial researchers themselves. Examining how and why their institution was conceived and nurtured may help deepen understanding of the industrial research process in ways not always possible with analytical studies of present-day research programs. With a few lessons from history, then, American industrial research may become more efficient and effective in the contributions it makes to the companies and the society that support it.

All authors incur debts, and I can claim more than my fair share. This study began as an American economic history seminar paper for Louis Galambos, then went on to become a history of science doctoral dissertation under the direction of Robert Kargon, both professors at The Johns Hopkins University. Dr. Kargon wisely counseled me to leave the comparison of research at General Electric and Bell for my first book and to concentrate on the latter alone for the dissertation, which I did. Research on the dissertation was supported by a predoctoral fellowship at the Smithsonian

Institution in 1975–6, where I benefited greatly from input by Bernard Finn, Paul Forman, and Eliot Sivowitch.

The cooperation I received from both companies was outstanding. At General Electric, George Wise guided me through the company's archives, making certain that I saw all pertinent materials, including the extensive oral histories he had compiled through interviews with retired GE researchers. In addition, Dr. Wise's own work on the history of industrial research at GE has been of great help to me in many ways. At the Bell Telephone Laboratories Archives, I received assistance from a number of people: M. D. Fagan, Deirdre LaPorte, George Schindler, Jr., Howard Pierce, Ruth Stumm, Norma McCormick, and Marcy Goldstein. The excellent job they have done in organizing their vast holdings makes these resources available to historians for the first time. At AT&T corporate headquarters, I was given important help by Viola Graeper, Robert Garnet, Alan Gardner, and Millie Ettlinger. Dr. Garnet's insights into Bell System management policies were especially valuable. Both GE and Bell kindly permitted me to quote from company documents and supplied me with photographs.

This book was largely written during 1982–3, when I had the good fortune to hold the Harvard-Newcomen Fellowship in Business History at the Harvard Business School. That fellowship was funded by Harvard, by the Newcomen Society of North America, and by my home institution, Rutgers University. I would particularly like to thank Alfred D. Chandler, Jr., Richard Rosenbloom, Richard Vietor, Thomas McCraw, Richard Tedlow, Jay Fell, Margaret Graham, Steven Sass, and Neil Wasserman for contributions to my work while I was there.

The following colleagues, at Rutgers University and elsewhere, read parts of the manuscript and offered their insights: Ronald Calinger, Robert Friedel, W. Bernard Carlson, Philip Pauly, James Reed, Paul Clemens, Keith Nier, Paul Israel, Robert Rosenberg, and Reese Jenkins. To David Cahan goes special thanks for his extensive comments on the three chapters concerning GE.

For help with the always bothersome – and sticky – final editing of the manuscript, I would like to express great appreciation to Robert Rosenberg and to my wife, Barbara Jane Allen.

Portions of three chapters have been published elsewhere, and I appreciate the editors' permission to use the material here: chapter two in Glenn Porter, ed., *The Encyclopedia of American Economic*

History (Charles Scribner's Sons, New York, 1980), vol. 1, pp. 281–293; chapter five in *Technology and Culture*, 24 (1983), pp. 199–221; and chapter nine in *Business History Review*, 51 (1977), pp. 208–235.

And, finally, a second note of thanks for Lou Galambos, coeditor of the series in which this book appears, who not only read the entire manuscript in its two incarnations, but offered me continuing encouragement and advice. I hope that this book meets his expectations.

L.S.R.

New Brunswick, N.J.
June 1985

1

Introduction: The Importance of Industrial Research

Industrial research has changed the way America does business. The first major American industrial research laboratory opened its doors in 1900, inaugurating a new century of profits and progress. But such catchwords do not tell the entire story. Industrial research labs are complex institutions. They have had considerable influence not only on the companies that supported them, but on competition between companies, on the relationship of science and technology, and on the structure of industry. In the study that follows, I examine the forces that brought these labs into being and try to explain why industrial research took root in America in the period from the turn of the 20th century to the First World War. I look in detail at the experiences of two companies and their research programs: General Electric (GE), formed in the merger of Edison General Electric with the Thomson–Houston Company in 1892, and the dominant force in the American electrical industry ever since; and American Telephone and Telegraph (AT&T), the commercial outgrowth of Alexander Graham Bell's 1876 invention of the telephone.

The laboratory that GE established in late 1900 brought to America a type of research institution pioneered by the German chemical and pharmaceutical industries several decades before.[1] Although the GE Research Laboratory was opened with strong corporate interest in the advance of diverse electrical and mechanical technologies – from dynamos to electric locomotives – expectations clearly focused on the technology most closely associated with the company since the time of Edison, the one that had brought much of its sales and profits – the electric lamp. During its first ten years, the Research Laboratory worked hard not only to maintain the company's dominant place in the electric lighting market, but to establish its own indispensibility to GE. Its ultimate success, after a somewhat difficult start, served as both a stimulus and an example for the American industrial research laboratories established in the years before the Great Depression of the 1930s.

The story at AT&T was in many ways similar. Founded in 1911 because of corporate concern over developing technologies that threatened the company's central market in wired-telephone service, the new research laboratory worked to advance and control those technologies. It later went on to supply the Bell System with opportunities for commercial exploitation while continuing to defend the System's telephone interests. Like GE's laboratory, AT&T's served as both a stimulus and an example for those that followed.

And follow they did. By 1931, more than 1,600 companies reported that they supported research laboratories, employing nearly 33,000 people in all. The Depression brought some cutbacks, but expansion began again during the second half of the 1930s; by 1940, more than 2,000 companies maintained laboratories, with a total of almost 70,000 employees. The largest laboratories grew the fastest. In 1940, for example, 82% of the research personnel in the electrical industry were employed by one-quarter of the companies. Although precise figures are not available, total expenditures for American research laboratories were in the range of $100–$160 million in 1930, and $225–$250 million in 1940. Research activity actually expanded faster than the economy, even when the economy itself was growing rapidly during the 1920s.[2]

Not all corporate laboratories, however, were of the industrial research type, and these figures undoubtedly overstate the number of labs, workers, and resources committed to industrial research activities. Most of them were, in fact, testing or engineering labs, where scientists and engineers labored to assure consistency and efficiency in production. While researchers may have been very effective in this restricted role, close association with manufacturing and testing activities usually limited the scope of their work and the range of contributions they could make. For companies to realize all the advantages of industrial research required that laboratories be set apart from production facilities, with no direct responsibilities to them; that scientists and engineers be hired for the purpose of conducting long-term projects that depended heavily on the development of deeper understandings of related science and technology; and that the laboratories be carefully organized and administered to keep them insulated from most immediate demands, while remaining responsive to business needs in the long term. Until the 20th century, such labs did not exist in America, and even then the majority of industrial laboratories were not of this type. In fact, the two laboratories considered in this study did not start out that way. They had to prove themselves before securing the level of autonomy needed to become industrial research institutions.

Industrial research can thus be characterized as follows: industrial laboratories set apart from production facilities, staffed by people trained in science and advanced engineering who work toward deeper understandings of corporate-related science and technology, and who are organized and administered to keep them somewhat insulated from immediate demands yet responsive to long-term company needs. Many research laboratories in industry did not fulfill these three basic requirements – for example, most general engineering labs – so, by this definition, they were not practicing industrial research. Although such laboratories did contribute to the development of industrial technology, they were the direct outgrowths of the analysis, testing, and engineering labs that took root in American industry during the years after the Civil War. Their limited roles and approaches to research and development restricted the type of contributions they could make.

It is clear from the figures given above that, by the end of the 1920s, a large number of American companies had become committed to research of some sort. Even though this activity spread throughout the economy, industrial research *per se* concentrated in those areas that were most technologically sophisticated, whose products were most closely associated with the scientific disciplines, and which showed promise of continuing to advance – areas like chemicals, electric power and communications, petroleum refining, photography, and rubber.[3]

The growth of research activity in general – and industrial research in particular – had substantial impact on the American economy. It increased productivity, brought forth new products, and changed the competitive environment. Some of the most important results from industrial research laboratories were the specialized knowledge, technical expertise, and patent rights that enabled companies to improve their products and processes, to protect their markets, and to threaten the interests of competitors.

Not surprisingly, industrial research had a profound effect on the competitive environment and on the structure of American industry. Companies that supported well-funded and well-organized industrial research laboratories developed significant advantages over their competitors. They became the centers of power in their industries, and only those other companies with similar operations could compete with them on equal terms. This relegated to a lesser position those unwilling or unable to maintain such laboratories and made it exceedingly difficult for independent inventors to gain a foothold in the market areas of interest to companies supporting industrial research.[4]

With the advent of industrial research, large companies could begin to control the rate and direction of technological change. Because science and technology had internal dynamics of their own, and no person or corporation could foresee or direct exactly how they would develop, complete control remained elusive. Yet through their laboratories' extensive research and development activities, orchestrated to produce not only new products and processes but also patents and technical expertise relating to important market areas, companies could circumscribe technological development so that it did not undermine their commercial positions or threaten their investments. A company maintained a strong position by staying in the forefront of research activity in areas germane to its primary markets, developing new products there, and gathering patents to prevent others – even those with new and revolutionary products – from being able to do the same. This could be accomplished through ownership of numerous "secondary" patents, which were almost always needed for commercial production. Sometimes a company's possession of strong patent rights for technologies in which it had no direct interest could be used to threaten the positions of competitors, yielding important ammunition in wars for market control.

Industrial research provided many of the resources needed for the corporate management of change. Through their laboratories' efforts, research-oriented companies made manufacturing operations more efficient, developed new production methods, and exerted considerable influence on the evolution of the marketplace through the advance and control of technology. Industrial research contributed to the effort in a number of ways. Procedures established in the laboratories assured that significant new ideas and results in science and technology came to the companies' attention, so that they were not caught unawares by new developments. The laboratories supplied patents to prevent competitors from encroaching on the companies' commercial turf, and they used the expertise acquired in research to design new manufacturing operations, to improve existing ones, and to locate the sources of trouble when difficulties with materials or methods threatened fabrication processes.

Industrial research also brought to the companies that pursued it a benefit somewhat less tangible but no less important: the progressive image associated with the advance of science and technology. This proved very useful for advertising, through which consumers were directed to associate "progressive" firms with the most desirable products. The support of industrial research and the image that it brought also helped protect companies from antitrust prosecution because public benefits from research could be seen as outweighing the detriments of restraint of trade under the U.S. Supreme Court's "Rule of Reason."[5]

Naturally, what benefited some companies in a competitive environment posed difficulties for others. Companies that lacked the substantial resources to support industrial research, those that had large investments in established products and production methods and were unwilling to abandon them, or those without the stable internal structures that led corporate managers to look beyond their immediate organizational problems to the larger questions of market development and defense, ultimately found themselves in disadvantageous positions relative to their better-organized and more aggressive competitors who undertook industrial research.[6] And of course, independent inventors, faced with these so-called invention factories found important areas of development preempted and opportunities to exploit their own inventions closed off. Whereas their only competition in new fields had previously been rival inventors, now they faced the organized onslaught of industrial research.

As industrial research took form at a number of companies in the early years of the 20th century, it helped to change the perspectives of corporate managers. Companies usually established research programs to protect their interests in particular market areas, but soon found that their laboratories had far greater capabilities. Scientists and engineers, organized into teams and set to work in fields germane to company interests, frequently made significant advances in both science and technology, presenting their employers with entirely new products and processes to exploit. Researchers developed small-scale manufacturing operations for new products and then transferred them to the factory, providing considerable impetus to the companies' total innovative processes.[7] As industrial researchers took their work into fields beyond those directly associated with company needs, they tried to acquire patents that might in the future prove vital to their own company's ability to enter new markets or – sometimes just as importantly – that could help prevent others from doing so. Such patents might be used in a number of ways, from stymieing competitors to trading with them for other patent rights or commercial concessions. In short, these patents, along with the new products, processes, and technical expertise developed in industrial research, presented corporations with new opportunities for innovation, market control, and growth. Before long, corporate management took advantage of these opportunities by expanding into new product areas, rationalizing and developing new production processes, and attacking competitors who threatened to invade their markets.

Science, technology, and industrial research

The impact of industrial research in America reached beyond the realm of business, strongly affecting science and technology as well. Industrial research provided American science and technology both support and direction. It also offered career opportunities for scientists and engineers at a time when their other options remained quite limited. When the first laboratories were established early in the 20th century, most American scientists had little time or support for research. Many taught at colleges and universities oriented toward classical learning, where they received neither incentives nor facilities to pursue research. Others worked in state universities or engineering colleges whose teaching loads were so heavy and whose equipment was so poor that conducting original work proved to be almost impossible. A few graduate-level, research-oriented science and engineering departments did exist by the turn of the century, but the number of people who could be accommodated in them remained quite small.

Industrial research laboratories offered American scientists and research-oriented engineers a welcome new career path. While a few scientists had been employed by American industry even before the Civil War, in most cases their purview had been limited to the testing and analysis of materials. Industrial research presented a considerably better opportunity: Scientists and engineers could devote a major portion of their time to activities oriented toward gaining deeper understandings of science and technology;

they commanded substantial resources; and they were provided with trained assistants to carry out the more technical or more mundane tasks of research and development. Industrial researchers often had restrictions placed on them in matters of publication and participation in professional organizations, but those more interested in the methods of science than concerned with either the advance of scientific disciplines or the trappings of the profession could find a comfortable home in industrial research. Though they had to set aside some of the pressing questions of the scientific disciplines to concentrate on those areas of research of importance to industry, this was a deal that many willingly made.[8]

Working in industrial research thus presented personal and professional trade-offs. Once in the labs, scientists and research-oriented engineers escaped the pressures of the academic environment, including teaching and directing students. They could invent without having to act as entrepreneurs, yet be paid quite well – far better than in comparable academic positions – and higher pay held particular allure in a country where personal worth was often measured by the size of one's paycheck. As industrial researchers, they accepted the responsibilities of record keeping, providing consulting services, and working for patents. In return, they received large amounts of research time, considerable support and assistance, and substantial financial reward. For many, it was a satisfactory, even satisfying, alternative.

As the industrial research laboratories at a number of corporations took form, they became quite different from earlier American labs. The demands placed on industrial researchers and the way in which they approached their work were peculiar to the new environment. Industrial research scientists and engineers often worked on group projects, to which they contributed specified types of results under the direction of a group leader. Their leeway for digression was often quite small, and they sometimes faced schedules for the completion of their work. Because research directors had to be certain that a large portion of results coming from their laboratories would be commercially applicable, they frequently supervised projects themselves or placed them under the control of a senior staff member. Individuals did not have to be brilliant to make important contributions to a project's success. Administrators took advantage of the complementary capabilities of their researchers, sometimes setting theorists and experimentalists, abstract thinkers and "nuts and bolts" people working together. The power of such a team to find solutions usually surpassed the sum of the powers of the individuals taken separately. In instances when such team projects were not used, administrators relied heavily on the strong influence of the commercial environment, which made researchers aware that they were expected, one way or another, to make their work pay.[9]

In industrial research, science and technology were pursued together in order to improve technologies of corporate interest. Science and technology were perceived, not as they had been through much of history – as two endeavors separated by purpose, methodology, and even the social classes of the practitioners – but rather as complex, interrelated activities aimed at a common goal. In fact, science and technology became so fully intertwined in many industrial research projects that it is impossible for the historian to distinguish between them. In this new approach to research, science and technology were each informed by and closely related to the other; they benefited greatly, both individually and collectively.

Yet, with only a few exceptions, the results of industrial research have been advances of science and technology in preconceived directions, because researchers and research directors usually had to foresee the types of results coming from projects in order to justify their support. By the very nature of preconception, the results were rarely revolutionary. Commercial and financial exigencies made most companies unwilling or unable to give many of their scientists and engineers the research freedom needed to pursue revolutionary change. Rules, regulations, and red tape limited the researchers' initiative and the scope of their work, while the need to produce a regular stream of results for corporate consumption forced many research directors to favor short-term, low-risk projects over longer-term undertakings which were less certain of applicable results. Thus the control and bureaucratization of research had a profound impact. At the same time, the market power of companies supporting industrial research was often so strong that it inhibited research and development in smaller companies, in university laboratories, and by individuals. Under certain circumstances, then, industrial research had an adverse impact on the pursuit of science and technology.

But even when these limitations and inhibitions are taken into account, one can hardly help but conclude that industrial research has, on balance, strongly promoted the pursuit of science and the advance of technology. The tremendous power of the combined science–technology approach, along with the substantial corporate resources committed to research, assured that a considerable amount of new knowledge about and control over the natural and man-made world would come from industrial research. That, given their levels of funding, industrial laboratories contributed relatively little to solving the outstanding problems of the scientific disciplines was of no particular concern to the companies supporting them, nor should it detract from the value we ultimately place on their results.

Industrial research combined science and engineering to create much of what we today call "high technology." Yet, not everyone considers all of it – from electronics and computers to synthetic materials and "wonder drugs" – as advances. Some of these developments tended to cause social dislocations, exacting a price from their users in one way or another, or they created as many social and economic problems as they solved. Other developments worked to concentrate power in the hands of those who already had more than their share of it, including the companies that supported industrial research.[10] Thus we can say that industrial research has been extremely successful in the advance of technology only so long as we understand that advance to be in the directions desired by major corporations.

The advent of industrial research had considerable impact on the communities and professions of science and engineering, on American industry, and through industry, on the lives and careers of most of the nation's people. The study that follows is an attempt to come to grips with the reasons for and importance of this phenomenon. It will look at how and why conditions in the late 19th and early 20th centuries led to the establishment of industrial research and will then go on to consider in detail the laboratories at GE and Bell. It will also examine the research projects they undertook in their early years and will consider their organization and methods of research, the relationship of the laboratories to the companies of which they were parts, and the commercial value of their results.

The main purpose in studying these relationships is to understand how industrial research influenced developments in science, technology, and industry. I try to show the ways in which it affected the rate and direction of changes in technology as well as how companies introduced new technology into the economy. Given the various advantages discussed above, I consider how industrial research changed the ways companies approached market control, innovation, and growth, and how the industrial environment influenced researchers' conceptions of their projects, the methods that they used, and the kinds of results that they achieved. I also attempt to determine why the first American industrial research laboratories were established in the years between the turn of the 20th century and the First World War. There are a number of reasons, including changes in the content and methods of science and technology during the 19th century; increases in the quantity and enhanced capabilities of available researchers; commercial threats to American industry based on developments in science and technology, especially abroad; changes in the structure of American industry in the late 19th and early 20th centuries; and social and political forces, including antitrust legislation that forced companies to adopt new ways to innovate and compete.

Taking these factors into account and answering all of the questions set out above requires consideration of the type of business and the market position of each company establishing industrial research. Of course, every company was unique, so the answers will be somewhat different for each. Because the study that follows deals with a very limited sample, the conclusions for industrial research as a whole must necessarily be tentative. Nevertheless, I chose GE and Bell as the two major case studies because they had overlapping areas of interest in science and technology, but very different corporate structures, operating methods, and market positions. Hence an examination of these questions in relation to the two companies should provide results more closely related to differences in corporate structure, outlook, and opportunity than to the science and technology involved.

GE and Bell provide examples of research activity at two large technology-based corporations that took form in the late 19th century and have played influential roles in the American economy ever since. These companies gained and maintained their positions in large part through their research work, so this study will look at the many ways it proved useful to them. Although the two cases do not comprise the entire story of American industrial research, they provide good starting points because both laboratories were influential in the industrial research movement that followed the First World War, and because many companies learned from the examples that they set.

Before taking up the story of industrial research at GE and Bell, however, it is important to survey the American environment that made such endeavors both possible and, from the companies' points of view, necessary. In the chapter that follows I discuss the developments in science, technology, and industry during the 19th century that led these and other American companies to undertake industrial research.

2

Building the Foundations of Industrial Research: American Science, Technology, and Industry in the 19th Century

The 19th century saw tremendous strides in science, both in its ability to explain natural phenomena and in the development of its educational and organizational bases. However, American industry's involvement with science began rather haltingly. Although some early inventors employed available scientific principles and methods to solve problems of commercial importance, only after they had succeeded a number of times and after engineering became well established as a science-based profession later in the century did American industry regularly turn to science. In the decades after the Civil War, a number of companies began to use employees with scientific training to perform tasks such as the design of products and installations, the analysis of materials, and the rationalization of procedures. All of these were important, but the seemingly obvious *modus operandi* of using science – rather than *doing* it – severely limited the range of contributions that most scientists and engineers could make to their employers. Only with the coming of industrial research did this situation change fully.

Activity that can be identified as industrial research began in America early in the 20th century due to a number of related factors. First, science and technology had changed in important ways. Whereas in the 18th and 19th centuries most technology could be modified and advanced by individuals with little training in science or concern with scientific principles, during the latter decades of the 19th century and the early years of the 20th, newly sophisticated commercial technologies, especially in the electrical and chemical industries, required inventors and engineers to include components of scientific research in their technical work.[1] The creation of new scientific disciplines and subdisciplines during the 19th century improved the ability of those who pursued science to explain and manipulate natural phenomena.

Other factors that led to the creation of industrial research in 20th century America were institutional, economic, and social in character. The large-scale development of educational programs in engineering and the sciences in the decades after the Civil War made available to industry a corps of individuals trained in the methods and principles of science and mathematics. Having learned experimental and analytical techniques during their years of advanced training, these research-oriented scientists and engineers provided the expertise needed for the activities associated with industrial research. Industry itself changed dramatically during the course of the century, and a number of large, technology-based corporations took form in the 1880s and 1890s. These companies, which sought long-term security and growth, found that they required a means to protect their investments in technology and their control of established markets. At the same time, the Sherman Antitrust Act, passed in 1890 and seriously enforced after 1900, closed off some of their traditional ways to undercut competitors. Social forces, exemplified by the Progressive movement, led both to professionalization of the middle classes and to the expectation that the new professionals – including scientists – could and should use their knowledge to improve the operations of government and industry. These combined needs, opportunities, expectations, and interests led a number of companies to establish research programs oriented toward the development and control of commercial technology in conjunction with in-depth studies of the type associated with science. Many such programs ultimately became industrial research laboratories, bringing powerful competitive advantages to companies that supported and managed them well. These laboratories served as vital components of the business organizations that historians have recently credited with exercising very strong influence over American economic and political life.[2]

To understand the process that led to the establishment of industrial research, we must examine science, technology, and industry in America during the 19th century and evaluate their interaction. Doing this in so short a space means, of course, that what follows will necessarily be suggestive rather than conclusive.

American science and engineering

It is extremely difficult to define science and technology, distinguishing clearly between them. This is especially true in the context of 19th century America. The general conception of science during that era had a comprehensive character, closely relating the study of materials and processes in nature (and in the man-made environment) with the ability to transform human surroundings. Indeed, no consensus then existed – nor does one now – of what comprised "true" science. Distinctions between science as knowledge and science as practice were not always clear. Some people presumed that the gathering and ordering of data led inductively to fundamental truths about nature. Others believed that in the deductive construction of theories lay the route to understanding. Science comprised knowledge about the environment and several sets of questions and methods believed appropriate for advancing that knowledge. It encompassed numerous subjects, methods, and purposes.

During the 18th and early 19th centuries American social, economic, and institutional conditions discouraged the pursuit of knowledge for its own sake. On a harsh continent rich in natural resources but lacking the population, farming methods, manufacturing technologies, and transportation facilities needed to make full use of them, most efforts of the intellect went toward developing practical ways to control and utilize the environment. At the time of its founding in 1743, the American Philosophical Society showed great concern with geography, geology, and other studies that promoted agriculture and industry. In the words of its founder, Benjamin Franklin, the society hoped to "increase the power of men over matter, and multiply the conveniences or pleasures of life." Similarly, the American Academy of Arts and Sciences, organized in Boston in 1780, devoted itself to "improvements in agriculture, arts, manufactures and commerce," and its members attempted to find new uses for indigenous natural resources.[3] Benjamin Franklin, internationally famous for his research in electrical theory, did not rest until his studies led him to various instruments of use to mankind. The lightning rod, bifocals, and the Pennsylvania fireplace ("Franklin Stove") are the best known among his many contributions. While other Americans studying the natural world might have been less technically oriented than Franklin, they nonetheless ably applied their minds and methods to meet compelling needs. David Rittenhouse in Philadelphia observed the planets and constructed orreries to explain their motions, but when the Revolution came he naturally turned his attentions to telescopic gun sights and the manufacture of cannon.

Some important early American inventors made use of the content and methods of science. Oliver Evans, for example, showed strong concern for scientific principles. In his inventions of an amphibious steam-powered dredge, a high-pressure steam engine, and a completely automated flour mill, Evans employed these principles when they were available and developed them himself when they were not. Evans remarked:

> It has been by the most intense studies that I made discoveries. After having a faint glimpse of the principle, it was with many toilsome and tedious steps that I attained a clear and distinct view. I received great assistance from the results of experiments made by others, which are to be found in scientific works.[4]

Of course, not all inventors read the scientific literature. Indeed, one of the salient characteristics of early machine technology was that it could be developed by ingenious cut-and-try methods. Yet the strong Enlightenment philosophy then prevalent in America saw progress coming from rational procedures of the type associated with science. This credo, reinforced by the few instances in which science had been of direct value in the improvement of technology, made it an article of faith in the early 19th century that technology would benefit from scientific input.[5] Men like Joseph Henry, engaged in the study of mathematics and the pursuit of electrical science, assumed that their research would serve to inform and enlighten mechanics and inventors – if not immediately and directly, then later and in more general ways.[6]

This belief in the efficacy of science for directing inventions and improvements led to the establishment of mechanics' institutes whose main purpose was to bring the contents and methods of science directly to artisans and mechanics. In 1824, after the establishment of such organizations in Glasgow and London, the Franklin Institute opened in Philadelphia. It was soon followed by similar associations in other American cities. Supported by the artisans and mechanics themselves, these organizations provided lectures and instruction on scientific discoveries, principles, and methods. Institute directors believed that such knowledge helped members direct their work along more productive lines, though whether it really did so is unclear.[7] Members' concern with scientific principles was expected to advance their social standing by providing the air of learning that had become associated – even in "democratic" America – with the study and pursuit of science.[8]

The extensive American public education system provided artisans and mechanics with rudimentary instruction in science and mathematics. Their literacy enabled them to draw ideas and information from materials published by the mechanics' institutes and other sources. A team of British commissioners studying American manufacture and invention during the 1850s commented that the mechanics' education gave them a "vivacity" in "enquiring into the first principles" of their work, yielding a "theoretical knowledge of the processes" quite beyond that of their British contemporaries.[9] How great a value theoretical knowledge held for the advance of their work is moot, but the American mechanics' level of understanding clearly impressed the experienced commissioners.

Although these mechanics may have been informed by science, and inventors like Oliver Evans and Samuel F. B. Morse made good use of its principles, it was the development of the engineering professions during the course of the 19th century that brought scientific and mathematical concepts and methods into American industry.[10] Engineering as a coherent body of knowledge (used mostly in the design of machines and fortifications) dates back at least to early Roman civilization. However, not until the establishment of the French *Ecole des Ponts et Chaussées* (School of Bridges and Roads) in 1747 was engineering taught in an academic setting. The *Ecole Polytechnique*, founded in 1794, incorporated scientific and mathematical studies into the engineering curriculum for the first time and established an explicit connection between the study of physical and mathematical theory and the pursuit of practical ends.

Engineering in America began with undertakings like the dredging of harbors, building of roads, and digging of canals. The Erie Canal, which opened the port of New York to the Great Lakes, was the first major American project requiring engineering skills. It served as an early and important school for the profession. When work began on the 363-mile waterway in 1817, the New York State canal commissioners could find no adequately trained engineers to take charge, so they turned the project over to four surveyors. Surveying required knowledge of many scientific and mathematical principles, and these four men adapted themselves to the unprecedented task they faced. Through further study and the inspection of existing works, they began an educational process that lasted throughout the nine years of construction.

More than sixty men learned engineering while working on the Erie. By taking part in a program of study and fieldwork, they rose from low-level positions to the ranks of engineer or assistant engineer during the course of the project, then went on to build canals, bridges, railroads, steel mills, and industrial facilities throughout the United States. These engineers' training may have been somewhat less than academic, but their uses of scientific and mathematical principles in the varied tasks of canal building guided them in the construction, invention, and design they subsequently undertook. In this way they helped bring a new level of sophistication to American technology.

In the same year that the Franklin Institute opened (1824), Stephen Van Rensselaer, patroon of vast lands on the Hudson River at the eastern terminus of the Erie Canal, established the school that became the Rensselaer Polytechnic Institute. Its initial course structure called for a single year of study in the sciences, including laboratory exercises, extensive field trips, and the preparation of student lectures and demonstrations. By 1835 the program had been enlarged and extended to three years in order to encompass engineering studies. Two other American schools also provided engineering education before the Civil War. The United States Military Academy at West Point, founded in 1802 and modeled in part on the *Ecole Polytechnique*, began to emphasize scientific studies and technical education after 1818; the American Literary, Scientific, and Military Academy, founded in 1820 at Norwich, Vermont, did likewise.

During the 1840s and 1850s a number of American colleges, including Union, Dartmouth, and Brown, inaugurated their own engineering curricula. In addition, both Harvard and Yale, as a result of substantial bequests, established scientific schools apart from their regular programs. Because Harvard and Yale were committed to religious and classical studies, neither placed much emphasis on training in science or engineering. Their scientific schools languished in their early years, with the exception of a few programs like Louis Agassiz's studies of natural history at Harvard.[11] In part because of Harvard's lack of commitment to scientific and engineering education, citizens of Boston founded the Massachusetts Institute of Technology (MIT) in 1861. It included a school of "industrial science" to provide a "complete course of instruction and training, suited to the various practical professions" and to meet "the more limited aims of such as desire to secure a scientific preparation for special industrial pursuits. . . . having their foundation in the exact sciences."[12]

It is interesting that this concept of the "exact sciences" providing a "foundation" for "industrial pursuits" was consonant with Joseph Henry's assumption that science lay at the base of invention and the crafts, and with the belief of the mechanics' institutes that instruction in the sciences would enhance their members' technical capabilities. The weekly journal *Scientific American*, founded in 1845, shared this perspective and attempted to bring to the attention of artisans, mechanics, and inventors those advances in science that the editors believed germane to their work. The journal's understanding of "science" clearly included the broad range of activities associated with taxonomy and description, experimentation, and even invention. The editors castigated as unworthy of attention and support those who worked only toward the development of theory. *Scientific American* had a very large and loyal readership. In its early decades it represented and promoted the synthesis of science and technology that had existed as an ideal throughout the American experience but was as yet largely unrealized. The founding of MIT and other engineering schools were significant steps in that direction. They soon provided an organiizational basis for the large-scale interaction of science and technology in America.

In 1862 Congress passed the Morrill Land Grant Act, which set aside 30,000 acres of public land in every state for each of its senators and representatives in Congress. That land was to be sold and the proceeds from the sale invested to support a college "where the leading object shall be . . . to teach such branches of learning as are related to agriculture and the mechanic arts." These land-grant institutions (which often became state universities) taught engineering, science, and agricultural studies to the increasing number of Americans who went on to higher education in the decades following the Civil War. Largely because of land grants, the number of schools offering science and engineering courses reached 70 by 1872, then increased to 85 in 1880, and to 126 in 1917.[13] Each of these institutions made the study of science an important part of its curriculum. Almost all of the more than 50 technically oriented colleges and universities that opened in the early 1870s put strong emphasis on physics and chemistry and on their relationship to engineering. By the middle 1880s, college-trained engineers outnumbered those who were self-taught or had learned their trades in apprenticeship programs.[14]

Engineering achieved professional status in America with the establishment of the engineering societies. The first of these, the American Society of Civil Engineers, was founded in 1852 and oriented toward all nonmilitary engineers. The further development of engineering disciplines after the Civil War led to formation of the American Institute of Mining Engineers in 1871, the American Society of Mechanical Engineers in 1880, and the American Institute of Electrical Engineers in 1884. Numerous subspeciality organizations, each representing a new branch of the growing profession, followed. The professional societies helped to assure the establishment and maintenance of standards in engineering education, with courses aimed directly at producing engineers who would be of service to industry.

Beginning in the period after the Civil War, academically trained engineers were hired in rather large numbers by American firms with interests in machine tools, metals fabrication, transportation, chemicals, and electrical equipment. They forcefully brought the content and methods of science to industry. While the type of work these engineers undertook for their employers was in no sense industrial research as defined in Chapter 1, they nevertheless helped to establish the usefulness of science for America's expanding economy.

The dramatic growth of the U.S. educational system after the Civil War created numerous teaching opportunities for scientists and engineers. Professors of the physical and biological sciences and of mathematics were employed by the thousands. However, their positions generally required them to spend long hours in the classroom and student laboratory. Hired to teach, not to do research, they usually received little time, support, or reward for research activities. A few individuals found other types of employment in which they could use their scientific education. The U.S. Coast Survey and the Patent Office hired physicists and chemists. State geological surveys, assay offices, state agricultural experiment stations, and the U.S. Department of Agriculture also employed chemists, geologists, biologists, and other scientists, but the number of positions was limited and the work often dull.[15]

During the 1880s and 1890s the scientific community in the United States began to expand and change character with the establishment of graduate education. Modeled on the German research-oriented universities, Johns Hopkins opened in 1876 with strong graduate departments in the physical and biological sciences. Its success at producing both science and scientists sparked the upgrading of graduate programs at Harvard, Yale, Princeton, and Cornell, as well as the creation of entirely new institutions devoted to graduate education and research, such as Clark and the University of Chicago. Previously almost all Americans who wanted to pursue advanced scientific studies went abroad, especially to Germany, but now opportunities were also open for them in the United States. As a consequence, many more went on to take advanced degrees.[16]

During the latter part of the 19th century a strong ideology of "pure" science developed in America. Taken in large part from Europe and based on graduate-level academic training and research, the pure-science ideology valued the advancement of knowledge for its own sake, emphasized the ever-more specialized scientific disciplines and subdisciplines, and held that scientists should only be evaluated by their peers. While a small cadre devoted to this type of pure-science professionalism had held positions of influence since the 1840s and 1850s – and even inspired Congress to create an honorary National Academy of Sciences in 1863 – their ideas had had little impact beyond a limited circle of elite colleges and government agencies.[17] Beginning in the 1870s, however, a substantial number of American scientists worked to establish their professional identities and prerogatives by changing existing organizations, beginning new journals, and, especially toward the end of the century, forming scientific societies with narrowly defined interests. The American Association for the Advancement of Science (AAAS), founded by and for amateurs in 1847, amended its constitution in 1874 to restrict office-holding rights to those recognized as among the scientific elite. In 1881 the association was divided into nine sections based on scientific specialities; yet it remained too general an organization and its members too mixed a group of amateurs, teachers, and interested laymen to satisfy the needs of the emerging class of professional specialists. The specialists thus formed such organizations as the American Chemical Society (ACS) in 1876. (Initially based in New York, it became a truly national organization in 1891.) The ACS printed the *Journal of the American Chemical Society* beginning in the late 1870s, at about the same time that the *American Journal of Mathematics* began publication. The *Physical Review* first appeared in 1893, and six years later the American Physical Society was formed to take it over. In the biological sciences, the American Physiological Society and the American Morphological Society both took form during this period. For the last quarter of the century, American professional science – characterized by graduate degree programs, research, publication, and specialization – was truly in rapid ascent. Its powerful disciplinary-based research programs and its production of research-oriented scientists and engineers soon helped establish close connections between science and American industry.

Henry Rowland, first professor of physics at Johns Hopkins and one of America's most highly regarded scientists in his time, spoke for professional science when he addressed the AAAS in 1883 and asked, "What must be done to create a science of physics in this country, rather than to call telegraphs, electric lights, and such conveniences by the name of science?"[18] Rowland represented a small but committed group of American scientists who believed that undue concern with application hindered the pursuit of knowledge. Yet Rowland had no argument with using science for commercial purposes. Like Joseph Henry, he assumed that most technological applications were based on earlier scientific work. However, expectations and demands by university presidents and trustees, government agency directors, and by the public at large (through such organs as *Scientific American*) incessantly pushed scientists to take up technically oriented studies, making their results applicable to solving agricultural and industrial problems. Rowland and other professionals argued for the autonomy to choose their projects and methods based on their own perceptions of the needs of the scientific disciplines. Application, they believed, would naturally follow. Fifty years after Joseph Henry, Rowland expressed many of the same sentiments, but he spoke for a larger segment of a dramatically expanded – and expanding – community.[19]

Yet even within the ranks of the professionals, Rowland's beliefs were not universally shared. Many members of the new breed, like chemist Willis Whitney at MIT, believed that one of the most important missions for American science (similarly to much of German science) was to bring a new level of sophistication to the products and processes of industry. A number of the new scientific societies, especially in the subspecialities and engineering-related fields, worked quite closely with industry. The American Electrochemical Society, of which Whitney was an officer and founding member, very strongly pursued contacts with the chemical companies. The major scientific societies sometimes did likewise. The American Chemical Society, for example, established the *Journal of Industrial and Engineering Chemistry* to address the proclivities of many of its members and the needs of industry. Further, the "purity" of even the most outspoken proponents of professionalism was not always certain. Rowland himself worked closely

Plate 1. Henry A. Rowland. Courtesy of the Johns Hopkins University Archives.

with the growing electrical industry and devoted a major part of his effort during the 1890s to the development and commercialization of a system of multiplex telegraphy.[20]

All in all, American science during the latter decades of the 19th century was a curious mixture of "pure" and "applied." Although the rhetoric of pure science caught the attention of many contemporaries – and recently, of many historians – the strong capitalist sentiments of the post–Civil War era and the democratic ideology that had pervaded the nation at least since the 1820s undercut attempts to divorce the support of science from demands that it address issues of utility. Practically minded university trustees, donors, and (in the case of state universities) legislators made certain that scientific research pursued on their campuses had practical value. Even the president of the research-oriented University of Chicago, William Rainey Harper, felt compelled during the 1890s to defend his staff's "pure" research on the basis of the applied work that would follow from it.[21] In 1883 the newborn journal *Science*, published by elocutionist–inventor Alexander Graham Bell and aimed at the broad range of professionals, amateurs, and concerned laymen, expressed American perceptions of science quite well when it editorialized:

> The science of today is in thorough accord with the spirit of the American people. They are proud of every achievement it makes, and are satisfied with the return it is giving them for their investments. To continue the *entente cordiale*, should be the object of every scientific worker. He may the more readily concede some practical return for the facilities for investigation which the people have furnished, since the march of discovery is not in the least hindered, but rather promoted, by the practical application of the new truth which it develops.[22]

That *entente cordiale* was most fully and successfully carried out in the new, scientifically oriented engineering disciplines which took form in the last three decades of the century. Unlike the mechanics' institutes, where studies of scientific principles and methods were presumed, *ipso facto*, to relate to the advance of members' work, the new engineering programs very carefully integrated courses in mathematics and the physical sciences into curricula intended to provide engineers with the intellectual tools for analysis and design. Electrical engineering, for example, built from bases of mechanical engineering, mathematics, and physics, developing into a discipline in its own right during the 1880s and 1890s while maintaining close associations with the "electricity and magnetism" branch of physics. As electrification spread across America during this period, and as several competitors of the early direct current electrical systems adopted the considerably more complex alternating current, the need for large numbers of highly trained people became clear. Since electrical studies had been the province of physics, early courses in the application of electrical science to practice came from academic physics departments. In 1882 MIT offered the first electrical engineering degree; many other schools soon followed.[23] Trained in mathematics, physics, and engineering practice, the new electrical engineers brought a synthesis of scientific methods and engineering know-how to the development of electrical technology. As one observer noted shortly after the turn of the century: "The trained man has shown the possibility of predicting results theoretically which previously had to be determined experimentally, at very great expense, and I am convinced that the entrance of the college man into electrical engineering has been the most important event in the history of the industry."[24]

However, American engineering practice rarely involved research. Almost all undergraduate engineering curricula stressed calculation, laboratory and shop work, and the solution of design problems – exercises of memory and computation that the Society for the Promotion of Engineering Education (founded in 1893) believed severely limited engineering graduates' capabilities and outlook.[25] Some new fields, like electrical and chemical engineering, might be perceived as scientific disciplines in their own right, but the emphasis among engineering practitioners was on applying their knowledge to the design of technical systems and on achieving limited technological advances as circumstances required. Engineers' understanding of the methods and content of science and mathematics permitted them to make important contributions to industrial technology; yet in only a few cases did they advance both the engineering disciplines and their employers' interests because industrial conditions still largely limited their work to finding solutions to design and implementation problems.

On the graduate level, engineering studies had become more fully integrated with the pursuit of science. At Johns Hopkins, Henry Rowland helped to train the initial generation of graduate students in electrical engineering within his department, sending the first physics/electrical engineering Ph.D. to work for the American Bell Telephone Company. One prominent American physicist of the early 20th century noted that to him "Rowland was the American Helmholtz of the new era of close co-operation between abstract science and engineering. . . . The scientific spirit of Rowland's laboratory and lecture-room was felt everywhere in the electrical industry."[26] This graduate research training in fields that encompassed both science and engineering produced researchers who would find their fullest application in the industrial research environment.

Science and industry

As understanding and codification of natural phenomena increased during the course of the 19th century, the value of science to industry became more apparent. Yet the relationship between industrial science and technology was in no way simple. Even though in a few instances scientific knowledge could be applied directly, far more frequently the analytical and deductive methods of science found use in experimental projects geared to the development of commercial technologies. The results served to inform both science and engineering. As historian Edwin Layton has noted, "engineers used experimental and theoretical methods in order to generate the sorts of scientific knowledge needed by technology."[27] The principles and methods of science also helped in testing the composition of materials, a task vital to the improvement of products and the rationalization of industrial processes. This positive – though limited – experience with science was an important reason for American industry's decision to establish ongoing research programs, which in turn led ultimately to the realization that the route to industrial security and growth lay in the corporate pursuit of carefully selected science.

The examples that follow give an idea of the ways in which American science, technology, and industry interacted during the 19th century. Many more cases could be cited, of course, but these few should serve to demonstrate both the power and the limitations of science in the pre-1900 American industrial environment.

In 1830 the Franklin Institute undertook research into the design and operation of waterwheels, a subject of great importance in a country where most industrial operations depended on waterpower. The institute solicited funds from mill owners and other interested parties and began research to determine "the mode of applying any given head of water, so as to produce the greatest ratio of effect to power expended." This proved to be a very complex problem. Variables included the head of water, wheel size, design, and velocity, and construction of the water entryway. The effects of friction and inertia had to be taken into account, and each experiment was run several times, so that mathematical correlations of varying results could be made. When the final results of this research were published in the Franklin Institute's *Journal*, scientific principles relating to engineering design became available to millwrights, thus enabling them to make better use of their water resources.[28]

Another research project on water power, undertaken in 1845 at the Merrimack Manufacturing Company of Lowell, Massachusetts, helped the turbine become considerably more compact and efficient than the waterwheel. James Francis, Uriah Boyden, and other company engineers studying turbine operations sought to go beyond the establishment of design parameters; they wanted to understand the flow of water through the turbine housing and to learn how the force of water reacted against the blades. Francis and Boyden based their work on the turbine flow theories of the Swiss Leonhard Euler and the Frenchman Jean-Victor Poncelet but recognized that idealized assumptions in the science and mathematics made these theories useful only as guides. The Lowell researchers developed what Layton called an engineering science of turbines – a detailed codification of knowledge, often expressed mathematically, based on careful experiment and analysis. Their work had important consequences, eventually replacing the millwright with the hydraulic engineer and making highly efficient, compact waterpower devices available to mills and factories throughout the country.[29]

These two research efforts on water power demonstrated that the advance of commercial technology could benefit greatly from the methods associated with science even if the content of science proved of limited value. Although the projects did not yield new understanding of nature itself, they provided important systematic information about the operation of man-made devices. Such knowledge directly aided industrial technology while contributing to new areas of related sciences, here hydraulics. Indeed, study of the actions, reactions, and fluid flows in waterwheels and turbines could reasonably be considered science in itself, though pursued in a nondisciplinary way. The principles and methods of science and the process of improving technology were so closely related in this case that to draw distinctions – especially to suggest that science was "applied" to technology – makes little sense.[30]

The steam engine had been developed well in advance of the areas of science that explained its operation, but as the first rudimentary engines gave way to more efficient ones, the need to understand their dynamics and thermodynamics became clear. In his pioneering work on the high-pressure engine, Oliver Evans studied the scientific literature on heat, pressure, and the structure of materials, using this knowledge in the significant advances he made. Charles Porter of New York, self-taught in the sciences and mathematics, worked outside the growing American scientific community, developing an understanding of engine operations that enabled him to make important improvements during the 1860s. Porter's dynamic theory of reciprocating engines led him to design machines that operated more smoothly at higher speeds, producing considerable increases in power along with reductions in weight. Although he derided the impracticality of scientists, especially those employed in the colleges and government agencies, Porter made generous use of scientific theory while developing his ideas.[31] His work serves as a good example of how some of the most important 19th century technological developments – often perceived as based on trial-and-error methodology – actually resulted from use of the theory, experimentation, and careful observation closely associated with science.

A number of individuals trained as scientists made significant contributions to American industry during the 19th century. James Booth studied chemistry in Germany, then returned to America, where he opened a consulting laboratory in Philadelphia in 1836. Over the following decades he analyzed iron and coal samples for mine owners, improved methods of sugar refining for local mills, and performed a number of services for Pennsylvania industry. Booth taught analytical chemistry in his lab, preparing students to do similar work.[32] A number of scientists also lent advice to inventors and industrialists. For example, Samuel F. B. Morse, a portrait painter by trade, received important help from Joseph Henry in the course of his work on the electric telegraph, as we have seen; George Corliss, the premier American builder of stationary steam engines, worked regularly with Alexis Caswell, professor of mathematics and science at nearby Brown University; and in making plans for the first transatlantic telegraph cable during the 1850s, entrepreneur Cyrus Field consulted with oceanographer Matthew F. Maury of the U.S. Naval Observatory, later with the great British scientist–engineer, William Thomson.

Beyond such desultory assistance, people trained in science sometimes took positions working directly for industry during the antebellum years. Perhaps the earliest case is that of Samuel Luther Dana, a physician and chemist employed by the Merrimack Manufacturing Company in its textile operations. During the 1830s

Dana experimented with the organic chemicals used for dyeing, which enabled him to improve the process of calico printing. He also undertook an extensive study of the chemical changes that accompanied the bleaching of cotton fabrics, further developing that process as well.[33] Significantly, Merrimack did not establish a full-scale laboratory under Dana's direction but let him work out his ideas with the aid of a few assistants until his death in 1868. The company did not conceive of a competitive strategy based on improving technology but simply used Dana's work to enhance efficiency and to lower costs.

By the later 19th century, corporate support of scientists became more frequent as companies grew larger and more profitable and as industrial products and processes took on greater complexity. This occurred in part from cumulative technological development, in part from scientific inputs such as those described above. The well-known success of chemists in establishing a synthetic dye industry in England and Germany after mid-century alerted American businessmen to the benefits that could arise from employing scientists, especially chemists. Thus in 1875 the Pennsylvania Railroad hired Yale Ph.D. chemist Charles B. Dudley to organize a laboratory for the testing and analysis of materials purchased from suppliers. The railroad initially intended the laboratory to determine which materials best suited its needs, to prepare specifications, and to run tests before it accepted materials from suppliers. In his first major project, Dudley formulated an acceptable composition of lubricating oils for locomotives. The railroad had previously encountered serious problems with the rapid corrosion of valves and other locomotive parts, but the application of Dudley's recommendations ended them. As the laboratory grew, Dudley's chemists turned their attention to the composition and properties of steel rails, which were then being introduced in place of iron. Their results were incorporated into supply specifications and saved the Pennsylvania Railroad considerable replacement costs over the following decades. By the time he retired in 1905, Dudley supervised a staff that had grown to thirty-four trained chemists and numerous assistants.[34]

Yet Dudley's laboratory effected no major innovations. Though its careful analysis of needs and its recommendations on purchases served the Pennsylvania Railroad well, the company saw no value in extending its activities to the invention of new products and processes. In this restricted role, scientists could help to increase efficiency and decrease costs, but they could not develop the types of knowledge that might take the company into new fields or gain it competitive advantages with advanced technology covered by patents.[35] Support for such a laboratory required a very different corporate perspective – one that recognized the possibilities of disruptive technical change and sought to direct and control that change for corporate purposes.

At about the same time that Dudley began his study of steel rails, the large and successful Carnegie Steel Company hired German Ph.D. chemist Ernst Fricke to analyze the process of steelmaking and to determine the preferred composition of ores. Until that time American iron and steel producers had been satisfied with traditional methods, seeing little reason to turn to science. This recalcitrance began to give way during the 1870s. With the introduction of the Bessemer–Kelly process of steelmaking at the time of the Civil War, analysis and control of raw materials became extremely important, so the acquisition of a trained chemist brought a significant advantage to Carnegie. Fricke found that some ores, generally considered of low quality and therefore cheaper, actually produced better iron and steel. He discovered that pig iron could be made at a lower cost by using fly ash and other waste products mixed with "inferior" ores. Carnegie soon regretted his tardiness in resorting to chemistry and noted in his autobiography: "What fools we had been! But then there was this consolation, we were not as great fools as our competitors." In order to keep up with Carnegie, his competitors also turned to chemistry. As a result the industry's efficiency, consistency, and product diversity improved dramatically over the next thirty years.[36]

Concern with science and engineering developed in several industries during the last third of the 19th century. For example, petroleum refiners looked to chemists for help in reducing unacceptably high proportions of sulfur in new supplies of midwestern crude oil. The electric communications and power industries hired mathematicians, physicists, and engineers to improve their increasingly extended and complex systems. The heavy chemicals and rubber companies likewise employed chemists, often as consultants, in an attempt to increase yields and to standardize products and processes. In almost all these cases, the problems were clear, the relationship of research to application close, and the results limited, though often commercially important.

Some companies, of course, were founded by scientists and engineers. Such firms usually depended on the knowledge and abilities of their scientist– and engineer–entrepreneurs to develop products, processes, and markets together.[37] Chemist William Nichols established an innovative acid-manufacturing firm in 1870; it became one of the first American chemical companies to introduce advanced methods of sulfuric acid production. Leo Baekeland, also a chemist–industrialist, invented and produced a number of important new plastics, including Bakelite. Mechanical engineer Frank Sprague had interests and expertise in electrical power. He established and directed the company that, during the late 1880s, built and installed the world's first successful electric street railway system.

In the field of electric power and traction a substantial list of people could be cited whose talents in experimentation, invention, and business led to the establishment of important new companies, including General Electric and Westinghouse. However, it is important to realize that while science, engineering, and technology were closely associated in the late-19th century electrical industry, the majority of electrical engineers did not attempt to advance understanding and technique but to apply known methodologies to the analysis of materials and operations and to the design of new installations. Significant advances came mainly from individuals fired by the spark of genius, such as Nicola Tesla and Charles P. Steinmetz, or from scientist- and engineer-entrepreneurs driven by the need to innovate – men like Charles van Depoele, Frank Sprague, and Charles Brush.[38] Only with the creation of large, technology-based corporations and their establishment of ongoing research programs would the advance of knowledge – combined with the development of new methodologies to make use of that knowledge – become a regular part of many scientists' and engineers' role in American industry.

American industry in the 19th century

So far, I have discussed American industry only in order to analyze its evolving relationship with science and engineering, but there were many other forces affecting it during the 19th century. We must carefully consider these forces and the changes that resulted from them in order to understand why and how American industrial enterprises were transformed from small in size, local in orientation, and usually short-term in duration early in the century to large, national, and often indefinitely long-term less than 100 years later. The two sections that follow describe the development of American industry during the 19th century, emphasizing the factors that brought about domination of the economy by large corporations. It was in those corporations, many of which sought long-term security and growth in technology-based markets, that the new type of industrial research programs first appeared.

During the early part of the 19th century, American business was composed mostly of small, locally oriented firms with limited interests and opportunities. The cost of entry into the majority of businesses remained low, and many failed. Single proprietorships and partnerships prevailed. It was not unusual for an individual to create and abandon a number of enterprises over the course of his career. In manufacturing establishments, owners often served as managers; as a result, owners and employees usually maintained close working relationships. Most manufacturers bought their raw materials from middlemen and sold their output to wholesalers, who took care of distribution in local or regional markets. Industrial operations in the antebellum years tended to be so small, and the business horizons of owners so limited, that few firms recognized the value of undertaking their own research efforts. Even those that did, like the Merrimack Manufacturing Company, usually established projects to accomplish narrowly defined goals, then disbanded the research groups when the goals had been achieved.

The introduction of stationary steam engines transformed American industry. The earliest manufacturing establishments had chosen sites along streams and rivers where they found adequate water power. This meant that factories were spread out in the countryside, so that it could be difficult for them to transport raw materials and finished products or to procure an adequate labor force. The development of industrial steam engines along with the mining of anthracite coal during the 1840s and 1850s began to make steam power readily available. This freed manufacturers from the tyranny of location, enabling them to site their mills so as to take advantage of transportation facilities, sources of raw materials, pools of available labor, and markets.[39] Many new business organizations situated their factories and mills in the growing cities, which were the foci of transportation networks and home to thousands of new immigrants seeking work. As a result, the nation's urban centers grew considerably, and the largest ones usually grew fastest. This development of urban centers and the dramatic increase in population during the 19th century created exciting marketing opportunities for business.[40]

The fast, reliable transportation facilities provided by the growing railroad system, combined with the high-speed telegraph communications networks of Western Union and other companies, gave businessmen new abilities to produce and sell more, since both the supply of raw materials and the market for sales encompassed wider areas. Whereas wagons, canals, and steamboats had been slow and weather-dependent – the Erie Canal, for example, froze solid about four months each year – the railroad ran year-round on published schedules. The railroad's much higher speeds meant that supply orders, sent long distances by telegraph, could be filled and delivered in days rather than weeks or months; and that perishable items like butchered meat could be shipped halfway across the continent to their ultimate destinations. As consumer of iron, steel, coal, lumber, lubricating oils, and other products on a vast scale, the railroad itself provided a significant stimulus to the American economy.

Railroads were actually the first "big business" in America, as almost everywhere else. In 1855, when it cost under $500,000 a year to operate the largest textile mills, the Pennsylvania and Erie Railroads had budgets of $2 million and $3 million, respectively. The high number of financial transactions and the far-flung nature of their complex operations led the larger railroads to regularize and bureaucratize their methods of administration. Trains needed to be routed, scheduled, and run full in order to hold down costs and maximize profits. Fares and fees had to be collected and accounted for. Thousands of suppliers, creditors, agents, and employees had to be paid. All these activities required the continued attention of a centralized organization, and the career manager – skilled in accounting, finance, and the management of operations – made his appearance in railroad administration.[41]

The number and complexity of industrial products increased dramatically in both Europe and America during the 19th century. Improved transportation and communication made possible large-scale national markets for such technically sophisticated products as electric motors and generators, firearms, sewing machines, reapers, and bicycles, as well as services like telegraphy and telephony. In every one of these cases, competing manufacturers turned to the advance of commercial technology to maintain or increase their market shares. Early in the century most industrial uses of science and engineering had been oriented toward enhancing efficiency and lowering costs; by the 1870s, however, it became commonplace to concentrate on improving products in order to gain competitive advantage and increase profit.[42]

Declining prices and rather severe economic cycles during the last third of the century made many businesses insecure. This led to new forms of organization. Competition, which appeared to work for the benefit of all during good times, brought numerous failures or near-failures during the economic downturns of the 1870s, 1880s, and 1890s. Following the lead of the railroads (whose overbuilding often led to "ruinous competition"), many industries formed cartels in an attempt to control output and to maintain prices. By 1895 this had taken place in textiles, iron and steel, petroleum, sugar refining, tobacco, lumber, anthracite coal, leather, liquor, glass, paper, gunpowder, and other industries. Such arrangements rarely worked well for long, however, so many companies chose to consolidate, at least in a legal sense. During the early 1880s John D. Rockefeller created a consortium of petroleum-refining companies, thus forming the nation's first large "trust," Standard Oil. The trust arrangement, in which a group of directors held controlling stock in several companies and administered the combination, provided a way around the common prohibition of one corporation's owning shares in another. When New Jersey passed a general incorporation law in 1889 that permitted one company to control others, the holding company quickly took the place of the trust, though the term "trust" remained in public use to describe any business organization that dominated an industry.

By the 1880s a number of companies had grown large and powerful by developing continuous-flow-process methods of production while exerting control over their own sources of supply and means of distribution and marketing.[43] As producers grew in size, they generally found that the costs and uncertainties of raw materials supply and the loss of sales due to dependence on wholesalers severely limited their operating efficiency and profitability. Large, innovative metals producers like Carnegie Steel therefore began to purchase and work their own ore fields, buy steamboats or even railroads to bring raw materials to their plants, and make special arrangements for distribution of their products. The Chicago meatpackers, anxious to develop large-volume sales in eastern cities, bought their own refrigerator cars for the railroads to haul, then built special depots to unload and distribute the meat. Rather than rely on salesmen who handled a number of companies' products and had no allegiance to theirs, the integrated producers hired and trained their own sales forces. Where appropriate, they followed up sales with service.

Operating such enterprises often proved to be more complicated than anticipated. Managers of the newly integrated firms soon realized that they had to eliminate some of the uncertainties inherent in Adam Smith's "invisible hand" of the marketplace, substituting for them the greater control and security of what historian Alfred Chandler later called the "visible hand" of management. To assure smooth, continuous manufacturing operations and to minimize costly inventory managers had to assimilate information from varied sources and locations, then coordinate raw materials supply, production, distribution, and marketing.[44] The level of complexity involved in running these businesses required that the authority, responsibility, and accountability of each manager and worker be clearly laid out and that several types and levels of managers work within a formal organizational structure. Yet each industry – and even each company – differed in significant ways, so the transition to this type of management system rarely came easily. In fact, several businesses that expanded and reorganized found themselves crushed under the weight of cumbersome management structures.[45]

The development of large business enterprises after the Civil War brought new levels of prosperity to Americans. At the same time it threatened some of the country's basic social and economic values. Between 1875 and 1900 both the number of manufacturing establishments and workers engaged in industry doubled, while the value of output tripled. Prices declined gradually but steadily over the three ten-year business cycles after 1870, largely as a result of the exploitation of new natural resources and the development of more efficient production technologies. Purchasing power increased for the average citizen, as businesses scrambled to maintain profits in a period of shrinking prices. Still, the growth of large corporations and "trusts" during the last third of the century aroused fear that opportunities were being closed off to small businessmen – that America was losing its character as the land of opportunity.[46]

The coming of "big business" brought a definite political reaction. By 1890 national sentiment had become so strongly opposed to the large combinations and their perceived domination of the marketplace that Congress passed the Sherman Antitrust

Act to limit cartel activity. A vague law, it prohibited "every contract... or conspiracy, in restraint of trade or commerce." However, court interpretations of the act during the 1890s only helped transform trust arrangements (which the courts considered to be illegal) into holding companies or other consolidated enterprises (which they did not).

The severely depressed economic conditions of the mid-1890s spurred first a populist revolt in the agrarian midwest and southwest, then an urban-based reform movement known as Progressivism. Both Populists and Progressives strongly opposed the emerging industrial and financial powers' growing control of the economy. Whereas Populists emphasized self-sufficiency and the decentralization of political and economic power, Progressives looked to a new group of professional "experts" who could, given the chance, rationalize both human and natural resources. Historian Robert Wiebe argues that the growing middle and upper-middle classes found prestige and security for themselves by professionalizing social programs previously undertaken by amateurs or politicians, or which had not been carried out at all.[47] This was clearly one of the sources for the appeal of Progressive solutions to contemporary problems.

In response to antitrust threats and economic forces, a wave of corporate mergers took place in the decade after 1895. Companies that joined together were less likely to encounter antitrust problems than those that attempted to control prices and output through cartels, so many of them sought consolidation. Finance of the railroads had helped to create a sophisticated national market for securities headed by several major brokerage "houses." Therefore, when expansion of the railroad system slowed considerably during the 1890s – first as a result and then as a further cause of economic contraction – funds became available to finance industrial mergers and consolidations. Mergers were facilitated by the great profits available to financiers and managers who arranged them. About 300 companies per year entered into mergers between 1895 and 1905, and much to the consternation of its foes, big business became bigger.[48] Concern grew that corporate giants would first crush competitors, then overcharge consumers for inferior wares: "trusts" had few incentives to rationalize production or improve products. Because of such sentiment, President Theodore Roosevelt invoked the Sherman Antitrust Act shortly after the turn of the century. In doing so, he broke up some of the more egregious offenders, but his efforts probably did more to placate an aroused population than to change business conditions in any fundamental way.

Some reformers and engineers believed that even the dominant firms might be made more efficient if scientific methods could be used to improve their operations. Frederick Taylor's principles of "Scientific Management," first developed and publicized in the late 1890s, were designed to increase the productivity of both capital and labor by reorganizing production processes along more efficient lines. Management secured the cooperation of laborers by rewarding those who accommodated themselves to Taylor's highly regimented system. Invoking the general principle of Scientific Management, Progressive reformers expected to make both industry and government run more efficiently.[49]

In this climate of reform and professionalization, American scientists found themselves perceived more than ever as rationalizers and innovators. The conception of science inherent in Scientific Management was that of a rational and disinterested activity which brought the methods of natural science and the content of social science to bear on industrial problems. Although the pure-science ideology had gained a certain foothold, most American scientists continued to think of science as an activity that included observation and codification, experiment, analysis, and application. With this outlook, and with the skills provided by their advanced studies, scientists and engineers appeared to have important places in rationalizing the production of society's goods and services. Columbia University physicist Robert S. Woodward expressed this sentiment in 1903 when he wrote in *Science* that "there never was a time when the talent, energy and enterprise of young [scientists] were so much in demand. . . . [What we need are] men who can study aright the mighty questions of industrial and social economy now confronting us."[50]

Of course, not all scientists shared this outlook, and some chose to remain aloof from social and industrial needs. However, many others – especially those from the generation that received Ph.D.s after 1890 – turned eagerly to the rewards offered by industry. Progressivism encouraged them to see their use of science for industrial purposes as contributing to the advancement of society.[51] Thus, as the 20th century began, a growing number of highly trained scientists were willing to consider working in American industry. Opinions in the scientific community differed as to the appropriateness of such employment, but social attitudes generally encouraged it.[52]

Science, technology, and industry at the turn of the century

The consolidations and mergers of the decade after 1895 produced a number of large, ambitious, technically oriented industrial corporations that dealt in national markets. Whatever advantage scientific and engineering research gave them could be exploited on a national scale. Sales and potential profits were substantial. The value of electrical manufactures, for example, rose from $19 million in 1889 to $335 million in 1914.[53] Because a large number of shareholders owned the corporations and a phalanx of managers ran them, the retirement or death of an individual rarely brought about dramatic change (which often happened with smaller, privately held firms). In fact as well as in law, they took on the character of corporate persons, concerned to maintain their own lives and to grow. Research became a vital activity for such companies. Product development formed a large part of their competitive strategy, and innovation by others often posed the greatest threat to their commercial position. As Willis Whitney, the first director of research for General Electric, commented, "Our research laboratory was a development of the idea that large industrial organizations have both an opportunity and a responsibility for their own life insurance. New discovery can provide it."[54]

A company could acquire "new discoveries" from outside scientists and inventors rather than develop its own, but that policy was dangerous. Important ideas and inventions might fall into the hands of competitors, or inventors and their backers might decide to become competitors themselves. Such a policy was also expensive: the more important or potentially disruptive an invention, the more likely it was that competitors would be interested in it, making its price higher. Either way, commercially important inventions in the hands of outsiders increased the costs of doing business and made large companies insecure.

The desire for corporate security led a number of American companies to consider supporting scientific and technical research on an ongoing basis. Their experiences with science sometimes reached well back into the 19th century, included work by both scientists and engineers, and strongly suggested that the content and methods of science and mathematics might help transform important commercial technologies. The quantity and quality of American scientific and engineering education had greatly increased during the last third of the 19th century,[55] and the combined science/engineering research programs at a number of universities were producing both the results and the types of researchers that these companies found attractive. The path to technical development and, ultimately, corporate security seemed to lie in the synthesis of scientific knowledge and methods with engineering know-how.

Important discoveries and new research programs in the physical sciences stimulated the development of industrial research by making scientists trained in some newly important areas especially useful to industry. European discoveries of radioactivity, X-rays, and electrons at the end of the 19th century aroused great interest and activity among scientists. Whereas research in the physical sciences had previously concentrated on chemical and spectral analysis, electromagnetism, and heat, the new century brought a shift of attention to the properties and actions of electrons and the composition of matter. These were areas of science that held great interest for industries concerned with the uses of electricity and the development of new materials. University courses on electrochemistry, X-rays, radioactivity, and the conduction of electricity through gases became commonplace in the better physical sciences curricula after 1900.[56] The available science was becoming attractive to industry during the first decade of the 20th century – and so were the available scientists.

Industrial research became a more desirable corporate investment as physical scientists advanced analytical methods and instruments by means of new research programs. The development of a framework for appropriately conceived theory in certain areas presented industry with opportunities for further, profitable work. In the case of research on vacuum tubes, for example, J. J. Thomson's work on electrical conduction through gases, O. W. Richardson's and Arthur Wehnelt's research on electron emissions from filaments, and J. E. Lilienfeld's examination of phenomena in vacuum prepared the way for the further advance of both knowledge and practice. Studies of electromagnetic waves by physicists like James Clerk Maxwell, Heinrich Hertz, and Oliver Heaviside laid the foundations for continuing research on the propagation and control of electric signals. French electrochemist Henri Moissan's development of a finely controlled high-temperature oven for the analysis of materials presented industry simultaneously with a useful analytical tool and with a means for modifying the properties of some commercially important substances.

Good business reasons also explain why the support of research laboratories began to appear worthwhile as the new century began. Establishing and maintaining labs were major expenses, but during most of the 19th century other investments were more promising. For corporations concerned with meeting competition in matters of service, price, and technical capabilities, research and development meant working toward straightforward technological goals. Investments centered on acquiring new plant or sources of supply, and on buying out competitors. Managers worked to prevent competition and to lower the costs of supply, production, distribution, and sales. Consequently their perspectives were usually limited to fairly short-term objectives.

Research necessarily competed with these other opportunities to invest; hence the final decision to institute a corporate laboratory rested on a comparison between the promise of research and the anticipated return from other alternatives. Research possibilities depended on the state of both technology and science, yet only as the 19th century drew to a close did technology become so sophisticated in a number of areas that the usual inventive and engineering development methods frequently proved inadequate. Although engineer-entrepreneurs such as Thomas Edison and Frank Sprague had made major contributions to industry, even they now began to find that the increasing complexity of technology required research into underlying principles. Those who, like Edison, could not or would not make the transition usually fell behind. In fact, industrial scientists abroad were taking advantage of recent advances in knowledge, and the products of European industry began to cause concern among American manufacturers.[57] Such threats from science raised the possibility that research might help usurp their traditional markets. This pushed American corporate managers and directors to consider establishing industrial research laboratories in order to control science and technology themselves.

At the same time, as the previous section has shown, the American business climate changed. The corporate consolidations of the 1890s and 1900s had established a number of large technology-based companies. Several years after merging, many of them were financially and organizationally stable – both of which were necessary to permit industrial managers to look beyond immediate needs and to consider establishing industrial research.[58] As investments, industrial research laboratories were likely to pay back their initial costs over periods exceeding normal business cycles. Unlike their 19th-century precursors, most postconsolidation firms took a long-range view of business. Only when they became committed to surviving in the long term – over the course of numerous cycles – were they willing to make investments in long-term research and development.

The passage of the Sherman Antitrust Act in 1890, and its more vigorous enforcement after the turn of the century threatened traditional methods of dealing with competitors. Because of the new law, large and powerful companies had greater difficulty in driving smaller ones out of business by localized price cutting, closing off their avenues to credit, or by other questionable means. As a result, big corporations sometimes saw their markets successfully invaded by smaller, more aggressive firms. Industrial research could provide a defense.

Because it gave large corporations new products, patent rights, and other advantages, industrial research promised protection of primary markets through means acceptable under the law. Development of new product lines and their shielding from competition through the legal monopoly conferred by research-generated patents also enabled large firms to control lucrative new market areas. Industrial research could thus help provide corporate security by opening and protecting avenues of growth.

Many factors influenced the decisions to undertake ongoing research programs in American industry. At a time when the content and methods of science made major advances in technology possible, the technological dependency of several large, integrated corporations meant that the establishment and support of research laboratories were reasonable investments. The broader vision resulting from commitment to long-term survival and growth, as well as the closing off of traditional means of competition, directed corporate leaders toward industrial research. The Progressive environment, in which both scientists and industrialists looked more favorably on each others' endeavors, further facilitated such a step. Decisions in favor of establishing institutionalized research efforts were made easier because many industrial leaders were themselves technical men, and because their companies usually supported research and development in several forms.[59] In addition, the precedent of industrial research had already been set in Germany. During the last third of the 19th century, a number of technology-based companies in the chemical, electrical, and pharmaceutical industries had established research labs, often in conjunction with universities and technical schools. Advances in organic chemistry led firms like Bayer, Badische Aniline- und Soda-Fabrik (BASF), and Agfa to support laboratories which developed anilin-based dyes for the highly competitive international market. By the 1880s the commercial successes of such firms rested predominantly on the results that issued from their labs. This was quite clear to all would-be competitors, including the Americans.[60] Several German electrical manufacturers also established laboratories, and the results issuing from them began to threaten American markets late in the century.

There is one other important reason why industrial research took root in the United States at this time. Stated simply, it is that research made *more* research imperative. A number of pioneering efforts had opened new fields or made major advances in established ones, demonstrating what economist Joseph Schumpeter referred to as the "creative destruction" wrought by advancing commercial technologies.[61] Once the pioneering work had been done, the climate changed. Even the companies that had initiated research could then ill afford complacency, so many of them decided to establish ongoing research efforts, often based on the types of studies long associated with science.

The two companies considered in the remaining chapters were among the first to undertake industrial research and to make major changes in the way they approached the advance of science and technology. An analysis of their reasons for pursuing research will make clear how the changing conditions in science, technology, and business prompted such corporate innovations. Consideration of the industrial research process itself will later reveal how commercial and organizational factors influenced the development of this new type of American research institution.

3

The Establishment and Early Growth of General Electric

Introduction

GE's industrial research laboratory first sprang from and then effected important changes in the company's technological and business environment. To comprehend both why GE decided to establish the laboratory and what differences in the company's capabilities and strategies resulted, it is important to understand the origins and operational bases of the company and of the American electrical industry itself. This chapter therefore analyzes the early history of GE and its competitors, beginning with the seminal work of Thomas Edison.

Thomas Edison – Combining science, technology, and business

During the last three decades of the 19th century, a number of individuals and corporations built the American electrical industry. First the Brush Electric Company developed and marketed arc-lighting systems during the 1870s.[1] Then Thomas Edison's invention of the high-resistance incandescent lamp in 1879 and his subsequent development of a complete system for the generation and distribution of electric power initiated rapid growth in the industry. Edison demonstrated the practicality of his system by opening a central power station on September 4, 1882 in lower Manhattan. It initially had fifty-nine customers, including the prominent banking house of Drexel, Morgan and Company, and the offices of the *New York Times*.

Edison influenced American industry in a number of ways. His use of team research at his laboratories in Menlo Park and, later, in West Orange, New Jersey, alerted businessmen to the potential value of science in general and to the profit-generating possibilities of coordinated work by scientists and engineers in particular. Edison's entrepreneurial activities drew financiers into the business of funding research, and his success in a number of ventures demonstrated that there was money to be made in the development and control of advanced technologies.

Born in Milan, Ohio, in 1847, Edison left school at an early age and spent his teen years as an itinerant telegrapher. He settled briefly in Boston in 1868, where he worked in the community of electrical inventors that, a few years later, nurtured Alexander Graham Bell. Edison's genius lay in his ability to conceptualize electromechanical systems; combined with his knowledge of telegraphy, it enabled him to design new ways of transmitting and recording messages. Unable to make any money from these inventions in Boston, in 1869 he went to New York, where he soon received inventive assignments from the powerful Western Union Company. Western Union intended to gain patent control of automatic and multiplex telegraphy in order to prevent smaller competitors from threatening its dominant position in the telegraph industry. Edison developed important advances relating to the duplex, quadruplex, automatic, and printing telegraphs – for which the company paid him quite well.[2] He soon went into business manufacturing telegraph equipment for Western Union, but gave most of his attention to further experiments at his Newark, New Jersey, factory.

At Newark, Edison gathered around him the skilled machinists and fellow inventors who would become the core group for his later research efforts. In 1876, using the profits from his telegraph work, Edison built a laboratory for himself and his staff in rural Menlo Park, New Jersey, about twenty miles south of Newark, situated on the train line between Philadelphia and New York.

Edison's Menlo Park installation has been called the first American industrial research laboratory, though in the sense that the term is used in this book, it was not. At Menlo Park, Edison expected to regularize invention, to turn out "a minor invention every ten days and a big thing every six months or so."[3] The number and importance of patents he received indicates that he succeeded. Between 1876 and 1879 Edison developed several advanced telegraph instruments and invented the carbon-button telephone transmitter as well as the chalk-drum telephone receiver (intended to enable Western Union to circumvent Bell's magnetic-receiver patent). At this time he conceived the phonograph, his most original invention. It was the first means ever for recording sound. Edison and his staff also developed the electric pen (a precursor to the mimeograph) and made numerous other minor inventions, from electric horse clippers and the aurophone (for hearing at a distance) to the "perpetual" cigar.[4] In a number of cases, like those of the phonograph and electric pen, Edison established his own companies to make and sell the products, then provided additional inventions and patents to keep them ahead of competitors.

In 1878 Edison became interested in the possibilities of incandescent electric lighting. For the first time he made full use of the research team and laboratory facilities he had been building since the early 1870s. The electric light presented a challenge Edison had not faced before. To succeed from both technical and economic perspectives, he had to develop, promote, and sell an entire *system* – not just a lamp, but an economically viable means of generating, distributing, consuming, and measuring electric power. Because such a project would be so large, he had to secure outside funding.

As Edison embarked on the electric-light project he expanded his Menlo Park facilities, adding a machine shop and an office. He purchased additional equipment, and acquired hundreds of scientific and technical books and journals. By late 1879 Menlo Park was probably the best-equipped electrical laboratory in the world. There Edison – soon lionized as the world's greatest inventor – directed a well-organized team effort that produced a working lamp in one year and an entire commercial electric direct-current (DC) system in just four.

Edison directed his work to the market. Large-scale use of gas lighting during the 1860s and 1870s had created a public expectation of inexpensive and easily controlled interior illumination. Edison carefully calculated that his electric system could profitably supply a superior light at lower cost. His technical fecundity and the practicality of his approach impressed a number of financiers, who advanced over $200,000 for the venture, expecting to make profits on the sale of patent rights when the system demonstrated its potential. By the time that he had completed work on his Pearl Street generating station in Manhattan, Edison had expended another several hundred thousand dollars of his backers' money, though there never seemed to be enough for all the work to be done.[5]

Edison's great advantage over inventor rivals rested on his ability to simultaneously pursue and manage several different types of activities within a highly complex innovative process. As Thomas

Hughes points out, Edison usually accomplished what he set out to do because he was neither ahead of nor behind his times – he made certain that his efforts were in harmony with both the scientific and technological state of the arts and the conditions of business.[6] Though American myths about Edison portray him as the cut-and-try inventor with little concern for science, he actually made very good use of both historic and contemporary scientific literature in order to understand the principles of his work. He was, moreover, careful to have on his staff men trained in science and mathematics. In creating an economical electric light and power system, he brought to the attention of businessmen the potential value and cost-effectiveness of organized research and development. Edison appreciated the importance of good public relations and of gaining support from those people powerful enough to smooth the way for his grand schemes. A master at manipulating reporters, he used the press to create public anticipation for his forthcoming inventions and to maintain the spirits of his investors who, Edison wryly noted, "naturally wanted to get rich faster than the nature of things permitted."[7] In some ways, Edison's approach to research, development, and innovation foreshadowed the early policies of the industrial research laboratories that would soon follow his pathbreaking work.

Early development of the electrical industry

To build the equipment for his Pearl Street station and for the other central power stations he expected to follow soon, Edison established a number of manufacturing companies. The Edison Machine Works made dynamos; the Electric Tube Company manufactured underground conduits; the Edison Shafting Company fabricated equipment for the power-plant drives; the Edison Lamp Works made incandescent lamps; and Bergmann and Company, run by Edison's former master machinist, Sigmund Bergmann, produced a variety of switches, junction boxes, lamp fixtures, and all the minor but necessary appurtenances of the system.

In 1883 Edison turned his attentions to the dissemination of electric light and power. "I'm going to be a business man," he declared. "I'm a regular contractor now for electric lighting plants, and I'm going to take a long vacation in the matter of invention."[8] For the next four years, he proved almost as good as his word. Working out of New York, Edison traveled around the country, helping with the installation of central power stations and smaller, "isolated" plants. He raised capital to manufacture equipment for sale to local promoters, who usually paid partially in cash and partially in the securities of their new ventures. By mid-1886, the Edison companies had installed 56 central power stations with a capacity of 150,000 lamps. A year and a half later, the number of stations had climbed to 121 and the lamp capacity to 325,000.[9]

Edison did not long remain alone in the field. The Thomson–Houston Electric Company (T–H) of Lynn, Massachusetts, founded in 1883 to capitalize on the arc-lighting patents of teacher-inventors Elihu Thomson and Edwin Houston, began building and selling electric lighting systems. In addition, George Westinghouse, manufacturer of air brakes and other railroad equipment in Pittsburgh, entered the electrical field in 1886 with an alternating-current (AC) system based on the transformer patents of the Frenchman Lucien Gaulard and the Briton John Gibbs. Thomson–Houston and Westinghouse supplied entire systems, including the lamps themselves, having acquired rights to the patent applications of Hiram Maxim and William Sawyer, both of whom claimed precedence over Edison on the invention of the incandescent electric light.

When, in 1888, Westinghouse developed a means of metering AC and acquired rights to immigrant inventor Nikola Tesla's AC motor, his system posed a serious threat to the Edison interests. AC had the distinct advantage that it could be transmitted over long distances at high voltage with considerably less power loss than DC. AC systems used transformers to lower the transmission voltages for local use.[10] A "war of the currents" ensued, during which Edison attempted to convince the public that AC posed serious dangers to life and limb (which, under certain circumstances, it did).[11] A dramatic increase in the price of copper for wires in 1888, along with decisions to use Westinghouse's AC system by the Chicago World's Fair and by the gigantic Niagara Falls hydroelectric power project in 1893, spelled the beginning of the end for DC central power. Unable to deal with the greater complexities of AC, Edison steadfastly maintained his personal commitment to DC and was ultimately forced from the field.

Promoter Henry Villard had been involved in helping Edison finance his ventures since the early 1880s, and in 1889 he reorganized Edison's electric light and power interests into a single corporate entity. Villard brought the disparate organizations together as the Edison General Electric Company (EGE), capitalizing it at $12 million. This permitted Edison to remove himself from the management of the electrical business and to devote his efforts more fully to his first love, inventing. EGE very quickly acquired the Sprague Electric Railway and Motor Company, which had recently installed the world's first successful street railway system in Richmond, Virginia.

Meanwhile, Thomson–Houston, under the technical leadership of Elihu Thomson and the aggressive management of former shoe-manufacturing executive Charles Coffin, developed its own AC capabilities and made a very strong showing in the electric power field. At the beginning of 1887, 171 systems of T–H equipment were in operation, powering 21,000 arc lamps. By the time that EGE took form in 1889, T–H had installed 419 systems with 51,000 lamps. Between 1883 and 1888, T–H's annual volume of business grew from $300,000 to $3.5 million, and the company acquired a number of smaller competitors who held important patents on electric generation, distribution, and use.[12]

Indeed, T–H gained such a strong patent position that EGE could not manufacture state-of-the-art traction, lighting, or power equipment without fear of infringement suits or injunctions. Of course, T–H faced the same threat from EGE. As EGE management contemplated adopting AC in the early 1890s, it realized that an agreement with T–H or Westinghouse would be necessary. Westinghouse had been a serious antagonist to the EGE interests, but relations between EGE and T–H remained reasonably cordial, so EGE president Henry Villard approached Charles Coffin.

With the exception of electric traction, the two rivals' capabilities and interests seemed to be complementary: EGE in DC, T–H in AC; EGE in incandescent lamps, T–H largely in arcs; EGE with extensive manufacturing facilities, T–H with a strong sales organization and an aggressive, efficient management. In traction, their combined position would be unassailable. The two companies were actually of equivalent size, both reporting gross incomes of between $10 and $11 million in 1891 – though EGE had 6,000 employees to T–H's 4,000. An agreement assigning various patent rights to each company might provoke antitrust action. A merger made sense.

In 1891 the two firms entered into negotiations. Financier J. P. Morgan, representing EGE, played a major role in the proposed refinancing and reorganization, a service for which he was very well compensated. The companies signed a merger agreement the following April, and on June 1, 1892, the new General Electric Company (GE) began operations. His name absent from the consolidated company, Edison soon removed himself entirely from the business.

General Electric during the 1890s

Thomson–Houston men comprised almost the entire upper-level management of the new General Electric Company, so it is not unreasonable to suggest that the smaller T–H actually absorbed EGE. Charles Coffin became GE's first president, holding that office until he "retired" in 1913 to become chairman of the board. However, Coffin did not have the same autonomy at GE that he had enjoyed as president of T–H. The board of directors, dominated by Morgan banking interests, established an executive committee to keep rein on the president. There were also several oversight committees, composed of operating officers from the various divisions of the company, which passed judgment on all important management decisions.

President Coffin merged the organizations of EGE and T–H into a unified structure. He liquidated the subsidiaries of each company, integrating them fully into GE. When finished, GE's management structure resembled that of a large railroad, with order imposed from the top. It had a central corporate office composed of the president and the vice-presidents in charge of major functional areas, each with a sizable staff. One vice-president took charge of sales, another handled the financial department (which included accounting for both internal and external affairs, collections, and credit), and a third oversaw manufacturing and engineering. The corporate office also included a patent department staffed by attorneys, and a separate legal department to handle other legal affairs. A public relations department to publicize developments both within the company and within the industry was soon added.[13]

The new GE bureaucracy was complex and slow-moving. Just as with many railroads, outside financial interests controlled the executive committee of the board of directors. The executive committee played a central role in setting corporate policy, assisted by large financial and advisory staffs. Each vice-president chaired a committee made up of the major functional officers under him. These committees met monthly to consider topics such as product pricing, customers' needs and concerns, standardization, and in-

Plate 2. Charles A. Coffin. Courtesy of the General Electric Company.

ternal operating problems. They had the right to refuse approval of major decisions affecting their areas of operation.[14] It is important to realize that this rigid structure of communication and oversight served to limit entrepreneurial activity within the company by making change slow and difficult. Because internal vested interests had veto power over potential changes in company products and processes, GE was inherently conservative in its approach to innovation. The management scheme that served the railroads well – with their complicated but rather narrow range of basic activities – did not promote the innovation and diversification a company would need to remain competitive in a burgeoning new industry like electric lighting and power.

As consolidation proceeded, President Coffin transferred GE's production to those plants with the greatest capacities and efficiencies for particular items. EGE's Schenectady, New York installation manufactured nonstandard machinery such as large generators and motors, the EGE plant at Harrison, New Jersey produced all of the company's incandescent electric lamps, and the T–H plant at Lynn, Massachusetts made arc lights along with a variety of smaller standard machinery such as motors and electric meters.

Because its production and sales dominated the industry, General Electric came to be known as the "Electric Trust" by both competitors and the public. This was true even though total sales and profits fell after the merger.[15] The Panic of 1893 quickly plunged the country into economic depression, and GE's business fell off sharply. The nationwide shortage of cash made collection of accounts extremely difficult; before long, GE had to borrow money at high rates of interest just to meet its weekly payroll. Even worse, bank notes of local power companies, which EGE and T–H had endorsed in order to receive partial payment for the equipment they sold, became the immediate responsibility of GE when those companies were forced into default.

GE faced a very serious cash balance problem that directly threatened its solvency. Coffin decided that the only way to keep GE afloat was to sell off many of the securities that EGE and T–H had accepted from the local power companies, even though this meant taking tremendous losses against their par values. In 1894 GE divested itself of securities supposed to be worth approximately $12 million, for which it received $4 million in cash. This moved carried the firm through its financial crisis. Sales for 1894 fell to less than $13 million, with profits of only $500,000, and business remained at that level for the next three years. Between the time of its formation in 1892 and the low point of its corporate fortunes in 1895, GE stock dropped in value from $115 to $30 per share.[16] Because most of GE's production at this time represented capital investment to its customers, poor business conditions – during which companies rarely purchased equipment – meant a severe cutback in GE's sales.

Coffin had learned a painful lesson. He never again permitted GE to get into a precarious financial position. Henceforth he appraised all assets at their lowest possible values for accounting purposes and made certain that the company always had a substantial cushion of cash on hand. He also became very cautious in matters of credit, granting even the best customers only short-term conditions on sales, with cash given preferential terms. The experience of shepherding a weak GE through the Panic of 1893 left Coffin a very conservative businessman. When he had run T–H, he had been willing to take substantial risks to stimulate the growth of the company and the industry, but as president of GE he exercised such extreme caution in the expansion of business that he often disconcerted the other officers. As a result GE produced far fewer innovations between 1892 and 1900 than had EGE or T–H individually in the years before the merger; it was also less innovative than many of its smaller competitors. Even as the economy picked up and GE sales rose to $16 million in 1898, $22 million in 1899, and $29 million in 1900, with concomitant increases in profits, President Coffin maintained his strongly conservative outlook.[17]

Because of this attitude, GE began entering into licensing and patent-pooling arrangements with its competitors. Just before the 1892 merger, the U.S. Circuit Court of Appeals had upheld Edison's patent on the incandescent lamp against the claims of Maxim, Sawyer, and others. This decision gave the new GE company the right to shut down its incandescent lighting competitors from 1892 until Edison's patent ran out in 1894.[18] GE pursued such closures half-heartedly, since so little time remained until the expiration of the patent. In 1894 it was faced with stiff competition from its great rival, Westinghouse, and from over thirty smaller companies. To gain a cost advantage, the superintendent of GE's Harrison Lamp Works collaborated with a group of his engineers to mechanize the production of electric lamps. Their accomplishments, along with certain economies of scale, permitted GE to maintain a price advantage over most of its competitors, so that it retained about 50% of the market. Given the company's outlook, including its conservative approach to research, invention, and innovation, the reasonable course was to improve lamp making and lower costs rather than attempt to effect significant advances in the incandescent lamp itself.

Uncomfortable with the competitive situation and concerned about the costs and uncertainties of litigation, GE instigated an agreement with sixteen other producers in late 1896 that fixed prices and alloted a share of the business to each company. Because GE's licensees – mostly local electric light and power companies – insisted that granting further licenses under company lamp patents violated their contracts, the agreement among the manufacturers was based on a number of improvement patents held by Westinghouse. Thus all producers, including GE, paid a small royalty to the Pittsburgh manufacturer. Under the agreement GE received 50% of the market, Westinghouse about 15%, and the others divided the remaining 35%.[19] Since compliance with the agreement depended on the use of nonessential patents, however, GE and Westinghouse could easily withdraw from it if they saw fit.

During the mid-1890s, when business was slow because of the country's economic condition, GE and Westinghouse came into conflict in many areas besides incandescent lighting. Both companies had rights to hundreds of electrical patents, posing frequent threats to each other. For example, Westinghouse's patent on the polyphase AC motor and GE's on the street railway trolley (electrical pickup) seemed to bar the other company from producing up-to-date equipment in fields important to both. By 1896 over 300 patent infringement suits were pending between the two. It became clear that if they wanted to control the electrical industry between them, they would have to work out some form of accommodation; otherwise, smaller and more aggressive companies would be likely to grab substantial shares of the market while the two large corporations held each other in check. After negotiations extending over several months, GE and Westinghouse reached an agreement in March 1896 whereby each granted manufacturing licenses to the other under all of its patents except those relating to electric lighting. The negotiators agreed that GE's patents represented five-eighths of the total patent value and Westinghouse's, three-eighths. If the value of manufactures covered by the patents did not conform to this 5:3 ratio, the company exceeding its share was to pay royalties to the other. The agreement clearly strengthened the positions of GE and Westinghouse relative to smaller firms, yet left room for competition between the giants, since the royalty rates were set below likely profitability.[20]

This agreement, combined with the incandescent lighting arrangement between GE, Westinghouse, and the smaller manufacturers signed at about the same time, stabilized the electrical industry. In electric lighting, a company optimized its position by reducing costs of production and distribution, not by making small improvements in the electric lamp that would benefit customers and that might, under other circumstances, bring it competitive advantage. Yet any major departure in electric lighting technology did present a threat, for a company could reasonably forego the improvement patents on which the agreement was based if it had control of a significant new technology. The patent-pooling arrangement between GE and Westinghouse, by covering all common commercial technologies except lighting, removed the stimulus for both companies to make major improvements in electrical technology because the main competitor of each would have the right to share them. This changed the nature of competition to that of providing the best equipment designs for particular installations and to giving that equipment the greatest perceived reliability and the lowest price.

Of course, as many old-time engineers of that era might have suggested, most of the major improvements had been made by then anyway. Wouldn't copper remain the best material for transmission lines and motor windings? Wouldn't motor brushes and lamp filaments always be made of carbon? Wasn't iron the best magnetic material? During the 1890s, these apparent truths led to a certain sense of complacency among American electrical manufacturers. Only when major technical advances from abroad threatened their commercial positions did they begin to realize that research into fundamental questions of materials and methods would be necessary.

In 1894 GE made the first major installation of electric motors in a factory environment, though not because the company's top management actively sought new areas to enter. The pressure to innovate came from the field. GE salesman Sidney Paine had convinced the owners of a textile mill under construction in Columbia, South Carolina that their power needs could be best served by the use of electric motors. He proposed an AC system with seventeen sixty-five-horsepower motors, all mounted on the mill ceiling where they would be out of the way of machinery and workmen on the floor. He further proposed that GE construct a hydroelectric station at a nearby river to transmit the power required for mill operations.

Persuading the mill owners to buy this GE system was only the first of Paine's sales jobs; he then had to convince GE to make it. Paine's proposal initially went before the sales committee. The sales supervisors saw an entire new field of opportunity being opened to them, so they approved. However, the executive committee of the board, with President Coffin in accord, hesitated. "We have never yet manufactured an ac motor larger than ten horse power and have never sold any larger than five horse power," Coffin wrote to Paine.[21] He suggested using DC, even though AC motors were clearly preferable for this installation because of their constant speed operation (a DC motor changed speed with fluctuations in line voltage), and because they did not spark, which could be disastrous in the fiber-filled mill air. Paine then appealed to E. W. Rice, vice-president in charge of manufacturing and engineering. Former assistant to company founder Elihu Thomson and one of the most technically aggressive managers at GE, Rice convinced Coffin and the executive committee that the proposed installation was not only feasible but that its successful completion would open up a major new line of business for the company. In this instance Rice saved Coffin and the GE committee system from committing a serious mistake due to their inherent conservatism. Largely as a result of this pioneering work, GE dominated the electrification of American industry during the early 20th century and helped bring about major productivity increases in almost all its factory installations.[22]

During the 1890s, GE and Westinghouse competed strongly in matters relating to street railways. Both developed systems of electric transmission and pickup for moving trolley cars, but they put their greatest efforts into the design and production of electric motors for street railway use. Westinghouse entered the field in 1890, when it introduced a single-reduction-gear motor, known as the No. 3. In 1893 GE responded to Westinghouse's substantial erosion of its business by marketing a system based on a motor similar in many ways to the Westinghouse No. 3, but which, at 1,450 pounds, weighed about half as much, was totally enclosed, and completely waterproof. During the first year of production, GE sold over 3,000 of them. In their competitive battle, each company came out with a number of improvements, and together they dominated the market for street railway motors. GE sold about 6,000 motors per year compared with Westinghouse's 2,500 to the rapidly expanding urban and interurban transit systems of the era.[23]

GE became involved in producing electric motors for railroad switching locomotives and for locomotives used to haul trains through long tunnels (like the Baltimore tunnel on the New York-to-Washington main-line railroad), where the exhaust smoke from steam power created severe problems. In 1896 GE installed electric

Plate 3. Edwin W. Rice. Courtesy of the General Electric Company.

trains on the Brooklyn Bridge to replace the steam locomotives that had been in service since the bridge opened in 1883. During the late 1890s it also began supplying motors, cars, and electric controllers for elevated urban railways after engineer-entrepreneur Frank Sprague had demonstrated the feasibility of using a multiple-unit system of control. Each such elevated-railway car had its own drive motors, and the entire train could be run by a single engineer using Sprague's control device. Unfortunately, GE's system was very similar to Sprague's, and Sprague sued for patent infringement. In order to dominate the lucrative elevated-railway business, GE bought him out in 1902, paying Sprague over $1 million for his company and controller.

In electric power, GE produced both AC and DC systems, marketing its equipment to local power companies around the country. By the end of 1896 it had sold more than 9,000 generators with a total capacity of about 400,000 horsepower. After the initial contract awards at Niagara Falls went to Westinghouse, GE was able to obtain orders for a substantial portion of the hydroelectric power equipment used there. First it built the transformers and transmission line to Buffalo, New York, then it designed and constructed generating systems at the Falls. By 1905, when there were twenty-one generators in operation, GE had supplied eleven of them.[24]

With business and profits picking up substantially in the late 1890s, GE purchased several smaller competitors. One, the Fort Wayne Electric Company, was already partially owned by GE through an earlier T–H acquisition. More importantly, in 1900 GE bought out the new American subsidiary of the powerful and innovative German electrical firm Siemens and Halske. This eliminated a potential source of serious competition. In 1903 it acquired valuable transformer patents when it purchased the Stanley Electric Manufacturing Company. With these and other acquisitions, combined with the patent-pooling and market-sharing agreements made during the 1890s, GE management placed itself in a position to dominate the American electrical industry.

At this same time, GE became involved in the development of steam turbines for use in electric power generation. In principle, turbines had much greater efficiency than the large reciprocating engines then in use. With far fewer moving parts, they also required less maintenance, and their higher power-to-weight ratios promised more compact installations. In 1895 GE turned down the chance to buy the patent rights to the steam turbine of the Englishman C. A. Parsons because its engineers reported inherent design difficulties. However, American inventor Charles Curtis approached GE in 1896 with a more promising concept and a proposal that the company provide facilities and manpower for his research in return for rights to buy the patents. GE agreed. Development went more slowly than envisioned, and only because E. W. Rice championed the project did Coffin and the executive committee permit work to continue. They took responsibility away from Curtis, however, and gave it to William Emmet, a GE engineer who had been very effective in his work on AC machinery but who had no experience with turbines. Under Emmet's administration, engineers designed and built a 500-kilowatt turbine by 1901, quickly following it with a 1,500-kilowatt unit. In 1903 GE installed the first commercial steam turbine. Made for Chicago Commonwealth Edison and rated at 5,000 kilowatts, it produced far more power than any steam turbine previously built. It was also very efficient. Whereas in 1900 Commonwealth Edison had used an average of almost seven pounds of coal to generate each kilowatt of power, the turbine required less than three for the same yield. GE licensed turbine patent rights to the large German electrical firm Allgemeine Elektrizitäts-Gesellshaft, agreeing to exchange information with it as turbine development continued.[25]

This project reveals much about research, development, and innovation at GE during the 1890s. When it came to major deviation from established product lines, the company frequently waited for outside developments to establish the direction and provide the stimulus.[26] Although aware of the potential of steam turbines, GE hesitated to undertake a development project until an outsider approached the company with a promising proposal. The project that ensued was directed by an inventor and a practical engineer – and the engineer initially knew little about turbines. Together they experimented with turbines, working to gain an understanding of how steam traveled through the various stages of expansion within the turbine housing. Then they built a number of test designs with the aid of machinists and mechanics. The engineer in charge, William Emmet, described his approach to research and development well when he commented, "There is only one sure way to get at the exact knowledge needed for new undertakings, namely, experimentation." His experimentation involved little resort to theory and very limited use of mathematics.[27]

Engineers at GE were organized into groups located at the company's installations. Sections of each group took responsibility for different production operations. The engineers worked to improve designs of company products and to implement changes in manufacturing processes. At GE's largest and most sophisticated manufacturing facility, in Schenectady, New York, a separate group of engineers known as the Works Laboratory performed functions similar to Charles Dudley's laboratory at the Pennsylvania Railroad, testing materials supplied to the company and occasionally

Plate 4. GE Standardizing Laboratory, c.1896. Courtesy of General Electric Research and Development Center.

developing improved composition specifications for items like electrical insulation and magnetic steel.[28]

In 1896 GE established the Standardizing Laboratory at Schenectady for the purpose of cleaning, repairing, and calibrating electrical measuring instruments. At a time when many electrical experimenters still made crude, inexact measurements, E. W. Rice and the GE engineering management realized that engineers needed to have confidence in their instruments' readings. The laboratory also established company-wide values for important measurements such as the ohm, a unit of electrical resistance which had not yet been standardized. The lab had its own building, isolated from the noise and vibration at the main works and constructed entirely of nonmagnetic materials. Begun with a staff of one in 1896, the Standardizing Laboratory employed sixteen people by 1900, an indication of how important its functions had become.[29]

The most important research organization at GE during the 1890s was the Calculating Department, headed by the electrical engineering genius, Charles P. Steinmetz. Steinmetz arrived in America in 1889 with advanced training in mathematics and engineering. Two brilliant papers on magnetic hysteresis presented before the American Institute of Electrical Engineers (AIEE) in 1893, as well as highly innovative work for a New York electrical manufacturer, brought him to the attention of GE engineers. When GE bought the company in 1893 – some said in order to acquire Steinmetz – he was asked to join the Calculating Department. During his first year at GE, Steinmetz developed a powerful method of complex-numbers algebra for the analysis of AC circuits, which he presented to a very enthusiastic audience at the International Electrical Congress in Chicago.[30] He taught this method to the first generation of GE engineers, greatly advancing their capability to design complicated and innovative AC systems. Steinmetz excelled at bringing the theories of electrophysics to bear on problems in engineering design. Using knowledge derived from the work of scientists like Ohm, Faraday, Maxwell, and Rowland, Steinmetz worked out formulas that related electric motor performance to such complex variables as winding resistance, exciting admittance, and leakage reactance. However, because of what he called "commercial interests," Steinmetz was not able to publish all of his results.[31] Yet his work proved so outstanding and his rise to prominence so rapid that the AIEE elected Steinmetz president in 1901, at the age of thirty-six.

As head of the Calculating Department, Steinmetz took charge of the group that designed GE's new alternators (AC dynamos), motors, transformers, and transmission systems. His engineers used many of Steinmetz's concepts and design methodologies. They ran experiments either in the Standardizing Laboratory or in an area at the Schenectady Works set up with special experimental and measurement apparatus, known as the Testing Room. Largely through their efforts, GE's capabilities in AC power improved significantly during the mid-1890s. Steinmetz himself also worked on developing new products for the company. The high-efficiency, magnetite-arc lamp, for example, absorbed much of his interest during the late 1890s.

For technological developments GE considered vital to its commercial interests but that lay beyond the range of the Calculating Department or the other engineering groups, outside inventors and consultants were often hired. In doing this GE followed the *modus operandi* of George Westinghouse, who had hired immigrant inventor Nikola Tesla during the late 1880s to develop an AC

Plate 5. Charles P. Steinmetz in his laboratory, c.1900. Photograph courtesy of Schenectady County Historical Society.

(induction) motor and had provided funds for inventor William Stanley to establish a laboratory where he could advance transformer design. Both men left Westinghouse's employ after brief but successful experiences. During the mid-1890s, GE hired inventor Charles Bradley to bring his patents and expertise to help develop a way to efficiently transform AC to DC. As a result of Bradley's work, GE was able to produce the "rotary converter." Because Westinghouse held an important edge in electric power through its ownership of rights to the Tesla AC motor, GE hired Swedish engineer Ernst Danielsen and electrical engineer–physicist Louis Bell (trained under Rowland at Johns Hopkins) to design an AC motor that circumvented Tesla's patent. They succeeded, thereby demonstrating the value of their talents for corporate invention; yet neither remained in the employ of the company for long.[32]

As GE's approach to these research-and-development projects demonstrates, the company had very little concern with *continuity* of research, at least when work was oriented toward *discontinuity* in the technology involved. Coffin and Rice believed that major technological departures generally came from individuals who did not work well in the engineering environment of large corporations. For these advances they depended on the temporary services of outside inventors and scientist–engineers; or, like their competitors, they attempted to buy patent rights to the most important new electrical inventions from all over the world. In 1898, for example, they dispatched lamp works superintendent John Howell to Italy to purchase inventor Arturo Malignani's patent rights for a means to improve the vacuum in incandescent bulbs. GE used these patent rights to close down several bothersome competitors.[33]

As the 19th century drew to a close, GE dominated the American electrical industry, but the technological basis for its continued success was by no means assured. Almost all of the patents on which the electrical industry was built would expire by the turn of the century, opening the way to new competition in electric lighting and power. Advances no longer came as easily, in part because the technology had grown more sophisticated, in part because much of the knowledge of electrical phenomena developed by scientists like Faraday and Maxwell had already been used extensively. Although patent-pooling arrangements with a number of smaller American companies temporarily stabilized the electrical industry, European scientist–inventors and European electrical companies were beginning to make significant technological advances that directly threatened GE's American markets. At the base of GE's dilemma lay its approach to research and development. Content to make measured advances in established directions, the company could expect to maintain its technological edge only so long as the basic forms of electrical technology remained the same. Yet advances in science and changes in the relationship of science to industry, especially in Germany, made this most unlikely. GE might attempt to purchase threatening patents before they fell into unfriendly hands, but continued pursuit of such a strategy held significant risk. By the new century, a fresh approach, one that included a strong component of scientific research, was clearly needed – and Steinmetz would lead the way.

4

Origins and Early History of the General Electric Research Laboratory

The need for industrial research

Although GE dominated the American market for electric lighting during the late 1890s, serious competitive threats had begun to appear, both in America and abroad. Scientists and engineers continued to make advances that threatened to relegate the carbon-filament electric lamp to obsolescence; gas lighting, never fully displaced by electricity, seemed to be on the verge of a comeback.

When Edison invented his electric light and power systems during the late 1870s and early 1880s, he benefited from the demand gas lighting had created for large-scale interior illumination. Candles and oil lamps were too expensive and produced too much smoke and soot for lighting large areas. By the 1850s, however, the gas-generating and -distributing systems introduced into many American cities had solved those problems, showing urban residents the advantages of illuminating large portions of their homes and businesses. Edison's electric light added the convenience of illumination at the touch of a switch (the gas lamp, of course, had to be lighted), and it eliminated the gas lamp's inherent flicker. Moreover, electric lighting appeared to be safer than gas and had the aura of the latest in scientific technology. It found quick acceptance among consumers.

In order to compete with the electric light as effectively as possible, gas companies lowered their prices, in some cases as much as 50%, so that during the 1880s and early 1890s, gas illumination actually cost less than electric. Then a major European development in gas light technology improved its competitive situation considerably. Austrian electrochemist Carl Auer von Welsbach invented a high-efficiency, luminous radiator "mantle" fabricated from cotton mesh impregnated with oxides of thorium and cerium. A gas flame heated the mantle, which radiated a bright, steady, yellow-white light. The Welsbach process, introduced into

America in 1893, reduced the cost of gas lighting by more than half, dramatically increasing its cost advantage over electricity.[1] Its invention and commercial development by a man with advanced degrees in science underscored the growing potential of such people to make major contributions to – and create serious dislocations in – the lighting industry.

Meanwhile GE's interests in incandescent lighting faced the possibility of direct competition from improvements to the electric lamp itself. The main problems with GE's carbon filament were that it remained, as one critic remarked, "too small, too red, and too hot."[2] This meant in practice that the lamps had limited output, requiring great numbers to illuminate large areas; that the light they emitted tended toward the lower (red) end of the visible spectrum, giving off a pleasant but unnatural red glow;[3] and that a very high proportion of the energy they consumed went not to visible light but to wave emissions in the infrared region, producing heat.

Heat production was the greatest concern. Even after a doubling of efficiency to 3.5 lumens per watt since Edison's early lamps, only about 5% of the energy went to illumination, the rest to heat.[4] In dispersing energy within the visible spectrum, a filament reached greatest efficiency at about 11,000°F. Yet carbon could not be operated above 3,000°F without evaporating quickly, making lamp life unacceptably short. Improvement might come in either of two ways: by using a filament material that operated for long periods at temperatures above 3,000°F, or by finding a selective radiator – a material that, when incandescent, concentrated its radiation in the narrow visible band of the spectrum.

Scientific advances during the 1890s made the likelihood of developing such materials much greater. In 1892 French electrochemist Henri Moissan had designed an electric-arc furnace that enabled scientists to work at higher and better-controlled temperatures. This led to an improved understanding of the composition and properties of many materials potentially useful for incandescent filaments, as well as for other electrochemical processes.[5]

Toward the end of the century, two new incandescent lamps developed in Germany caused GE great concern. The first was a somewhat different kind of lamp: an incandescent "glower" in air rather than a filament in a vacuum. Invented by Walther Nernst, a leading professor of chemistry at Göttingen University who was studying the light-emitting properties of the Welsbach mantle, the glower lamp was made from a small rod composed of rare-earth oxides. A wire coil heated the rod to about 1,750°F, then current automatically switched to flow through the rod itself, bringing it to incandescence at about 4,250°F. A selective radiator, the Nernst lamp achieved efficiencies about 50% greater than a carbon filament. Nernst himself did not wish to be tied down in technological and business pursuits. He sold his patent rights to Germany's largest electrical company, the Allgemeine Elektrizitäts-Gesellschaft, and to Westinghouse in America. Though the Nernst lamp was not yet ready for commercial production, GE soon realized that Westinghouse possessed the rights to what might become a highly competitive new type of lighting technology.

The other German innovation appeared to threaten GE's incandescent lighting interests even more directly. After his success with the gas mantle, von Welsbach undertook research in electric lighting; by 1898 he had developed a filament made from the metal osmium that showed selective radiating characteristics at an operating temperature of over 4,000°F. This gave his lamp an efficiency of about 5.5 lumens per watt, 60% greater than GE's carbon filament. It had a longer useful life as well. Osmium was rare and expensive, however, and filaments made of the metal proved to be quite fragile. Even though millions of the lamps were produced for sale in Europe, they never actually threatened GE's American market position.[6] But they did serve notice that high-efficiency metal filaments were possible and that the days of the too small, too red, and too hot carbon filament were numbered.

The last decade of the 19th century saw several independent American researchers at work developing electric-discharge lamps that emitted light through the ionization of gases and vapors at low pressures. Inventor Peter Cooper-Hewitt based his work on mercury vapor. Although he could make lamps with an efficiency of 12.5 lumens per watt, their blue-green light proved undesirable for general illumination. George Westinghouse financed Cooper-Hewitt's continuing experiments, acquiring the right to purchase his patents if they took on commercial value.[7]

During the late 1890s Charles Steinmetz visited Cooper-Hewitt's laboratory to assess the kind of competition GE might soon face. What he found reinforced his belief that GE should establish a new laboratory, separate from the incessant demands of production and design, where new types of technologies like electric-discharge lamps might be developed. Having pursued his doctorate in mathematics at Germany's University of Breslau and having studied advanced engineering at the Polytechnic Institute in Zurich, Steinmetz was thoroughly familiar with European research programs.[8] He felt very strongly that GE would be well served by a semi-independent research program of the type often found in the German chemical, pharmaceutical, and electrical industries. As early as July 1897, he began formally proposing that the company establish an electrochemical laboratory and enlisted the support of company founder Elihu Thomson, then serving as a GE "consultant" with his own laboratory at the Lynn, Massachusetts works. Steinmetz favored an electrochemical orientation for the proposed laboratory because of GE's expanding opportunities in this field and because of his own interest in arc lighting.[9]

By September 1897 Steinmetz had become frustrated with the attitudes of Coffin and the board of directors toward expending money on a research laboratory not clearly and directly tied into the company's business. In a letter to E. W. Rice he lamented, "Due to the extreme slowness with which we are moving in this matter it appears that the field will be exploited before we start to do anything therein and we shall be left behind."[10] Although Rice seems to have been in sympathy with Steinmetz's ideas,[11] the company's slow recovery from the economic depression of the mid-1890s, Coffin's resulting conservative approach to business and financial matters, and the lack of any unusual new product threatening GE's position in its primary markets precluded decisive action.

Steinmetz did not let his proposal die. Aware that GE's former consultant on the rotary converter, Charles Bradley, had recently established the Ampere Electrochemical Company to develop new processes that would be likely to threaten GE's commercial interests, Steinmetz again proposed that the company establish an electrochemical laboratory.[12] In a review of his own work for the year 1898, he concluded:

> It may . . . be desirable to resuscitate the recommendations which I made some years ago regarding the establishment of an electro-chemical laboratory in connection with the factory, to be put in charge of a good chemist. It appears to me that our Company would have in such work a very great advantage over any other concern, not only in having an enormous power available but also by having Prof. Thomson's advice. . . .[13]

When this plea resulted in the usual inaction, Steinmetz decided that he needed another powerful voice speaking for his laboratory at the corporate level. Over the course of the following year, he subtly brought GE's head patent attorney, Albert G. Davis, into his camp. Davis later recalled:

> I was never able to make up my mind whether the first suggestion [for the Research Laboratory] came from Steinmetz or from myself. Looking back on it now [in 1933], I see that it may well be that Steinmetz originated the idea, and that in his efforts to get Mr. Rice and myself to endorse it he was astute enough to make each of us separately feel himself the originator.[14]

These three worked together to make a strong case for the establishment and support of a research laboratory. Given the growing threats to GE's position in electric lighting from the Welsbach gas mantle, Nernst lamp, osmium filament, and electric-discharge lamps, the strongest argument for a research laboratory was certainly the need to develop electric-lighting technology in advance of GE's rivals. Steinmetz and Davis wrote letters to Rice, which Rice then used in his attempts to convince Coffin and the board. In September 1900 this correspondence reached a crescendo when Thomson added his voice. First Davis wrote to Rice, explaining the necessity for the company to undertake research on the mercury-vapor lamp, research which Peter Cooper-Hewitt was already pursuing. He concluded by saying, "If someone gets ahead of us in this development we will have to spend large sums in buying patents or patent rights, whereas if we do the work ourselves this necessity will be avoided."[15] GE, of course, intended to remain in control of the American electric-lighting market.

Then, in a four-page letter to Rice, Steinmetz laid out in detail a research program for the laboratory, including work on mercury-vapor lamps, arc-light electrodes, glower-type lamps, and new filament materials such as osmium and uranium. He proposed that with whatever extra time remained, the lab investigate properties of materials because of the likelihood "that some substances would find an important commercial application by their electrical or physical properties." He further suggested that the laboratory be administered by a "practical chemist of considerable originality" and noted as "absolutely essential" that the laboratory be separate from the manufacturing works and insulated from the interference of production problems. Davis later recalled that Steinmetz wanted the research lab to be a place where "anyone who mentioned orders or selling would be thrown out."[16]

Three days later Elihu Thomson wrote two letters concerning

the laboratory, one to Steinmetz and the other to Rice. To the former he commented:

> The proposals you make as to the investigations to be undertaken are just in the line of what I would have suggested myself. It does seem to me that a company as large as the General Electric Company should not fail to continue investigating and developing in new fields. . . . I am sure that the company would gain greatly from such a laboratory properly conducted.

And to Rice, he reiterated:

> It does seem to me that a Company as large as the General Electric Company should not fail to continue investigating and developing in new fields: there should, in fact, be a research laboratory for commercial applications of new principles, and even for the discovery of those principles.[17]

Within a week the board of directors had acquiesced. Word of approval came down with a caveat, however. "Find the right man [to head the laboratory]," Rice was told. "With such a man this may be a fine thing, without him, it may be simply a machine for spending money."[18] This strong concern with costs and results helped establish the early tenor of the Research Laboratory and placed a very heavy burden on its first director. Even though the lab would be separate from the concerns of production, it was born with the expectation that it could bring the company important technological advances, especially in electric lighting. It had to accomplish this in a reasonable time or face the possibility of termination. Indeed, one early laboratory researcher claimed that the board of directors was reluctant to approve its establishment, and that several board members thought that after a few years they could show that the money had been wasted, and close the laboratory down.[19]

Establishing the Research Laboratory

Even before approval came from the board, Steinmetz wrote to Thomson, asking him to suggest a chemist who might direct the new laboratory. Thomson replied that he had no one immediately in mind, but added, "He needs, of course rather exceptional qualities, as he must be not only a chemist, but a rather broad minded man of general education and some experience, which would allow him to go directly to the mark in getting results."[20]

While Thomson considered, Steinmetz also contacted Charles R. Cross, a professor of physics and chemistry at MIT who had close contacts with industry. Cross put the proposition to his colleagues, then replied that "one of our best instructors in chemistry, Dr. Willis R. Whitney . . . is thinking seriously of the matter." Steinmetz asked Elihu Thomson to interview Whitney at MIT in order to "find out his qualifications . . . and let me know what you think about this gentleman."[21] By the time of the meeting, Rice and Davis had become interested enough in Whitney to take the train to Boston and sit in.

Willis Whitney graduated from MIT in 1890 with a degree in chemistry and remained on campus for several years as an instructor and laboratory assistant. He then went to Germany, where he acquired his Ph.D. at Leipzig University under the foremost physical chemist of the time, Wilhelm Ostwald. Whitney also studied organic chemistry at the Sorbonne in Paris before returning to the chemistry department at MIT. However, his position there as a junior member of the faculty turned out to be less satisfying than he had anticipated: he remained at the level of instructor, saw his requests for modest pay raises turned down, and was relegated to teaching lower-level courses to engineering undergraduates. In 1898 Whitney collaborated with his colleague and mentor, Arthur A. Noyes, on a consulting project for American Aristotype, a company which made photographic printing paper. Their invention of a process to reclaim production solvents earned the company great profits and brought them both substantial financial rewards.[22] Yet even after this quick and successful venture into industrial consulting, Whitney preferred to remain at MIT. Several of his friends had experienced great difficulties after leaving academia for industrial positions, finding their research too confined and the level of support inadequate for the work they were expected to perform. Whitney even turned down the offer of a lucrative position with the noted Boston consulting chemist, Arthur D. Little.[23]

By the fall of 1900, however, Whitney had become extremely frustrated in his position at MIT; so when offered the opportunity to help shape GE's new industrial laboratory, he expressed cautious interest. In the same letter to GE mentioning Whitney, Cross noted what were undoubtedly Whitney's sentiments: "The chief difficulty is as to what the position will be worth, not merely pecuniarily but otherwise."[24]

In their meeting with Whitney, the men from GE attempted to explain the "otherwise." Davis later recalled that they wanted to convince Whitney that "even though they were industrialists, they, too, possessed scientific ideals." Thomson stressed the opportunity to work with Steinmetz. Whitney demurred. Forsaking academia for an industrial position, no matter what the intentions of the industrialists, was too large a step for him to take at that time. Instead the four men worked out a compromise that permitted Whitney to retain his MIT post while spending two days each week at GE during the school term, and full time during the summer. For this GE would pay him $2,400 per year – the salary of a full professor – and he would remain on the MIT payroll as well.[25]

No doubt Davis and Rice were prepared to strike such a deal only because they believed that they had found the right man for the job. With his research for American Aristotype Whitney had demonstrated that he could do the type of work that led to quick results. His studies of corrosion and colloids at MIT interested the company. Moreover, sharing Whitney's services promised to strengthen ties with the MIT chemistry and physics departments, facilitating GE's use of science in its development of commercial technology.

Ambivalent about his industrial commitment, Whitney began as GE's first director of research that December. Although he soon extended his stay in Schenectady from two to three days per week, he very carefully maintained his presence at MIT, both through teaching and research. Whitney intended to continue with this dual assignment until the opening of the 1901 fall term, when he would decide whether to make his career in industry or return to the academic fold.[26]

Early days of the laboratory

For lack of space in the rapidly expanding GE works, Whitney initially set up shop in a building on the property of Steinmetz's Schenectady home. There he went to work on the recalcitrant mercury-vapor lamp, which both Steinmetz and Davis had cited in their pleas to establish the laboratory. He set out to transpose some of its radiation from the blue-green to the red region of the visible spectrum, and to simplify start-up procedures, which then required an exact tilting of the lamp to initiate current flow. The work went slowly as Whitney and his untrained assistant, John Dempster, added impurities to the mercury and coated the bulb with various fluorescent materials, all to no avail.[27] Whitney also began an analysis of magnetite, an oxide of iron with properties that suggested its usefulness in a number of electrical applications, particularly arc-light electrodes. Steinmetz had a strong interest in magnetite, so he probably promoted Whitney's research on it.

Within a few months fire damaged the small laboratory, and Whitney prevailed upon Rice to find him space at the Schenectady Works. That spring, having launched several projects and acquired a more satisfactory laboratory facility, Whitney felt that it was time to bring in more staff. With Rice's approval, he hired four men, all from MIT. The first two, Ezekiel Weintraub and Julius Ober, had, like Whitney, taken European Ph.D.s and later found themselves in unsatisfactory faculty positions. The other two, William Arsem and Howard Wood, had just earned their bachelor's degrees.

Whitney set his men to work on electric lighting, especially mercury-vapor discharge tubes. They soon made progress, but commercially viable results eluded them. Whitney knew that the Research Laboratory had to show a reasonable return on investment before long, so he very much wanted to produce some kind of "tangible and negotiable results." However, as he wrote home to his parents, "These men of mine are all at work but what they do is fail, fail, fail."[28] The first few years would prove trying.

When it became clear that significant results in lighting might take some time, Whitney moved to broaden the laboratory's areas of research. In doing so, he violated one of the basic premises on which it had been established – separation from engineering and manufacturing operations. When several company engineers approached him during the summer of 1901 with requests to develop special products, Whitney did not hesitate to seize the opportunity. He took on the first project himself, using his knowledge of electrochemistry to design a process for precisely controlling the physical properties of high-resistance rods used in the company's electrical meters. With a slight modification, this process yielded another product requested of the laboratory, lightning-arrestor elements that increased in resistance as a discharge flowed through them (rather than decreasing, which was normal). When the Meter

Department asked Whitney to provide it with a steady supply of his newly developed resistors, he saw a chance both to demonstrate the lab's value to the company and to earn some income against expenses. He set up a small manufacturing operation in the laboratory, the first of several that soon paid a significant portion of its costs.[29]

In 1902 Whitney began to collaborate with newly hired Ph.D. chemist William Weedon in a study of arc-light electrodes. Whitney and Weedon approached the problem using the theoretical constructs of electrochemistry. This initially caused them great difficulties; in fact, as a subsequent part of this chapter shows, it led Whitney to question the efficacy of the disciplinary approach to industrial research problems. After several years their work finally led to the use of the heat-resistant alloy titanium carbide to make a highly efficient and long-lasting electrode.[30]

Given Whitney's new policy of taking on jobs from the manufacturing and engineering departments, the laboratory's different lines of work increased rapidly. By the fall of 1902 more than thirty projects were underway, covering such diverse areas as platinum plating, paper for blueprints, AC electrolysis, wood distillation, magnetic iron, and copper casting. Meanwhile, Whitney's research staff had grown to fourteen.[31]

In early 1902 E. W. Rice decided that the time had come to announce to GE's stockholders that it had established America's first industrial research laboratory. At the conclusion of his message in the annual report for 1901, he stated:

> Although our engineers have always been liberally supplied with every facility for the development of new and original designs and improvements of existing standards, it has been deemed wise during the past year to establish a laboratory to be devoted exclusively to original research. It is hoped by this means that many profitable fields may be discovered.[32]

And, he might have added, controlled as well.

Shaping the institution

From Whitney's earliest days in Schenectady, Steinmetz took an active role in Research Laboratory operations. He initially served as an intermediary between Whitney and Rice, requesting equipment and new staff, while also attending to numerous small matters. However, Whitney and Steinmetz did not get along well.

Steinmetz clearly intended to exert strong influence on the laboratory, but Whitney would not permit it. A very uneasy relationship resulted. John Dempster recalled that "their methods were different. Steinmetz liked to start at the end of a problem and work back. Dr. Whitney liked to start at the beginning and work forward." They argued frequently; soon Steinmetz left Whitney and the laboratory to their own devices. "Then," noted Dempster, "we didn't often see him."[33]

But Steinmetz had other ways to exert his influence. When Whitney began severely compromising what Steinmetz believed to be the Research Laboratory's mission by undertaking numerous outside projects, Steinmetz and Rice acted to gain a measure of control over laboratory activities. Since GE operations often functioned under a system of committee review and approval, an effective rein could be placed on the lab by establishing an oversight committee. In August 1903 Rice sent letters to Steinmetz, Thomson, Davis, and John Howell, manager of the Harrison Lamp Works, asking that they be prepared to attend meetings of a Research Laboratory Advisory Council, since administration of the lab was "a very severe tax upon any one person who has it in charge" – that is, on Whitney. The first meeting of the council took place on October 5, 1903; thereafter it met monthly.[34]

As vice-president in charge of engineering and manufacturing, Rice did not object to Whitney's taking on projects related to engineering and production, but he wanted to be certain that informed judgment went into their selection, especially those that required substantial commitments of laboratory resources. Concerned with the precarious nature of the board of directors' support for the Research Laboratory, Rice told Whitney at the council's first meeting to keep careful records of all projects that made contributions to the company, along with estimates of their monetary value.[35]

The advisory council meetings continued regularly for a decade, serving a number of purposes. They enabled Vice-President Rice to bring to Whitney's attention important corporate concerns that he believed might benefit from laboratory attention. Input from Chief Patent Counsel Davis kept the lab informed of company patent needs in a number of areas. John Howell's presence assured that the Research Laboratory and the Harrison Lamp Works coordinated their efforts. Steinmetz exerted his influence by suggesting projects and by directing a stream of scientific and technical information at Whitney. Finally, as the chamber of advice and consent, the council decided on whether to approve particular laboratory projects based on the scientific and technical insights of Steinmetz and Thomson as well as the commercial and manufacturing knowledge of Rice and Howell. Decisions usually depended on expected costs and the perceived likelihood of success. Small projects, especially when timely solutions were important, could be undertaken at Whitney's discretion, without council approval.[36]

So, by the end of 1903, the fledgling laboratory that had begun with a half-time director and his assistant in an outbuilding at Steinmetz's home had its own quarters at the Schenectady Works, a staff of nineteen researchers and twenty-six support personnel, and a reasonably well-defined – if not necessarily secure – niche in the GE corporate structure. Whitney had requested leave from MIT in 1901, so it had a full-time director as well.[37]

Research on the incandescent light

While making high-resistance rods for the Meter Department, Whitney developed an electric high-temperature furnace which could be controlled to an exacting degree. Whitney based his design on the furnace developed by French electrochemist Henri Moissan in the 1890s. Whitney's device presented the laboratory with an opportunity to heat materials to previously unattainable controlled temperatures in order to observe changes in their physical properties. Because the processing of carbon incandescent filaments left a residue of mineral oxide ash, Whitney decided to see if the new furnace could eliminate the ash and improve the filament. He succeeded far beyond his expectations. Not only did the heat treatment remove the oxides, it also changed the surface structure of the filament, making it hard and tough like graphite and lending it several metallic properties: resistance that increased rather than decreased with rising temperature, and a higher melting point than untreated carbon. This enabled GE to make very rugged lamps that were 20% more efficient at the standard filament life of 800 hours, or up to 50% more efficient if the life expectancy were lowered somewhat by operating at higher temperatures.[38] The company called this its GEM – for GE Metallized – lamp and, thanks to the Research Laboratory's close cooperation with the Harrison Lamp Works, put it on sale by 1905.

This new lamp could be produced and sold inexpensively, so

GE was for the moment reassured in its control of the American lighting market. Its security there had been enhanced considerably in 1901, when the leading small producers of incandescent lamps, whose combined output was over half of GE's, decided to form a holding company under protection of the electrical giant. For an investment of $120,000 and promises of technical aid to bring the new National Electric Lamp Company's products up to par with its own, GE gained controlling stock in the holding company and rights to 75% of its profits. Using patent licenses as vehicles of agreement, GE and National established shares of the market and selling prices for lamps, thus making the smaller companies virtual subsidiaries of GE. This arrangement brought GE $600,000 in dividends over the next ten years in addition to enormously increased value for National's stock. At the same time it gave the appearance of competition in the American incandescent lighting market where none actually existed.[39]

Although the GEM lamp represented the major contribution to electric lighting that Whitney had been looking for, his sense of accomplishment was short-lived. In Europe, where the cost of electricity was far greater than America, intensive research for a high-efficiency incandescent filament centered on the use of metals. Welsbach's osmium had been the first, but its high cost and fragility limited its appeal. In 1902 and 1903 researchers in the Siemens and Halske Company's laboratory produced a ductile filament from the metal tantalum. The new filament made possible a highly efficient, rugged lamp, which gave very long life when used on DC and which cost considerably less than the osmium lamp. News of the tantalum lamp caused great concern at GE.[40]

Siemens and Halske offered GE the American rights to the new lamp for a high price in 1904. Because the tantalum filament quickly became brittle and lost one-half to two-thirds of its useful life when operated on AC, GE declined. Instead, it later acquired (for a payment of $250,000) American rights for itself and National to produce the lamps on a royalty basis, with tantalum wire supplied from Germany.[41]

This situation presented a severe threat to the Research Laboratory, since it had been established precisely to avoid paying others for the right to use lighting patents. Whitney's efforts to diversify research had paid off in numerous small contributions to the company, but his position remained insecure; another major setback in incandescent lighting could mean termination of the lab, or at least limitation of its work to those types of projects for engineering and production that it had already shown it could do well.

Accordingly, Whitney regrouped his forces for an attack on the metal-filament incandescent lamp. His knowledge of electochemistry led Whitney to choose a number of metals that promised high efficiency. Tungsten, zirconium, and molybdenum were the likely candidates. Tungsten had the highest melting point (6,100°F), but its extreme brittleness in pure form prevented its use. During the fall of 1904 Whitney directed Ezekiel Weintraub and other lab chemists to examine the structure and properties of tungsten to determine what, if anything, could be done to draw it into wire form. William Arsem made preliminary studies of other metals, and a number of researchers were soon attacking all the metals on Whitney's growing list. Between 1904 and 1906 the laboratory's professional staff increased from twenty to forty-four, as Rice approved the addition of scientists and engineers to take on the metal-filament work.[42]

In early 1906 Whitney acquired the brilliant experimentalist William Coolidge for his staff. Coolidge had been an undergraduate chemistry student of Whitney's at MIT. After earning his bachelor's degree in electrical engineering he had taken his doctorate in physics at Leipzig University. Since 1900 Coolidge had worked as a researcher in the MIT chemistry laboratory of Whitney's former colleague, Arthur Noyes. Coolidge rejected Whitney's first offer of employment, but a contract for twice his current pay and granting him one-third of his time to continue a project he was then pursuing at MIT swayed him to accept in mid-1905. Coolidge began work on tungsten even before reporting to Schenectady; once there, he found the job so consuming that he soon abandoned the MIT project.[43]

Before Coolidge got very far in his research, GE learned that a number of Europeans had succeeded in making metal filaments and that some of them were about to come on the market. Beginning with a carbon-based, gluelike substance such as wax or sugar, European researchers had mixed in a finely powdered metal. This resulted in paste that could be squirted through a die to form short pieces of wire. Treating the wire with heat removed the glue material, leaving a brittle metallic filament that contained many impurities, but that produced an incandescent lamp about 50% more efficient than tantalum.[44] Rice sent Whitney and Howell to Europe in order to assess the situation and to consider buying patent or production rights if necessary. Coolidge, meanwhile,

Plate 6. William D. Coolidge. Courtesy of General Electric Research and Development Center.

became assistant director of the laboratory, temporarily taking charge of the metal-filament work in Schenectady.

Whitney and Howell traveled first to Germany, where they toured the factory of Welsbach's company, the Auer Gesellschaft, which made a metal-filament lamp from a combination of osmium and tungsten. Impressed with the techniques used in fabricating these filaments, Whitney and Howell suggested to Rice that GE purchase the relevant patents from Welsbach. After some negotiation, the deal was completed at a price of $100,000. Whitney and Howell recommended against GE's buying rights to some other processes, including one developed by the Austrians Alexander Just and Fritz Hanaman. Just and Hanaman coated a very thin carbon rod with pure tungsten, then dissolved the carbon to yield a fragile, hollow metal filament. This method did not impress the GE representatives, even though it was then going into commercial production in Hungary.[45]

When Whitney returned to the Research Laboratory in September 1906 he faced a difficult situation. The Auer process to which GE had bought patent rights remained unsatisfactory: it would require considerable development to produce a lamp cheap and durable enough to be sold in America. Although Whitney had put his professional judgment behind the Auer process, its use – even if further developed by GE researchers – would demonstrate the Research Laboratory's failure to provide GE with the protection it desired. Of course there was no certainty that another type of process would not supplant Auer's. In fact, while Whitney and Howell toured Europe, Coolidge and the GE researchers had found a promising new way to work with tungsten. They mixed tungsten powder with an amalgam of the metals bismuth, cadmium, and mercury before drawing it into a filament, then drove out the amalgam through heat treatment.[46]

Work on perfecting a metal filament proceeded on several fronts in the Research Laboratory. Whitney undertook development of the Auer process himself, apparently feeling responsible for making it successful because he had recommended that GE spend a substantial sum for the rights – and Coffin was known to be concerned that the money might have been wasted! Meanwhile, Coolidge pushed ahead with his new process; and, under Whitney's direction, many other researchers tried new types of binders and methods for working the metals into filament form. The laboratory investigated at least thirteen different processes for making tungsten filaments during the next few years.[47]

Strong pressure came from corporate management to succeed quickly in what Coffin and Rice saw as a race with the Europeans to develop the controlling method of metal-filament fabrication. Should the Europeans win, GE would have to pay handsomely for patent or production rights, for Westinghouse had already signaled its intention of bidding for them in an attempt to gain control of the American electric lighting market. Reports now came in from GE's European agents of numerous filament developments – not only with tungsten, but also with other metals, from chromium and manganese to titanium and zinc.[48]

Whitney worried lest GE "lose its high place in the lighting field through some negligence or careless action of mine." Consequently, he pushed himself and his staff very hard. Coolidge reported that the work was indeed strenuous: Rice "wanted things pushed."[49] With stakes so high, failure could be disastrous, but as Coolidge noted in a 1906 letter to his parents, "Our success on [the] problem would make the Company give the lab anything Whitney sees fit to ask for. If we can get the metal, tungsten, in such shape that it can be drawn into wire, it means millions of dollars to the Company."[50]

In fact, that same year, GE sales of electric lamps reached $7.5 million, having climbed from $2 million in 1900 and $5 million in 1903.[51] Continuing improvements in electric power generation and distribution were lowering energy costs to the consumer. The company expected that this economy, combined with a much more efficient filament, would boost lamp sales significantly and lead to increased profits – if GE could maintain control of the market.

But by mid-1907 the laboratory's race appeared to be lost. Just and Hanaman's process, which Whitney and Howell had passed over, now showed itself capable of producing commercial-grade filaments. In fact, the Austrians' patents appeared to be basic to the metal-filament art, so GE decided to buy patent rights while the opportunity remained. This meant paying $250,000 to Just and Hanaman as well as another $240,000 to the Austrian chemist Hans Kuzel, who had patented a similar method. GE expended a great sum of money, but its purchase of patent rights kept potentially damaging weapons away from Westinghouse. GE's lamp works in Cleveland and Harrison began development work on the Just and Hanaman process in order to adapt it to their mechanized high-speed manufacturing methods. Coolidge's amalgam process still showed promise, however, and it continued to receive research attention.[52]

Steinmetz had never been happy with Whitney's management of the laboratory. In 1908 he wrote an extended memorandum to Rice, complaining that the Research Laboratory had (among other inadequacies) failed to do "pioneer work in the field of electrochemistry," which was "felt seriously . . . in the metal filament lamps." He lamented, "It appears shameful to me, that the successors of Edison should cease to be considered as the leaders in the development of incandescent lighting, and European engineers get the credit which our company should have retained, if its engineers had not been asleep."[53]

This apparent defeat in electric lighting, combined with the panic that struck American financial markets in mid-1907, spelled disaster for the laboratory. In 1904, at a time when it was demonstrating its usefulness to GE in a number of ways, an economic downturn that brought marked reductions to most parts of the company had left the Research Laboratory unscathed. In 1907, however, the result was far different. Coffin and Rice trimmed the Research Laboratory budget by 41% over the next year, causing the termination of thirteen of the forty-four professional staff members and a pay cut for the rest.[54] Whitney, whose sense of failure was acute, suffered a physical and mental breakdown. While he convalesced in Florida during the autumn of 1907 and the winter of 1908, Coolidge took over direction of the disheartened laboratory staff.

Recovery

The laboratory's salvation had its origin in Coolidge's 1907 research. While working with tungsten filaments made by the amalgam process, Coolidge discovered that they lost some of their brittleness when hammered or squeezed at temperatures of about 700°F, much cooler than either theory or experience had suggested. After GE's purchase of the European patents, however, Coolidge dropped this line of research to begin a study of tungsten oxide powders. When, in the spring of 1908, Whitney returned to his director's position, Rice sent Coolidge abroad to demonstrate the amalgam process to GE's British affiliates and to observe metal-filament research at a number of European laboratories. At the Auer facility in Berlin, Coolidge observed a process for thermal and chemical treatment of molybdenum that produced a filament capable of deformation without breaking, even at room temperature. Coolidge's earlier experience with tungsten led him to believe that mechanical working might be superior to chemical treatment. Upon Coolidge's return to Schenectady, Whitney encouraged him to take up new research on tungsten, which has many properties similar to molybdenum.[55]

As he progressed, Coolidge learned that tungsten became less brittle as it took on a fibrous internal structure. This behavior was the opposite of most metals, which are ductile in the crystalline state and brittle when fibrous. Coolidge became convinced that the right combination of heat treatment and mechanical working could elongate pure tungsten crystals into fibers, yielding ductile filaments. For several months he and other researchers under his direction attempted to work the tungsten in various ways and at different temperatures. Coolidge called in the most experienced hammerer at GE, a blacksmith from the Schenectady Works, but even his skills proved fruitless against the reluctant metal.[56] Still the battle with tungsten had just begun. Over the next two years, Coolidge and his co-workers attacked the problems of heat-treating, working, and fabricating tungsten into ductile filaments. Their ultimate success in 1912 gave GE the commanding commercial advantage in electric lighting that it had always sought.

Coolidge did not achieve success alone. Filament research at the laboratory involved about three-fourths of the staff at one time or another between 1906 and 1910: Coolidge later noted that a total of forty researchers and assistants had worked with him on ductile tungsten. Meanwhile, resources flowed back into the Research Laboratory. The annual budget, at a low of $105,000 in 1908, climbed to $163,000 in 1911, which was almost as high as it had been before the 1907 debacle. In 1910, when total expenses were $162,000, the lab's summary of work noted that over half of its efforts had gone into making ductile tungsten. It thus expended substantial resources on the ductile-tungsten lamp. But the total was considerably less than GE had already spent in purchasing nonductile-tungsten patent rights, and the end result proved to be far more valuable.[57]

Using thoria oxide as an agent to inhibit crystal growth, Coolidge and his co-workers designed a process for fabricating ductile-tungsten filaments on a commercial scale. They worked closely with the engineers at Harrison, and GE was able to place the ductile-tungsten lamp on the market by late 1911. Adopting the new filament meant discarding several hundred thousand dollars' worth of newly designed and installed equipment for the Just and Hanaman lamps, but increased automation and speed of manufacture made possible by the ductile filament justified the expenditure. Furthermore, the ductile-tungsten lamps had two major advantages for the consumer that significantly increased sales: they were far more rugged, and their output, at 10 lumens per watt, gave an efficiency almost 25% greater than any incandescent lamp yet made.[58]

Ductile-tungsten lamps quickly took over the profitable American lighting market, as their share rose from 25% in 1911 to 71% in 1914. The profit margin on these lamps was considerably higher than that on most other GE products. It ranged from 50% to 200% of costs, on lamp sales of $21 million in 1913, $36 million in 1917, and $58 million in 1920. Profits on incandescent lamps reached over $30 million annually during the 1920s, a figure which the *New York Times* calculated to be a 30% return on investment. Up until the Second World War, incandescent lamps brought the company one-third to two-thirds of its annual profit, although they represented only one-sixth of its sales.[59]

In addition to increased sales and profits, development of the ductile-tungsten lamp improved GE's commercial position in several ways. Ductile tungsten made GE a licensor of European patent rights, rather than a licensee. The company granted rights to a number of European producers and entered into a patent-pooling arrangement with several German companies. This permitted GE to use improvement patents on the ductile-tungsten lamp, while preventing the Europeans from entering the American market, thus assuring GE's virtual monopoly.[60]

Even more importantly, the ductile-tungsten patents enabled GE to maintain control of the American electric lamp market in the face of a consent decree forced upon it in 1911. Prosecuting GE, National, and a number of smaller producers who stood under the GE pricing umbrella, the Department of Justice contended that relationships within the industry only purported to be competitive, but in fact amounted to close cooperation, both in production and pricing. This restrained free trade in violation of the Sherman Antitrust Act. At first GE intended to contest the suit. But then it saw that its interests could best be served by agreeing to abandon these arrangements because it could still retain control of the market through patents. As part of its consent agreement, GE purchased the remaining 25% of National stock, making National a wholly owned subsidiary, and abandoned all market-sharing and price arrangements with other producers. However, the decree did not prevent GE from using its patents to control the industry, so the overall situation remained unchanged. GE licensed its patents to other manufacturers, who agreed to quotas based on GE lamp sales. The licensees paid small royalties on lamps they produced within the quota and considerably larger royalties on additional ones. They also agreed to share all technical information with GE and to make available to it all of their lamp-related patents. GE even found a way to control the price of lamps for the customer by retaining ownership of the product until the final sale had been transacted.[61] "Progressive" attempts to break up concentrated economic power notwithstanding, GE found a way to use the products of its research to maintain hegemony over the American lighting market for many years to come.

Diversifying research

By developing the ductile-tungsten filament, the laboratory finally accomplished the basic mission for which it had been established – to provide GE with controlling technology in incandescent electric lighting. Ductile tungsten produced the rugged, high-efficiency filament that science and industry in both Europe and America had sought since before the turn of the century. GE's now supreme position in incandescent lighting brought it profits enough to pay the expenses of the Research Laboratory many times over.[62]

The laboratory's decade-long struggle to secure its place within the corporation had ended, and subtle but important shifts in attitudes toward research took place: direction from the Research Laboratory Advisory Council became less rigorous; expectations concerning the immediacy of payoffs from research softened; and, in general, Whitney acquired a freer hand in his choice of projects and administration of research. Such changes occurred in part because E. W. Rice took over the presidency from Coffin in 1913. Rice had been an early supporter of research, considerably more sympathetic than Coffin to Steinmetz's original conception of a laboratory unencumbered by commercial exigencies.[63] Rice saw to it that the lab received adequate backing. Nonetheless, Whitney made certain that the laboratory continued to meet GE's needs on a number of levels, from support of manufacturing operations to the development of new products. As he explained in response to a query from Eastman Kodak: "It is not safe to assume that we are indespensible to the Company."[64] For the next ten years, at least, Whitney operated by this credo.

In 1909 the man destined to become the laboratory's most renowned scientist joined its staff. Irving Langmuir had taken an undergraduate degree in metallurgical engineering from Columbia University, then a Ph.D. in physical chemistry at Göttingen University, where he studied under Walther Nernst. In his doctoral research project Langmuir analyzed heat transfer and the dissociation of gases at the surface of incandescent filaments, work that prepared him well for dealing with incandescent lamps and, later, vacuum tubes. From 1906 to 1909 Langmuir taught chemistry at the Stevens Institute of Technology. However, as a result of his heavy teaching load, his students' and colleagues' lack of interest in research, and what he considered to be inadequate pay, he was discontented there. Accordingly, he was happy to accept Whitney's offer of a position. Langmuir initially intended to leave industry after a year or two for a "good" university appointment. But, finding everything he wanted at GE, he stayed for his entire career.[65]

In his first project at the Research Laboratory, Langmuir undertook a long-term research effort to assess the physical and chemical processes that took place in ductile-tungsten incandescent lamps. Whitney tolerated this apparently disinterested activity because he believed that gaining knowledge about the operation of incandescent lamps held out the greatest promise for improving them. After Langmuir had been engaged in this research for some time without any tangible results, he asked Whitney whether he should persist. Langmuir later recalled Whitney's responding that

> he would like to see me continue working along any fundamental lines that would give us more information in regard to the phenomena taking place in incandescent lamps, and that I should feel perfectly free to go ahead on any such lines that seemed of interest to me. For nearly three years I worked in this way with several assistants before any application was made of any of the work that I had done.[66]

When application came in 1912, however, it not only solved long-standing problems with bulb blackening, but also resulted in considerably greater lamp efficiency. Based on his understanding of heat transfer and other physical processes taking place within the lamp, Langmuir designed a special filament configuration that could be used in a gaseous environment. By inhibiting evaporation of tungsten atoms, the gas retarded bulb blackening; it also permitted higher operating temperatures, which gave greater efficiencies. Full development of the new lamp required six months of intensive effort on the part of about twenty-five lab workers before it was turned over to the lamp engineers. During all this

Plate 7. Willis Whitney and Irving Langmuir demonstrate GE apparatus for Guglielmo Marconi, c.1920. Courtesy of General Electric Research and Development Center.

time, the Research Laboratory worked closely with the lamp factories to be certain that designs would be amenable to cost-effective mass production.[67] GE placed nitrogen-filled lamps on the market in 1913, though only in the larger sizes, whose increased efficiency compared to vacuum lamps was most dramatic. In fact, high-

Plate 8. Meeting of the Lamp Vacuum Committee of the General Electric Research Laboratory, c.1915. Whitney is third from left; Lawrence Hawkins, fourth from left; Langmuir far right. Courtesy of General Electric Research and Development Center.

powered, gas-filled tungsten lamps were so efficient and, compared to arc lighting, so inexpensive, that they almost completely displaced arc lighting and any remnants of high-power gas lighting from the market. When the inert gas argon became available on a commercial scale after the First World War, GE made nitrogen-argon lamps in sizes as small as fifty watts. The improved efficiency and longer life of this new line further strengthened GE's already substantial control of the American electric lamp industry.[68]

Even after such major advances, the Research Laboratory continued incandescent lamp work on many fronts. To help in directing lamp research, Whitney established the Lamp Vacuum Committee in 1912. Made up of laboratory researchers, lamp works engineers, and company administrators from a number of departments, it met weekly to consider and coordinate GE's development of incandescent lamp technology. In 1914, for example, under the committee's guidance the lab pursued projects on lamp-bulb glass; methods of lamp construction, testing, and exhaust; lamp bases, lead-in wires, and cements; machinery for making lamps; and, of course, lamp filaments. Accounting figures show that the laboratory spent about $90,000 on lamp-related projects that year, when its total budget had grown to $360,000.[69] Many of these projects were aimed at making minor improvements in the techniques of light-bulb fabrication and in methods of manufacture. The Research Laboratory worked very closely with the lamp engineers and production divisions; together, they slowly brought down manufacturing costs while improving the quality of the product. As a result GE was able to lower the price of its lamps steadily, while increasing its profits on each one sold.[70] Through the 1910s, the laboratory continued to expend considerable effort on lamp-related research, much of it to make certain that no one got ahead of GE in lamp technology. One report from the Research Laboratory noted:

> Investigation of possible high melting alloys [for use as filaments] is being started, with the idea that while there is probably not one chance in a hundred that anything will be found to compete with tungsten, it will be worth what the investigation costs in the assurance that no one else is likely to discover such an alloy.[71]

As this statement explicitly acknowledged, the laboratory had moved into a new type of defensive research for GE. Ductile tungsten was the lab's breakthrough into rugged, high-efficiency, metal filaments. That innovation had assured GE's domination of the American market. Now the lab would help GE cover the field, assuring that it controlled not only improvements to ductile-tungsten lamp technology but also any other filament materials that might compete with tungsten. This was one important means for the Research Laboratory to bring GE its greatest security, providing the "life insurance" that Whitney and his bosses believed so vital. The laboratory's broadly based lamp-research and -development program continued for many years and helped protect GE and its licensees from competition. In 1928 the GE group accounted for 96% of U.S. incandescent lamp sales. As late as 1939, well after the basic tungsten patents had expired, improvements in the lamps and methods for manufacturing them – many of which came from the Research Laboratory – enabled GE to retain control of 87% of the American market.[72]

Besides electric lamps, one of the laboratory's major areas of activity during its second decade was vacuum-tube electronics and radio. The transmission of "wireless" telegraph signals had become commonplace with Marconi's commercialization of ship-to-shore communication in the 1890s. Since then various inventors, including Reginald Fessenden and Lee de Forest in the United States, had attempted to transmit voice-carrying signals. Fessenden approached GE in 1903 with the request to build a high-frequency alternator to produce carrier waves for his experiments. Steinmetz designed the first alternator for Fessenden, and, over the next decade, Ernest Alexanderson of GE's Engineering Laboratory improved upon it. In 1906 physicist–inventor Lee de Forest made an important modification to British physicist Ambrose Fleming's two-element vacuum tube rectifier by inserting a third element to more effectively control current flow. However, de Forest's "audions," as he called them, were poorly constructed, inconsistent in their performance, and able to handle only very low levels of power before breaking down completely in a highly ionized state called "blue-haze." In late 1912, as Alexanderson was working on improvements to the high-frequency alternator, he came across the audion in use as a crude, low-power amplifier. He realized that this vacuum-tube device might possibly find use as a modulator – or controller – in alternator circuits.[73] Alexanderson brought the audion to Langmuir's attention, and the man who had just devoted several years to studying the emission of electrons in vacuum and gases very quickly found ways to improve upon de Forest's device. Realizing that the audion did not require the presence of gas to operate, as de Forest had believed, Langmuir designed and built a high-vacuum electron tube that operated effectively at much greater power levels without "blue-haze" problems.[74] His patent application on the use of high vacuum would become the basis for extensive negotiations and maneuverings between GE and AT&T, as they later attempted to control the very important rights to the three-element vacuum tube and, through it, to radio.

Over the following years Langmuir spearheaded the Research Laboratory's efforts to develop vacuum tubes and radio. He worked with several assistants and a number of colleagues, including electrical engineer William White and Ph.D. physicists Albert Hull and Saul Dushman. Together these men provided GE with technologies that the company used to enter a number of new fields, including high-voltage rectifiers and radio transmission services. Dushman developed the two-element, "kenotron" rectifier, which found extensive use in high-voltage power transmission systems. Hull used his expertise in the emission of electrons to design entirely new types of vacuum tubes – ones that had negative resistance characteristics. This permitted them to act very efficiently as amplifiers and oscillators, important functions for radio transmission and reception.[75] Langmuir directed White in numerous experiments that led to vacuum-tube improvements, from better exhaust to more effective element design and configuration. Langmuir's ability to synthesize information and rapidly conceive new operational theories led to highly efficient circuit and tube combinations. By September 1914 work had progressed so far that Langmuir felt confident in assuring Whitney that, with an improved alternator, transatlantic radio communication was within reach. In fact, the alternator itself soon proved to be unnecessary, for Dushman succeeded that November in designing vacuum-tube oscillating circuits which could handle over 500 watts at frequencies up to 200,000 cycles per second.[76]

The Research Laboratory soon became involved in radio design and production. In mid-1915 Whitney suggested that it was time to develop an operational radio system for demonstration purposes, and the entire group of radio and vacuum-tube researchers went to work on the project. By October they had designed and built two all-tube sets that gave "excellent performance" between the laboratory in Schenectady and GE's Pittsfield Works, a distance of about fifty miles. With war raging in Europe, the U.S. military had begun to consider modernizing its forces, and Whitney's request to test the laboratory's radio systems between two battleships met with enthusiasm. Prospects for selling radio sets to the military seemed so encouraging that during the spring of 1916 Whitney established a small manufacturing operation for electron tubes in the lab; it was producing about sixty tubes per month by that fall.[77] When Congress declared war in April 1917, the government removed restrictions on patent use, so the laboratory was able to supply the military with radio communications systems for high-powered transmissions and for use by airplanes, ships, and soldiers in the field. The GE lamp factories, taking over from the Research Laboratory, produced about 200,000 vacuum tubes. When the war ended in late 1918, GE found itself with substantial profits from its radio research and with an advanced technology of radio transmission and reception, including an improved Alexanderson alternator and the circuits needed for its use. However, the confused patent situation, especially in relation to AT&T, meant that GE was not yet able to take advantage of opportunities for further profit in radio.

During the same time that Langmuir led research efforts on vacuum tubes and radio, William Coolidge experimented on another new technology of commercial interest to the company, the X-ray tube. X-rays had been discovered in Germany during the 1890s. They held great interest for physicists and chemists because they brought into question many theories about the nature of matter. X-rays also had obvious medical value because they enabled doctors to observe bone and tissue structure without (or before) operating on a patient. Two-element, partially evacuated tubes generated the X-rays. The tubes' functions depended on internal gas pressure, yet as they operated more gas was produced, changing the pressure and making them erratic. Coolidge substituted tungsten in place of platinum for the positive electrode and achieved higher-powered and longer-lived tubes: tungsten could be heated to a greater temperature without melting, while emitting less gas than platinum. Making such tubes required considerable development work in order to increase the heat conductivity of the tungsten electrodes to prevent them from cracking. By 1913 the lab was manufacturing Coolidge's X-ray tubes on a small scale, selling 3,000 that year and 6,500 in 1914.[78]

Still, these tubes remained "cranky" in their operation, failed unexpectedly, and provided levels of radiation barely adequate for diagnosis. One way to solve those problems was to supply electrons from incandescent filaments in high vacuum, an idea that came from Langmuir's work on electron emissions.[79] By avoiding the use of ionized gases entirely, GE researchers made X-ray tubes that were both more powerful and more reliable. After lengthy development work – which included cooling the positive electrode, "degassing" all metallic parts during the evacuation process, and designing low-weight, high-powered transformers – Coolidge demonstrated the new X-ray tubes to a number of medical radiologists. As a result the laboratory received strong encouragement to bring them into production. However, a study by Research Laboratory engineers suggested that, because the new tubes were considerably more complex and expensive than the earlier ones, the market for them would be too small to warrant manufacture. Nevertheless, GE management insisted that production go ahead, though not for the usual commercial reasons. Patent counsel Albert Davis noted:

> Mr. Coffin and Mr. Rice have expressed the opinion very strongly that the tube should be exploited in such a way as to confer a public benefit, feeling that it is a device which is useful to humanity and that we cannot afford to take an arbitrary, or even perhaps any ordinary commercial position with regard to it.[80]

The new X-ray tubes went into production in early 1914, but, as foreseen, sales remained low because of high costs, while limited

Plate 9. Langmuir and Coolidge show X-ray tube to discoverer of the electron, British physicist J. J. Thomson, c.1920. Courtesy of General Electric Research and Development Center.

production kept prices up. Whitney wanted to shift production from the Research Laboratory to the Schenectady Works, telling Rice, "I think we could make something like $100,000 per year without any trouble if we had 100 square feet of floor space." He may have been overly optimistic; not until the military began ordering tubes on a large scale for portable X-ray units during the First World War did GE increase production and make a significant profit. At that time the laboratory established a new factory department to make the apparatus. After the war, Rice decided that the company should become a full-line X-ray equipment supplier. GE bought the Victor X-ray Company, switched its production of Coolidge X-tubes to Victor, and soon held a dominant position in the profitable medical equipment supply business.[81]

Work in the laboratory diversified after 1911. Many projects occupied researchers, from magnetic steel, electric heating elements, and corrosion-resistant turbine blades to electrical and thermal insulation. And, of course, the staff remained on call to solve any problems that cropped up in engineering or production. Ever mindful of maintaining the laboratory's indispensability to GE, Whitney at this time established a firm policy that a call for assistance from another department took precedence over research in progress. He called this "Trouble Work." For instance, the laboratory saved GE's electric railway department from an embarrassing difficulty by analyzing its motor brushes to find out why they had begun to behave erratically, then supplying a remedy. A little later, Langmuir left his research in surface chemistry to use his knowledge of heat transfer in solving difficulties with GE's new line of refrigerators.[82]

Yet of all of this activity, the results from radio and X-ray tubes were in one important way the most significant. They pointed the Research Laboratory in a new direction, one foreseen by its founders but until then largely unrealized: providing technology to take the company into new product areas. Although its defense of GE's market position in electric lighting may have been the Research Laboratory's most profitable service, the lab did not reach its full potential until research results began to open up entirely new commercial opportunities. While Rice's 1902 report to the stockholders had stated, "It is hoped by [establishing the laboratory] that many profitable fields may be discovered,"[83] not until it achieved recognition as a necessary and hence secure part of the company could the lab break free of immediate corporate needs. Only then could it open up the new fields to which Rice had referred. Part of the reason may have been the perceptions and methods of Willis Whitney, whose great concern to serve the company initially overshadowed his proclivities to let his scientists and engineers pursue research in their own way. The laboratory's outstanding success with ductile tungsten permitted Whitney to reduce the rigor of his direction, which led within three years to another major advance in incandescent lighting, the gas-filled lamp.

At about the same time, the Research Laboratory Advisory Council loosened its grip. Steinmetz had begun the experiments with artificial lightning that occupied him for the rest of his life, and, as his interests diverged from those of the laboratory, his desire to influence it decreased. In 1913 Rice assumed the GE presidency, leaving him less time and inclination to delve deeply into lab affairs, though he did "drop in every month or so" to have the executive engineer show him around. In the period from 1910 to the World War, the advisory council met four to six times per year, mainly to hear Whitney's summary of accomplishments and of work in progress.[84] The council was moribund by 1919, and the Research Laboratory, then secure in its position and very well connected within the company, made its own way. Numerous committees, from the (radio) Condenser Committee and the Mazda (lamp) Engineering Committee to the Lamp Vacuum Committee and several standardizing committees, helped keep the Research Laboratory in touch with company needs.[85]

The Research Laboratory fared quite well in the decade after 1910. Its budget went from $162,000 in 1910 to $250,000 in 1913, and to $553,000 in 1916. The number of professional workers climbed from 47 in 1910 to 65 in 1913, 78 in 1916, and 134 in 1919. Even during the hard financial times that GE faced in 1914 and 1915, the laboratory budget held steady while the company cut back almost everywhere else.[86]

In 1915 the laboratory moved into a large, well-equipped building constructed for it at the Schenectady Works. The new facility had over 60,000 square feet of floor space and central systems to supply compressed air, illuminating gas, vacuum suction, hydrogen, oxygen, distilled water, and steam. Generators and transformers in the basement delivered electric power at frequencies from 25 to 2,000 hertz, at currents as high as 12,000 amperes, and potentials as great as 200,000 volts. Carpentry and machine shops as well as a specialized library were located on the premises. All told, the company spent about $300,000 on the new laboratory, a third of it for equipment.[87] By 1916 GE had the most fully equipped research laboratory in America, if not in the world.

The First World War presented the General Electric Research Laboratory with an opportunity to demonstrate the power of organized research and development in solving pressing military

Plate 10. Buildings housing the General Electric Research Laboratory, 1926. Building 5, on left, was first occupied in 1915. Courtesy of General Electric Research and Development Center.

problems. At the request of the Naval Consulting Board, the laboratory became involved in submarine detection.[88] Langmuir and Hull went off to the navy's research station in Nahant, Massachusetts, while Coolidge led a team working on the problem in Schenectady. Through their combined efforts, two acoustical systems, dubbed the C-tube and the K-tube, were placed aboard U.S. ships by 1918. Another group in the lab adopted the Coolidge X-ray tube for military use, producing an entire field unit that weighed less than 900 pounds, including electrical generator. GE made these for the U.S. Army and the Red Cross; it even supplied some to England and France. Other researchers worked with the GE lamp division at Cleveland to develop means of mass producing vacuum tubes for radios supplied to the navy and the army's Signal Corps. Overcoming numerous problems, they built about 200,000 tubes of five different types during the short course of America's involvement in the war. The laboratory also worked on several other military projects, from searchlight electrodes and incendiary bombs to gas masks and submarine mine detonators, in each case making good profits for GE under government contracts.[89]

By the end of its second decade, the Research Laboratory had demonstrated its value not only to GE, but to the nation as a whole. This gave the company opportunities to capitalize on the positive image of research. Whitney served on the Naval Consulting Board as representative of the American Chemical Society; in that position he strongly promoted industrial research as part of a national preparedness program. His activities brought the General Electric Research Laboratory a high level of visibility among businessmen, industrial managers, and the public, helping to identify "science" and "progress" with the company name. As early as 1915 GE promotional materials featured lab accomplishments to enhance the image of company products. An advertisement in the mass-circulation *Saturday Evening Post* extolled the virtues of "Mazda" incandescent lamps, produced by GE and its licensees:

> The mark of MAZDA on the bulb indicates that the services of the extensive Research Laboratory of the General Electric Company of Schenectady have been available to the maker of that lamp. Great corps of physicists, chemists, metallurgists and other scientists, besides electrical engineers and lighting experts, test, select, compare and systematize all available knowledge which may assist in improving incandescent lamps.[90]

Yet GE put more money into advertising than into research! Well aware of this, Whitney wrote to Rice in 1921, "As long as the cost of advertising Mazda service is much greater than the research behind it, we ought to do more."[91]

After the World War, GE publicity emphasized the role of research in developing company products. Stories about Langmuir, Hull, Coolidge and other lab members found their way into magazines and newspapers, almost always with favorable comment about the value of industrial research in general and GE's efforts in particular. During the 1920s, popular newsman and radio commentator Floyd Gibbons dubbed the Research Laboratory the "House of Magic." His broadcasts describing its research, as well as GE publicity using the "Magic" name, brought so many requests for tours that the lab set up permanent exhibits with hired demonstrators. The company even made a "House of Magic" exhibit for display at the 1933 World's Fair, which was subsequently taken on tour around the country during the 1930s. Over 3 million people saw it. GE had learned the many values of industrial research, and associating the company name with science in an era when science had captured the public imagination was clearly one of them.[92]

Moving into the 1920s

When Rice stepped down in 1922 to make way for GE's new president, Gerard Swope, the Research Laboratory had come to serve many functions. It provided important technical support and assistance for the production divisions, solving all kinds of problems and improving methods of manufacture. It worked with the engineering labs to develop new materials for meeting difficult service conditions and made numerous "little" inventions, many of which were incorporated into existing GE products. It functioned as a small-scale manufacturing facility for some of the products it had developed, especially those that required sophisticated fabrication techniques. It consulted with the production divisions in designing its manufacturing operations, then worked with them to transfer production to the factories once methods had been fully established.

The laboratory also defended important company patents. Whitney, Langmuir, Coolidge, and several other laboratory researchers spent hundreds of hours preparing case records and testifying in patent-interference and -infringement suits, most notably on ductile tungsten and the high-vacuum electron tube. Laboratory researchers even performed studies and wrote papers to bolster the company's position in these cases.[93]

Every few years, the Research Laboratory was expected to bring forth a major product to open the way for GE's exploitation of new markets. During the 1920s these would be "Carboloy," a tungsten-carbide cutting material that had profound impact on the machine tool industry, and "Glyptal" resins, which found use in glues, lacquers, paints, plastics, and photographic film. Glyptal resins led GE into chemical production, an important market area for the company ever since.[94]

Finally, as described in the last section, the Research Laboratory served as a powerful means of advertising the company's high-quality state-of-the-art products and "progressive" spirit. Although the higher sales and increased good will that resulted are hard to measure, they were surely substantial. Maintaining and promoting such a laboratory raised a company's value in the eyes of investors, usually increased the price of its stock, and made it easier to sell bonds or otherwise raise money.[95]

When Gerard Swope took over, then, he had good reason to give the Research Laboratory his full support. Swope had acquired a bachelor's degree in electrical engineering during the 1890s at

MIT, where he studied chemistry with a young instructor named Willis Whitney. During his working life, Swope had devoted himself to management and sales, first at Western Electric (the manufacturing arm of the Bell System), then at GE. Even with his engineering background, Swope's technical expertise had become quite limited by the time he assumed the presidency of GE. So when it came to research, he confidently placed his faith in his former teacher. Whitney, for his part, was quite happy to have the full and unquestioning support of a president who forcefully asserted his control over the corporation.[96]

Operations went smoothly in the Research Laboratory through the 1920s. Except for a brief cutback during the severe recession of 1920–22, the funding and staff of the laboratory continued to grow. Although budget figures are not available for this period, the number of professional workers climbed from 133 in 1922 to 174 in 1925, and to 223 in 1928.[97] In 1928 Swope promoted Whitney to GE vice-president, in charge of research. This gave divisional status to the Research Laboratory and marked the culmination of a journey which had begun in an out-building at Steinmetz's Schenectady home, where its half-time director had worked with one assistant. There had been problems at first, and the lab had suffered setbacks; but hard work, careful management, and a little good luck had paid off handsomely – both for the company and for the scientists and engineers who staffed its Research Laboratory.

5

General Electric: The Research Process

By the end of its first decade, the General Electric Research Laboratory had become different from any laboratory, either academic or industrial, that preceded it. The research laboratories in the German chemical and pharmaceutical industries, established during the 1880s, were tightly organized, very secretive in their operations, and content to leave to the universities all scientific research not directly applicable to their work.[1] American laboratories tended toward analysis of materials and engineering development. These were extremely important activities for the growing technology-based corporations, but they lacked the scientific components that could often bring revolutionary advances in industrial technology.

As Chapter 4 has shown, only after the GE Research Laboratory achieved success with the incandescent lamp was it able to diversify the scope and methods of its research. This change marked the transformation from corporate engineering and analysis to industrial research as defined in the first chapter: activity set apart from production; undertaken by people trained in science and engineering who worked toward deeper understanding of corporate-related science and technology; and administered in such a way as to keep researchers at least partially insulated from short-term business demands but responsive to long-term corporate needs. In this chapter I will discuss that transformation at GE and the policies that made it possible.

Willis Whitney and the administration of research

Willis Whitney began as the laboratory's chief researcher, but he soon added so many new staff and projects that he spent more time on administration than research. As late as 1907, however, Whitney was still undertaking projects himself, his last being an attempt to perfect the Auer tungsten-filament process. Whitney's physical and nervous breakdown convinced him that pursuing research as well as directing the laboratory placed him in too many different and potentially conflicting roles. After his return in 1908 he concentrated on administration, placing all of his attention on getting the most out of the lab's research – and out of its researchers.

Whitney's policies strongly influenced laboratory operations, for he clearly dominated both the choice of research problems and the actual direction of work. His philosophy harked back to Francis Bacon's 17th century utilitarian, experimental approach, which forswore analysis based on preexisting theory. Bacon believed that the accumulation of data, combined with observation and experience, would eventually lead to the solution of almost all research problems.[2] Whitney did not come to GE with this Baconian approach; his experience there directed him to it. During the laboratory's early years, Whitney failed to solve an important problem relating to arc lighting because the theoretical constructs of electrochemistry he brought to his work proved ineffective.[3] This finally led him to question the value of disciplinary approaches when applied to industrial research and to urge his staff to leave aside disciplinary-based theory in order to concentrate on understanding phenomena through observation and experiment. Of course, theory and experiment went hand in hand, but Whitney very strongly suggested that the latter precede any attempt at detailed theoretical analysis. He believed that chance favored the prepared mind, and he wanted to maximize the chances while keeping the minds open to new interpretations. Unanticipated discovery and understanding of new phenomena, often coming from one or more researchers piecing together seemingly unrelated results, was called "serendipity." By the 1920s it had become part of the laboratory's ideology.

Although the Research Laboratory maintained a scientific and technical library which Whitney encouraged researchers to use, he actively discouraged them from depending on results they found in the scientific literature. One staff member later recalled that the library "was well stocked with back and current numbers of periodicals, but woe to the man who ventured in to do more than grab a book and rush out again. . . . If a person had a new idea, Whitney's comment was apt to be, 'Fine, but try it out first before you read about it.' "[4]

Physicist Saul Dushman once commented that the surest way to anger Whitney was to use preconceived theory to suggest the impossibility of achieving a particular result. Dushman knew about that; he and Whitney often argued about the efficacy of theory. Another lab worker remembered Whitney calling Dushman a "damned schoolteacher" to drive home his disdain for the theoretical approach to problem solving.[5] Yet Whitney permitted his researchers considerable latitude, and some of the most productive, like Dushman and Langmuir, placed great emphasis on theoretical analysis. Nevertheless, as I show in this chapter, they frequently tied theory very closely to application, for they knew that their primary duty was to support the commercial interests of GE.

By the Research Laboratory's second decade, Whitney had come to perceive his role as that of a leader rather than an administrative director. In the early years he had tried to be both, perhaps even leaning toward the latter; but the strain had been too great, and the lab's successes too limited. No single individual could deal effectively with the Research Laboratory Advisory Council, coordinate the activities of a number of research teams, and still keep in touch with all of the activities underway in the lab and in other parts of the company. Furthermore, the laboratory's greatest accomplishment, ductile tungsten, had come not as a result of some project that he had carefully organized and administered but because one well-prepared and imaginative researcher had taken a new approach based on experience and observation.

In 1908 Whitney created the position of Research Laboratory Executive Engineer to remove some of the administrative burden from himself and to institutionalize the lab's liaison with the engineering laboratories and production operations. Significantly, the first person to fill this post, Samuel Ferguson, came to the Research Laboratory from Steinmetz's engineering group. Ferguson helped coordinate activities between the laboratory and engineers in other parts of the company, handled much of the lab's routine correspondence, prepared budgets, and took responsibility for maintaining its facilities. He also collected materials from researchers in order to draw up summary reports for presentation at advisory council meetings. In 1912, Lawrence Hawkins, an MIT engineer who had worked for nine years in the GE Patent Department, took over the position and held it until 1945.[6]

After the laboratory's early experiences, Whitney began to view research administration as potentially counterproductive. He came to believe very strongly that too much organization was worse than none at all. He found dealing with the advisory council burdensome and its oversight intrusive, so he put an end to the meetings as soon as he could. He tried to make the Research Laboratory's organization as informal as possible, minimizing red tape, and proceeding on a generally ad hoc basis.[7] To a 1912 query about lab administration, Whitney responded: "It is perfectly conceivable to me that a laboratory could go to pieces and still have very systematic arrangement. . . . I dread organization and system so much that I want to warn others from expending much time and effort upon it."[8]

Yet there was careful thought given to the "disorganization" of the Research Laboratory. Small groups met regularly to discuss common concerns; scientists and engineers, often with the help of the executive engineer, carefully maintained liaison with other parts of the company; and Whitney got his researchers to work on those types of problems he believed most closely related to GE's commercial interests. Whitney directed with a light hand, suggesting projects to researchers rather than assigning them; but he directed nonetheless, and he did it very effectively.[9]

Whitney showed a personal concern for each researcher in the laboratory. When, in 1908, he decided to devote full time to directing, he developed a management style intended to get the best results from every member of his staff. Whitney gave constant encouragement and direction to some researchers, while others received more leeway, along with constructive criticism. Whitney could be quite subtle in his approach. Regarding one man, he commented, "I must show that I expect the goods but also that I expect to see him deliver them easily." To foster close personal contact, Whitney toured the lab almost every day and encouraged researchers to seek him out at any time. In 1909 a sign appeared over his office door that read "Come In Rain Or Shine," and he meant it. Whitney had chosen to lead rather than direct. Consulting chemist Arthur D. Little, who knew him very well, remarked, "Whitney can talk to a man for three minutes and inject into him enough enthusiasm to last three months."[10]

But leading the Research Laboratory did not entail simply drawing forth each researcher's best efforts. Work had to be coordinated within the lab and between it, engineering departments, and production facilities. Projects needed to be initiated and, what was often more difficult, terminated. Results had to be patented and put to use within the complex engineering, manufacturing, financial, commercial, and legal entity that comprised General Electric. Whitney could leave some of this to the executive engineer, but he still had to do much of it himself.

Whitney facilitated research on a daily basis. During his regular rounds of the laboratory he offered numerous suggestions. "He made a lot more inventions that way than anyone realized," one researcher commented. "Some of them were good – some of them weren't so good." If a project were at a critical stage or in difficulty of some sort, Whitney often brought along Coolidge, Langmuir, or Hull to advise both him and the researcher.[11] Later, he sent in other staff members whose expertise might be useful. They not only advised on current problems but made suggestions as to how the project could yield new or improved products. Whitney believed strongly in the value of cross-fertilization – that, for example, "knowledge gained along the line of insulation" by one researcher "would be of use in [the study of] conduction" by another.[12] Such contacts, he believed, engendered serendipity.

Whitney also used Coolidge, Langmuir, and Hull to help him wean staff members from projects that no longer showed any likelihood of being productive, at least as far as the company's needs were concerned. They even counseled each other in these matters. Hull recalled that in 1918, after he had been working on X-ray crystal analysis for some time, "Langmuir advised me that there was no end to it, and that I could do something *more interesting*. So I dropped the crystal analysis work and went back to electronics."[13]

After the World War, Whitney came to depend on Coolidge, Langmuir, Hull, Dushman, and a few of his other best researchers as informal group leaders. Each took responsibility for loose oversight of five to ten staff members, though without actually directing their research. Langmuir, for example, served as a sounding board and a synthesizer of information but limited his formal role to preparing the group reports of work, which were periodically submitted to Whitney.[14]

Whitney based his philosophy of research management on the belief that, first and foremost, researchers' morale and motivation had to be kept high; that enthusiasm was more likely to breed results than even the most carefully organized research effort. The problem he faced was to supply encouragement and permit a reasonable amount of independence while keeping researchers at work on what he considered to be appropriate projects. For this reason, some sidetracking – and hence some scientific research with little chance of being useful to GE (like Hull's X-ray crystal analysis) – had to be tolerated. But when this type of research had gone too far, staff members needed to be brought back on track. Whitney tried to make certain that this was done gently so as not to lower morale and ruin motivation. He often interested researchers in other projects and saw to it that they were encouraged about them. Most took the "suggestion," so Whitney got the work he desired, at least after a short time.[15]

In some cases Whitney wanted highly developmental projects undertaken – ones that, for example, required considerable effort to transform a device from prototype to commercial reality. Researchers usually did as he requested, but they sometimes believed this kind of work to be a poor use of their time. Albert Hull, in reflecting on how he had missed receiving credit for important scientific discoveries because he became extensively involved in development work, remarked that, "The philosophy behind that incident, which is typical of all the experience I've had, is that whenever I've been diverted into spending time on development, it turned out to be a poor investment of time."[16] Yet Whitney clearly believed that development work paid the Research Laboratory's "dues" to GE, and that without it, none of the scientific research Hull cared so much about would have been possible. The pursuit of science had an important place in industrial research, but advancing commercial technology remained its *sine qua non*.

During his early years as research director, Whitney attempted to maintain some control of the information flow within the laboratory and between it and other GE departments. In 1903 he directed a "General Notice" to the managers at the Schenectady Works:

> Will you kindly recognize the propriety and importance of addressing all correspondence intended for any of the investigators of this Laboratory, or the various development departments under its direction in the factory, to me, and not to other individuals therein? The necessary system for filing new suggestions, and for properly directing the details of the work, make this absolutely necessary.[17]

Whitney also carefully controlled interaction between the laboratory and the GE Patent Department. Researchers submitted monthly reports on their work that he combed for patentable inventions. When he found something promising, Whitney sent a memorandum to the Patent Department along with the relevant report. The reports of work themselves helped Whitney keep track of lab activities. They also forced the researchers to compile and analyze their results. Finally, they served as dated records for establishing inventive priorities. Researchers were of course expected to keep records as they worked, though Whitney placed more emphasis on the formal reports.[18]

In 1908 his approach changed. Whitney began issuing consecutively numbered notebooks, carefully keeping track of their ownership. This was part of a program to stress the autonomy and responsibility of each researcher. Every notebook entry was to be dated, signed, and witnessed. "Write something in your notebook every day," Whitney told his staff, "even if it's only 'I didn't do a damn thing today.' " However, not everyone kept up his entries as desired. By 1920 Whitney acknowledged that careful record-keeping had "always been desired – used to be expected – but it has not been attained and therefore is not required. . . . Some of the best men are the poorest record keepers."[19]

Nevertheless, the records of the laboratory were quite good. All reports of work spelled out both methods and results. Whitney supplied researchers with standardized sheets to record data in a form that was useful to them and clear to outsiders. He also made certain that the apparatus and even the rooms themselves were photographed frequently.[20]

During the 1910s the Research Laboratory – Patent Department relationship changed. Whitney no longer reviewed reports of work in order to send letters suggesting patent applications. Instead, the Patent Department assigned several attorneys to follow laboratory research by reading reports of work and visiting research in progress.[21] Patents could be derived in a number of ways by these means. Albert Hull, discussing his work on X-ray crystal analysis, related the following example:

> It was necessary to smooth out the fluctuations of this rectified voltage, which I did in the way that any physicist would do, by using a pair of condensers across the line with an inductive choke between them. I had no idea of making an invention and when a young patent attorney, Mr. W. G. Gartner who was following the work of the Laboratory for the General Electric Patent Department, came to see if there was anything patentable in my apparatus, I told him, "No." But in looking it over, he noticed this filter circuit and patented it for me.[22]

This shows that the patent attorney following Hull's research had adequate technical competence to understand the circuit and to recognize its commercial value, even though Hull himself did not. It also shows that important results – in this case a patent that was later licensed to every manufacturer of radio receivers[23] – could emerge from research not oriented toward commercial application.

This is certainly an unusual example, but such cross-connections did occur, and the Research Laboratory – Patent Department relationship was structured to find most that did.

The Patent Department kept the Research Laboratory informed of company patent needs, and lab workers often undertook or extended research projects in an attempt to meet them. For example, when Hull discovered the power of magnetic fields to control current flow in vacuum tubes, he spent considerable time on the idea because it presented an opportunity for GE to circumvent the de Forest grid-control (audion) patent, to which AT&T held rights. His "magnetron" vacuum tube, though never used commercially, bolstered GE's position in its 1920 negotiations with AT&T over rights to radio production.[24]

Laboratory relations within GE

The Research Laboratory was only one of a number of laboratories maintained by GE. Rapidly changing technologies in electric power generation and distribution, in electric motors and traction, and of course, in electric lighting, required the company to maintain several development laboratories as it pushed its technological advantages over competitors. In addition to the works labs at each manufacturing installation, there were a number of more specialized labs: the Standardizing Laboratory (later known as the General Engineering Laboratory), which, after the turn of the century, added substantial engineering development work (especially on high-voltage phenomena) to its standardizing function; the Schenectady Works Testing Laboratory for testing materials; the Illuminating Engineering Laboratory, which attempted to find the best type and arrangements of lighting units for varied installations; the Insulations Laboratory, specializing in high-power insulation problems; lamp development laboratories at the Harrison, New Jersey and (later) Cleveland production facilities, for developing and standardizing new processes, materials, and designs for lamp making; and the Consulting Engineering Laboratory run by Steinmetz and devoted to projects he deemed of importance even though they had not been taken up by the Research Laboratory.[25] The company established other specialized development laboratories as need arose, like the Radio Engineering Department (1918).

The presence of these laboratories in the GE organization relieved the Research Lab of routine investigations and strictly developmental work,[26] but also created problems of coordination and, in certain cases, jealousy. Steinmetz, unhappy with the disparity in resources allocated to the Research Laboratory and to his own Consulting Engineering Laboratory, often complained. Other engineering organizations sometimes attempted to wrest responsibility from the Research Lab for important areas of company research work, but they usually failed.[27]

Under the circumstances, coordinating research among the laboratories, and, in the words of Executive Engineer Hawkins, "having thoro [*sic*] and cordial cooperation" between them, sometimes presented great difficulties. To facilitate that cooperation, the executive engineer maintained contact with all labs and manufacturing departments whose interests overlapped those of the Research Laboratory. Under his direction, laboratory workers provided research services and supplied the company's engineers with advanced apparatus like vacuum tubes. He also maintained close relations with the GE Sales Department and informed researchers of salesmen's perceptions of market opportunities as they related to technologies under development.[28] In addition to the executive engineer, certain individuals within the laboratory were assigned the tasks of following company needs and production problems, discussing them with engineering and production personnel, and bringing them to the attention of appropriate people in the laboratory.[29] Beginning about 1912, Whitney sent all divisions of the company a regular "Progress Report" about the lab's research accomplishments and about the status of work under way.[30]

Laboratory researchers were also kept well informed and integrated into GE operations on a somewhat less formal basis. Engineers and managers from all over the company spoke at Research Laboratory meetings to discuss their needs.[31] Perhaps one of the most effective ways of integrating the lab into company operations resulted from its proximity to the Schenectady Works. As one staff member later recalled:

> Since the Research Lab was right down at the works, I had a lot of contact with the other operations of the company. I used to go across the street to the Standardizing Lab quite often, to see what was going on there. I got a real education in what was really happening in the company. Also, Langmuir used to take me down to the big shops, especially the turbine shops.[32]

Laboratory workers with such contacts were not likely to believe that their research was an end in itself. Made fully aware on a daily basis of operations at the works, they thought in terms of how their research could be useful for meeting GE's engineering and manufacturing requirements. As one researcher put it, "There were always needs in the General Electric Company, and one way or another, we knew about them."[33]

To further its efforts for full integration with company operations, the Research Laboratory worked closely with the engineering and manufacturing divisions. In certain cases it even took people in, trained them in areas related to its research, then placed them in various works laboratories, thus facilitating the transfer of technology from Research Lab to production. During their early work on incandescent lamps, lab scientists and engineers made frequent trips to the Harrison Lamp Works to gain a fuller understanding of manufacturing operations. Lamp works engineers came regularly to Schenectady as well.[34] As a result of this close working relationship, materials and techniques developed in the laboratory were appropriate for mass manufacture, while the lamp works was able to gear up for changes in production as smoothly as possible.

In some cases, the Research Laboratory set up pilot plants or experimental production lines in preparation for full-scale manufacture. Responding to a query from a company in the process of establishing its own research program, Whitney explained the lab's approach to the development of production processes:

> The extent to which the men engaged in scientific research have to do with practical development work and ultimate production varies widely in different cases. In the case of new devices, it depends largely on the novelty and interest of the engineers in charge of the department or factory in which the device is to be produced. For instance, in the case of Coolidge [X-ray] tubes, the thing was so new, and required such novel apparatus and methods in its production, that we not only first put the tube on a production basis in the laboratory, but when it outgrew our available space, we started a new factory department, with laboratory men in charge, to make the tube. . . . In other cases we carry the thing in the laboratory to the extent of small scale production, simply to eliminate production troubles, or to develop the technique, and then turn the thing bodily over to the factory department. In still other cases we carry the device no farther than the experimental stage, and then turn it over to factory engineers to complete the development, and to initiate production. The whole thing

> may be summed up in saying that we do what we think is necessary to get the productive activity properly started, but the extent of productive activity which we consider necessary in a given case may vary from zero to one hundred per cent.[35]

Whitney preferred to keep some production work in the laboratory because it served as a source of income to offset expenses. For example, receipts on tungsten electrical contacts (sold to automakers for use in ignition systems) amounted to a total of $472,000 for the years 1912–16 against itemized manufacturing expenses of $202,000, giving a $270,000 "profit" that amounted to 15% of the laboratory's total budget over the period. Whitney justified this manufacturing activity by claiming that it made use of equipment not found elsewhere in the company; that it was on such a small scale no other company divisions had any interest in taking it over; that certain products called for low quantity and extremely high quality, which only the lab could provide economically; and that "this profit has been . . . an important help, since it is a relief to all of us to feel that the money is not all going out, but that some is coming back." For the years 1912–16, the proportion of the Research Laboratory's budget compensated by manufacturing credits on items sold both outside the company and to divisions within GE ranged from 25% (1912) to 79% (1914).[36]

This use of income from in-house manufacturing suggests the complexity of the Research Laboratory's budgetary process after 1910. Like other GE divisions, the lab was treated as a "profit center," judged in part on whether it showed a profit or loss at the end of each year. Every major project was supported either by the division that requested it or by the laboratory itself. In the latter case, the lab recouped expenses if it sold the results within GE. Unsolicited projects with unsaleable products appeared on the books as losses, so there was a very strong concern that projects initiated within the lab should produce useful results. One company official confirmed that this arrangement was "unquestionably a great incentive to Dr. Whitney and his principal assistants."[37]

This transformation from a simple corporate stipend for the lab to a complex accounting system took place at the same time Whitney made many of the other changes in administration discussed in the first section of this chapter. Whitney also began to have the executive engineer prepare an annual report of "articles made regularly by this Company which had their origins in the Research Laboratory," along with an estimate of their total sales or other value to GE. This demonstrated the continuing importance of the lab's research and helped justify its regular "losses" as a corporate division.[38]

Tying the Research Laboratory into GE's other divisions by financial means helped bring lab operations into harmony with manufacturing and engineering needs. In order to minimize unrecouped expenses, the laboratory constantly appraised its research efforts in light of their value to other corporate divisions; this meant that only a small amount of "unproductive" research could be tolerated. It was a measure of Whitney's genius as a research director that he kept his staff at work in potentially useful directions at the same time that he gave them the feeling they had at least limited freedom to pursue research as they saw fit.[39]

Researchers and the lab

Whitney looked both for bright, highly motivated researchers and for those who worked well in a cooperative environment. During the lab's early years – when he had been much more directive in his approach – the latter characteristic did not seem so important. A number of the men whom Whitney hired then, schooled in the more secretive atmosphere of German academic and industrial labs, had been less than fully cooperative with Whitney or with each other. This led patent counsel Albert Davis, one of the early advocates of the Research Laboratory, to refer to it as the "menagerie" and the "bear pit." By 1910 most foreign-born researchers had left, probably because of Whitney's policy of paying them less than American staff members.[40]

In order to attract and keep first-rate people, Whitney had to be able to compensate for the inevitable loss of independence researchers suffered in GE's corporate environment. He did this in a number of ways. In the early years Whitney generally offered potential employees a salary about 15% greater than they could command in an academic position; later that was increased. Special people, like Langmuir or Coolidge, might get as much as 50% to 100% more as an incentive to join GE, then receive considerable raises afterward. Whitney based researchers' annual salary increments on their value to the lab, which included cooperation and contributions to the work of others. He steadfastly rejected a bonus system to reward outstanding results as being counterproductive, at least in terms of cooperation and *esprit* within the lab.[41] To

Whitney – especially after 1908 – *esprit de corps* was the most important ingredient in the mixture that made for successful industrial research.

Professional staff members were accommodated in other ways as well. In general, Whitney tried to emulate the university environment through means that also helped orient the researchers toward company problems. A regular colloquium, begun in the fall of 1901, brought laboratory researchers together to hear about important discoveries and issues in the world of science and technology, as presented both by staff members and by outsiders. Company engineers and managers often addressed the colloquium on problems and opportunities facing GE. In reformulating his approach to research direction in 1908, Whitney put new emphasis on the importance of the colloquium. He hoped to do away with any vestiges of secrecy by making researchers discuss their projects before the entire group. This would encourage teamwork and engender cross-fertilization. Such a colloquium, he noted, "affects the personnel by effecting closer and more friendly intercourse (not one against the other but we against the world) Utmost importance."[42]

The Research Laboratory's library was another means of accommodation, and an important research tool as well. By 1915 the library held a substantial scientific and technical collection of 1,400 volumes and sixty-five periodicals, overseen by a full-time librarian. During the next six years its holdings more than doubled. Even though Whitney claimed in 1910 that "the most useful and fertile of our investigators use the library the most," his assertion must be balanced against the staff member's statement, quoted above, that the director discouraged researchers from referring to the scientific and technical literature before they began new projects for fear that they might be misdirected by their predecessors' conceptions and results.[43]

GE researchers also had access to far better support in terms of equipment and assistants than they were likely to find in academia. After 1915 the laboratory was supplied with various gases, steam, flexible power supplies, and shop services. The most advanced electrical and electronic apparatus were brought in from the engineering labs or built in-house. Whitney did not hesitate to buy special equipment like vacuum furnaces or hydraulic presses, which, after they had become "part of the equipment . . . it seemed [im]possible to proceed without."[44] The Research Laboratory employed skilled craftsmen, such as glassblowers and mechanics, as well as numerous assistants to handle routine matters. For anyone serious about research and development work, the lab offered unsurpassed facilities.

Torn as he was between the calling of science and the opportunities of industrial research, Whitney realized that in order to attract and keep good people, he had to allow them to take part in the scientific community by publishing some of their research results. But publication could create difficulties, since the company did not want its rights to inventions compromised. Thus, researchers always had to wait until all related patent applications had been filed before submitting their articles, and complete disclosure was not always possible. Laboratory staff members often missed receiving credit for their work because outsiders published results first or more fully. They even had to get prior approval from the Patent Department to present papers at scientific and technical meetings.[45] Still, Whitney permitted – even encouraged – his people to prepare their materials for publication. By 1920 the GE laboratory had acquired a strong reputation as a scientific institution, even though, judging by the number of papers published annually per researcher, its output was rather low compared to a good university lab.[46]

Sometimes, however, secrecy was strictly enforced. In such cases, Whitney cautioned staff members not to talk about particular projects to anyone, not even to other GE employees. These measures could be quite effective. For example, the laboratory's ductile-tungsten research remained unknown in Europe until GE demonstrated tungsten wire there in late 1909.[47] Up to that time, Coolidge had been unable to publish any of his results, which left him quite discouraged about earning a scientific reputation. Some laboratory researchers, at least, believed that much of their work was kept secret "for company reasons."[48]

Even with these restrictions on communication and publication, Whitney had little trouble finding researchers willing to work at GE. He recruited them from a number of places. In the early days, he took many from MIT, mostly Ph.D.s without entirely satisfactory staff positions or undergraduates just finishing their degrees. MIT's influence on the Research Laboratory during its first decade was marked at a time when the institute retained a very strong engineering and applied-science outlook. Although most of the staff were recruited directly from college or graduate school, a few did leave faculty positions to join GE because they were unhappy with their opportunities to do research in an academic setting. As Albert Hull noted, "After finishing my postgraduate work, I taught for five years [1908-1913] at the Worcester Polytechnic Insititute. During those years I spent all the spare time I could snatch from sleep in research work. . . . After five years I was getting a bit discouraged about the future prospect of teaching. I couldn't see the way ahead."[49] Irving Langmuir, who joined the faculty of Stevens Institute of Technology in 1906, assisted there in several courses as well as teaching his own. To his chagrin, he found few students with an interest in science. His attempts to upgrade the laboratory facilities and the quality of student work met with hostility from students and indifference from his colleagues. To make matters worse, he had little time for research. When he left in 1909 to join the GE Research Laboratory, Langmuir found a position that met his needs far better.[50]

In looking for accomplished researchers, Whitney often used invitations to address the colloquium as means of determining how well people would fit into the laboratory. In one case, Whitney decided not to hire a physicist – even though his research on incandescent lamps was "interesting and suggestive" – because he did not understand the language of the lamp engineers in dealing with lamp efficiency. To Whitney, this suggested a lack of serious interest in technological problems. Some researchers, like Saul Dushman, decided to accept offers of employment in part because they were impressed by the caliber of discussion at their colloquium presentations.[51] Whitney also hired a number of graduate students and university faculty to work for a few months over the summer; in this way he could look them over as potential employees. In fact, that was how he hired Langmuir and Hull. In general, Whitney sought people with decided experimental bents who were well prepared in the fundamentals of chemistry, physics, and mathematics. Individuals who had earned undergraduate degrees in engineering and Ph.D.s in science often proved to be the most fruitful researchers; Langmuir and Coolidge both had this background.

As part of its program to give engineers exposure to a number of company organizations, GE rotated them through several different operations, in some cases including the Research Laboratory. A few fit in well and stayed on. One such person was Vincent Shaeffer, who began as Langmuir's assistant and later did important research of his own.

Whitney encouraged Research Laboratory staff members to join scientific and engineering societies. He himself was very active in the American Electrochemical Society and the American Chemical Society. The latter organization elected both Whitney and Langmuir as president, and Hull became president of the American Physical Society, high honors for all of them. Laboratory researchers regularly attended meetings of the various societies, but they were restricted as to the subjects they could discuss, and, as mentioned earlier in this chapter, they needed company clearance to present papers.[52] Nonetheless, they used these meetings to maintain important professional contacts. They took part in an interchange of information and ideas that benefited not only themselves and the Research Laboratory, but also the outside community of scientists and engineers, including employees of their competitors. Whitney realized that to cut off this type of exchange would make his laboratory very insular. He was therefore prepared to provide some help to GE's competitors in order to be certain that his researchers remained open to new developments in science and engineering.

The rate of turnover in the laboratory was low, but some researchers did leave. A number went to other divisions of GE, often following developments through the engineering and production phases, then settling in one of the places where they had worked. Others decided that, lucrative pay scales and opportunities to do research notwithstanding, they preferred academic positions. Wheeler Davey, a Ph.D. physicist from Cornell who joined the Research Laboratory in 1914, left during the 1920s for a position at Pennsylvania State University. Others took jobs at Harvard, Yale, and MIT. Such losses were the price that Whitney paid for permitting his researchers to publish results and make professional names for themselves. Some staff also left to take jobs with other companies, often in research management positions.[53] Whatever the reasons, these departures from the Research Laboratory suggest that not everyone found there what he sought. The lab as Whitney ran it, especially after 1908, was a peculiar kind of place; not everyone fit in. For those who did, however, it provided a satisfactory – even satisfying – alternative to the usual academic and industrial careers.

By the second decade of its operation, the GE Research Laboratory had become a full industrial research institution according to the definition I set out in the introductory chapter. Staffed by scientists and research engineers who worked toward deeper understandings of physical phenomena; set apart from engineering and production operations; largely insulated from the company's immediate demands, it was nonetheless responsive to GE's business needs in the long term. The laboratory had been molded by a director vitally concerned with meeting those needs but also chary of losing his scientific identity in the corporate environment. The laboratory operation he developed could be characterized as both organized and disorganized, for researchers were carefully directed while seemingly free to pursue their work as they saw fit. A strong institutional culture had been developed: with a minimum of organization and bureaucratic control, a clearly defined set of values and boundaries directed researchers' work along the productive paths that led to commercially valuable results.

Science and technology in the research lab

To better understand the process of research and development in the laboratory it is useful to consider the work of two of its outstanding scientist–engineers, William Coolidge and Irving Langmuir. With similar educational backgrounds but dissimilar orientations, these two men approached their research in very different ways. Both had undergraduate degrees in engineering and German Ph.D.s – Coolidge in physics, Langmuir in physical chemistry. Although each retained a technological orientation from his engineering background, Coolidge approached problems directly, setting goals and confronting difficulties one at a time until he had accomplished his ends. Langmuir, by contrast, first undertook fundamental studies in order to obtain a full understanding of physical processes, then used this knowledge to make technical advances.

These methods proved effective for the types of projects that each man undertook. Coolidge employed his imaginative and precise experimental approach to overcome numerous obstacles in the fabrication of ductile tungsten. Langmuir studied the phenomena of electrical emission in gases and vacuum to learn how incandescent lamps and electron tubes could be improved. An examination of Coolidge's work on ductile tungsten and Langmuir's on incandescence suggests how these very different approaches to problem solving could, in the end, lead to very similar types of results.

William Coolidge and the development of ductile tungsten

William Coolidge was an ingenious designer of equipment and a gifted experimentalist. He had a way of making things work, perhaps as a result of his boyhood on a struggling Massachusetts farm. As a doctoral student at the University of Leipzig, Coolidge had been Professor Gustav Wiedemann's special assistant. Arthur Noyes gave him the most complex experimental work in the MIT physical chemistry laboratory.[54] Whitney had become acquainted with him during the days when Coolidge was an undergraduate at MIT and Whitney still taught there. Whitney believed that Coolidge possessed the experimental skills the Research Laboratory needed to make progress in its metal-filament work. While doing postdoctoral research at MIT, Coolidge had developed a high-pressure "bomb" apparatus for the study of chemical reactions under extreme conditions, a task that required knowledge of the properties of metals at high temperatures and pressures. This introduction to metallurgy served him well in the battle with tungsten. Coolidge began his research on tungsten during the months before he left for Schenectady. Once at GE, he ignored the "bomb" he had brought along because the research on tungsten became all-consuming.

At the time there was little knowledge of tungsten upon which Coolidge could draw. Metallurgy as a discipline was still more concerned with improving traditional methods of fabrication than with understanding internal structures of materials, though such studies were getting under way. Without an established scientific basis for dealing with the problem, Coolidge had to use his training in chemistry and physics to help him understand what took place within and between the crystals of the extremely hard, brittle metal. His careful observations of changes in tungsten's crystalline structure guided him throughout the work. No one had yet achieved noncatastrophic deformation of tungsten, and it was the almost unanimous opinion of chemists and metallurgists that the metal displayed an inherently brittle character.[55] Had Whitney accepted this assessment, of course, he would not have devoted the laboratory's resources to Coolidge's project. However, Whitney's growing belief that preexisting theory provided more of a roadblock than a signpost suggested that substantial work be done before dismissing the possibility of fabricating ductile tungsten.

Coolidge began his research by studying the effect of impurities on tungsten. He first produced the purest metal possible, then deliberately added other elements to study their effect. Finding little difference in the results, he concluded that brittleness was an inherent characteristic of the metal. This work gave him important clues. In testing for brittleness, he carefully hammered several specimens and found that, if heated to certain exact temperatures, they could be slightly deformed without shattering. This led him to believe that the metal might somehow be made ductile entirely by mechanical and thermal means as he worked its crystalline structure into a fibrous state.

Meanwhile a number of experimenters in Europe had found ways to fabricate tungsten filaments by mixing the powdered metal with carbon-based binders. They squirted the resulting paste through a die, then vaporized the binder and sintered the metal to leave a brittle tungsten filament. Coolidge's experience with a number of metals suggested to him that a better binder might be made from a highly ductile metal like gold, silver, or cadmium. After considerable experimentation, he settled on an amalgam binder of cadmium, bismuth, and mercury because it held its plasticity over a wide range of conditions. At carefully controlled temperatures, Coolidge could bend amalgam-impregnated filaments into closely spiralled coils, then vaporize the amalgam to leave almost-pure metal. This coiled configuration, which concentrated the source of light, gave more effective filaments for lamps used in conjunction with a lens or reflector.[56]

Coolidge's visit to the Auer laboratory in 1908 rekindled his interest in making ductile tungsten by thermal and mechanical means. When he returned to Schenectady he developed a complex process for drawing filaments through a series of dies to change their crystalline structure and, he hoped, to improve their ductility. First, in order to introduce the filament into a die that was smaller than the filament itself, Coolidge had to narrow its entering end, so he electrolyzed the tip in a concentrated aqueous solution of potassium cyanide. The process reduced the diameter without pitting the surface (which would have made the filament weaker at the point where the hot pliers grasped it). Coolidge's experience in chemistry at MIT led him to this chemical solution to a physical problem. The drawing process had to be done at carefully controlled temperatures, so Coolidge developed means to supply exact amounts of heat to the die, to the pliers, and to the filament, both before the filament entered the die and after it left. Numerous experiments were required to determine appropriate specimen and apparatus temperatures. Coolidge learned that tungsten became more ductile only when worked below its annealing temperature – the opposite of other metals – and that the annealing temperature itself decreased as the metal was worked. Of course, if he hammered, rolled, or drew the metal at more than a few degrees below its ever-changing annealing temperature, it cracked or shattered.[57] Thus, the amount of working had to be closely correlated with controlled decreases in temperature throughout the process. No existing theory or analytic technique could predict the appropriate temperatures and amounts of working. That came only through painstaking experiment.

Whitney hired a special lapidary expert to work on the design and lubrication of the diamond dies. With his help, Coolidge succeeded in drawing tungsten filaments through a series of five progressively smaller dies in late 1908. This made a partially ductile form of the metal that could be permanently deformed at room temperature without fracture.[58] However, its ductility was not great enough for use in high-speed lamp-making machinery, nor was the process expandable to a commercial scale because of the limited length of the brittle filaments used to initiate the process. So research continued. Nevertheless, Coolidge and his co-workers had accomplished something very important: through applications of chemistry and physics, using careful observation, analysis, and the imaginative design of experimental processes, they had finally demonstrated that pure tungsten could be made ductile.

In order to develop a method for use on a commercial scale, Coolidge next turned to creating ingots of the pure metal. The process that yielded tungsten from ores left it in a powdered form, and Coolidge compressed this powder in a steel mold to fuse it. He found that to make crack-free ingots he needed extended study of the mold's design, the amount of pressure and the speed with which it was applied, and the use of lubricants for extraction. To give the finished ingots much greater mechanical strength, Coolidge first baked them (in an atmosphere of hydrogen to prevent their picking up impurities), then sintered them electrically at high temperature. This later operation caused considerable problems, such as explosions when air leaked into the treatment vessel during cooling. Coolidge and his staff worked several months on the sintering process to make it consistent and safe.[59] Even then, the finished ingots proved to be completely brittle, not only cold but also hot. They could not be worked in any way without shattering.

Coolidge called in the Schenectady Works blacksmith, but his techniques were no more successful than the others.

During the attempts to hammer the hot tungsten ingots, Coolidge noticed that the first blow to a spot rarely caused difficulties, while the second or subsequent blows induced failure. Because he knew the importance of maintaining exact temperatures when working tungsten, Coolidge deduced that heat flowed from the metal to the hammer during the first blow, chilling the metal and making it unworkable. If he could maintain a precise temperature at the point of contact, mechanical methods might be possible. Coolidge and his co-workers built a rolling mill that passed a strong electric current from one roll to the other through the tungsten workpiece, heating it at the point where it was being compressed. They discovered that at exactly the right temperatures a considerable amount of deformation took place before shattering. In the samples he examined under his microscope, Coolidge found that the rolled tungsten had begun to take on a marked fibrous character.[60]

At this point Coolidge decided to learn more about how other industries dealt with problems in fine metalworking. He visited wire- and needle-making factories, where he was impressed with their rapid-hammering swaging machines. He acquired one for the lab, but initially found it to be no more effective with tungsten than any other form of working. However, Coolidge's hard-won understanding of the metal served him well. He realized that if the hammers were redesigned and the rate of movement of the workpiece regulated so that blows did not overlap; if the temperature of the tungsten and of the hammers were carefully controlled; then the metal would be amenable to working. With these and other minor modifications, he pounded his tungsten ingots into rods about one-quarter of an inch in diameter. Attempting to work them beyond that point, however, caused them to crack or shatter. Coolidge then tried using molybdenum, a metal similar to tungsten but slightly less brittle. Laboratory chemist Colin Fink, who had been studying the properties of molybdenum, helped him in this effort. In May 1909, using his modified swaging methods, Coolidge succeeded in transforming a block of molybdenum into a ductile wire entirely by thermal and mechanical means.[61]

At Whitney's urging, Coolidge procured a much smaller swaging machine, which could be run at higher speeds, with smaller hammers and dies. Using this device, followed by treatment with special compressing rollers, he reduced the tungsten rods to diameters of thirty-thousandths of an inch – small enough to begin the drawing process. With the tungsten rods, dies, and rollers heated to carefully controlled temperatures; with special lubricants baked onto the rods to prevent excessive wearing of the dies; and with a gradual reduction in temperatures as the working proceeded, Coolidge made ductile tungsten.[62]

But still more work was needed to create a commercial process, and a large number of researchers took part in the next stage of development. First they strove to assure consistency in the tungsten ingots used to make the wire. Many ingots had proved to be unworkable because they absorbed impurities during the baking and sintering processes. The GE researchers developed new types of furnaces, along with special ways of transporting the tungsten so that it would not come in contact with contaminants. Inconsistencies in ingot behavior still remained, however, and Coolidge finally determined that they resulted from trapped oxygen. The ingots had been made from fine-grained tungsten powder; when sintered in hydrogen gas, their surface fused before residual oxygen could be expelled from the interior by the hydrogen. This suggested to Coolidge that the solution might lie in starting the process with coarse-grained tungsten powder, so he put several lab researchers to work on methods of preparing it.[63]

Even with the achievement of consistency in producing ductile-tungsten filaments, one very serious problem remained. When most of the filaments were operated with alternating current, crystalline structures recurred. Where the edges of crystals lined up across the filaments, offsets developed, causing failure. But filaments whose coarse-grained tungsten powder had been made in crucibles coated with refractory oxides usually did not fail. Coolidge discovered that some of the oxides entered the tungsten as impurities. Even though they had no effect on working the tungsten, refractory oxides impeded crystal growth. The solution, then, lay in adding a controlled amount of an appropriate substance to the coarse tungsten powder. After prolonged experiment, Coolidge decided to use thoria, a rare-earth oxide.[64]

As a result of four years of effort and expenditures totalling well over $100,000, the Research Laboratory finally succeeded in producing ductile tungsten by a process that could be used on a commercial scale. After filing all the related patent applications, Coolidge and several of his co-workers published papers on their experiences with tungsten and other metals like molybdenum.[65]

Plate 11. William D. Coolidge explains the process of making ductile tungsten to Thomas Edison, 1914. Courtesy of General Electric Research and Development Center.

Coolidge's work on ductile tungsten aroused considerable interest among chemists and metallurgists and brought him the prestigious Rumford Medal of the American Academy of Arts and Sciences in 1914. GE attorneys later cited this award to emphasize the original nature of Coolidge's work in their defense of his ductile-tungsten patents.[66] Coolidge not only led GE researchers in the development of an important new commercial technology, he and his co-workers also made major contributions to the field of metallurgy in general and to powder metallurgy in particular.

Coolidge's careful, controlled, precise experimental style and his ability to identify critical problems were well matched with the tasks he undertook for the Research Laboratory. The process for making ductile tungsten could not have been determined by scientific or mathematical analysis alone. Of course, such analyses were needed to understand why certain changes took place in the metal and to suggest new methods of working it. But knowledge about metals was then so incomplete that Coolidge's only recourse was to experiment persistently as he further developed his understanding of the chemical and physical processes involved. Even then, the processes often proved to be so subtle or complex that his ability to predict behavior remained quite limited.

Coolidge used his considerable skills as an experimenter along with his excellent understanding of chemistry and physics to successfully attack a problem that many scientists had thought insoluble. Coolidge's method was actually reminiscent of Edison's determined efforts with the incandescent lamp during the late 1870s. Both encountered problems that were beyond the power of contemporary science to explain. With substantial resources at their command, both headed large teams of skilled researchers and craftsmen. Both experimented persistently until they achieved their goals, although Coolidge made more frequent use of theory and analysis, as befitted his training in science and engineering. Although Coolidge's approach was thus not really new in the annals of American technology, his project to develop ductile tungsten marked the first time that an American company had devoted substantial resources within a well-established, ongoing research program to make a preconceived breakthrough in an area of strong commercial interest. Its successful completion marked the beginning of a new era at the GE Research Laboratory.

Irving Langmuir at the GE Research Laboratory

Irving Langmuir joined the lab in 1909 after unhappy experience as a faculty member at Stevens Institute of Technology. His personal ambitions at that time were to make a scientific reputation for himself and a substantial income for his family. Employment by GE permitted him to do both.[67]

When Langmuir first reported to the Research Laboratory, Whitney told him to look around for a few days at work under way, then to decide on a project of his own. Langmuir chose to study the operation of GE's new ductile-tungsten filaments in vacuum. There were a number of practical problems associated with these filaments, primarily that they failed quickly when used with alternating current (soon to be solved by the addition of thoria) and that they gradually caused the inside of lamp bulbs to blacken. Langmuir set out not to solve these problems directly, but to understand the basic principles of lamp operation. He wanted to determine what reactions went on inside the bulbs and how variations in temperature and pressure affected them. With the help of three assistants, including a skilled toolmaker, he studied the dissociation of gases near the filament and the transfer of heat from it; the transportation of molecules between the filament, envelope space, and glass bulb; and the buildup of electrical charge within the lamp. His research took him into the general study of electrical discharge in gases and vacuum.[68] Langmuir undertook this study to gain a general understanding of the physical processes inside the lamp, not only to improve it. Indeed, he himself later claimed that "nearly all those experiments would have seemed quite useless, or even foolish, to a man who was making a direct and logical attack on the problem of improving tungsten lamps."[69]

Although Langmuir soon began research on other projects as well, this undertaking served as the focus of his interests for the next four years. Using the incandescent tungsten filament as a research tool, he discovered that at a temperature of about 3,600°F, hydrogen molecules underwent dissociation to atomic form. He used this knowledge to develop atomic-hydrogen welding, a means to apply intense heat to small areas. After experimenting for several years on the dissociation of molecules at high temperatures, he concluded that the lamp-blackening problem could be solved by introducing an inert gas into the bulb envelope, provided a specially configured filament were used. His research had shown that the light radiated from a filament was a direct function of its surface area, but that filament shape significantly affected heat loss. Knowing this, he designed a closely spiraled filament that emitted light from its total surface but lost heat only from the surface of the spiral. After all related patent applications had been filed, Langmuir published extensively on this work, both in scientific journals and in journals of the engineering societies.

Langmuir's research led him to a study of the thermionic emission and transportation of electrons in vacuum, a subject of great concern to physicists. Experimenters had found results so apparently inconsistent that contemporary theories of electron emission had been cast into doubt. Some physicists actually believed that electron emission in vacuum was impossible, that ion formation in a residual gas was necessary to bombard the filament, knocking off electrons. From his own carefully analyzed experiments, Langmuir concluded that "pure" electron emission *did* occur and that the anomalies resulted from a buildup of electric charge in the space around the filament. This, he believed, inhibited further emissions. He mathematically analyzed several shapes of emitter, showing that what he called "space charge" accounted for discrepancies from the results predicted by theory. In so doing, Langmuir was said to have "saved thermionic emissions for physics." He also acquired the knowledge needed to design better incandescent lamp filaments and to improve the emission characteristics of the electron tube then being developed in the Research Laboratory. Langmuir's scientific paper published in 1913 brought his results to the attention of the physics community. It also served as evidence for the originality of his ideas when GE attorneys defended his crucial high-vacuum tube invention against claims that it was a minor improvement rather than a conceptual breakthrough.[70]

In some phases of his thermionic emission work Langmuir required very high vacuum. Although GE already commanded the best vacuum techniques in the world, he improved upon them. He designed a new vacuum pump, developed a special oven for baking bulbs in order to disperse occluded gases, introduced the use of tungsten as a "getter" in the evacuated space (to remove any gas traces), and invented a sensitive, high-vacuum "molecular gauge" to measure the concentration of the remaining molecules.[71]

In this, his first major research project at GE, Langmuir showed that he was a powerful industrial researcher. He was able to recognize areas of research and types of experiments that promised knowledge valuable to his employer's commercial interests. He undertook this work not to improve the technology directly but to find "the scientific principles underlying these peculiar effects."[72] So much the better. Langmuir's research yielded significant results for GE in part because it absorbed his interests as a scientist. He did not stop when he had the answer to a predetermined question but drove on for as complete an explanation as he could find, often answering many previously unasked questions – and finding unexpected applications, such as hydrogen welding – along the way. Other researchers in the laboratory, like Albert Hull and Saul Dushman, operated similarly.

During his early years at GE Langmuir also undertook projects aimed directly at improving technology. He developed techniques for fabricating incandescent lamps, including the design of a machine to make tungsten paste. He worked closely with E. F. W. Alexanderson of the General Engineering Laboratory on the development of modulators for high-frequency alternators, including their application in radio systems. One day each week for several years he travelled to the GE works at Great Barrington, Massachusetts, where he helped veteran inventor William Stanley design an efficient electric stove.[73]

Langmuir also pursued research on heat transfer, a subject that had interested him greatly since the time it had played an important role in his doctoral research project. Drawing upon his experiments with incandescent filaments and with Stanley's stove, as well as upon his experience constructing bulb-baking ovens, he published several papers in the field. In each he attempted to extend or qualify earlier work and to tie theory closely to application. He took great pains to make his work available to engineers, presenting it at a convention of the American Institute of Electrical Engineers and publishing a separate paper to show how his results could be applied to technical problems.[74] Work of this type served to keep Langmuir in touch with the engineering community. It also brought him recognition from the engineers: both the electrical and mechanical engineering societies eventually awarded him their highest medals.

During this same period Langmuir played a major role in GE's development of radio and vacuum tubes. Indeed, in the improvement of the balky de Forest audion, he and a few colleagues accomplished almost as much as the large, well-organized team of scientists and engineers in the Bell System. However, the GE researchers never worked out methods to match service conditions with tube design, nor did they "cover the field" nearly so well, for their company's interests were more exploratory than defensive in character. Langmuir spearheaded the radio effort at a time when GE had expectations of going into the radio market. Through his efforts and those of his assistants and colleagues, the company was able to provide some of the very best radio equipment for the U.S. government when it began placing military orders in 1915.

But this was not the type of work upon which Langmuir built his reputation. The same research on incandescent filaments that contributed to his understanding of heat transfer led him to further analysis of gases at extreme temperatures and to a study of adsorption phenomena on filament surfaces. All of this ultimately yielded application, but first Langmuir pursued underlying principles. An abnormaly high heat loss from tungsten filaments in hydrogen gas led to his discovery of hydrogen molecular dissociation. For several years he studied how the hydrogen molecules split, how they interacted with the surface of the filament, and how they recombined, publishing a number of papers on the subject. This work brought him widespread recognition from physicists and chemists, including Ernest Rutherford, G. N. Lewis, and Niels Bohr.[75]

Langmuir went on to further studies of adsorption, the nature of atomic bonds, the structure of crystals, and the processes involved in condensation and sublimation. He attempted to demonstrate that, in general, the forces involved came from chemical bonds rather than from Newtonian attraction. In 1916 and 1917 he published two extensive papers on this topic titled "The Constitution and Fundamental Properties of Solids and Liquids." In the first paper Langmuir reviewed theories of the chemical bond. But because he was concerned with forces operating between molecules in crystals and surface films, and not with the chemical bond itself or the structure of molecules, he failed to understand fully several of the theories he rejected.[76] Langmuir's approach to science was strongly influenced by commercial concerns. He concentrated on molecular interaction in crystals and surface films in part because these phenomena might find application in technologies of interest to GE. Understanding surface phenomena, in particular, promised to be useful in the design of incandescent lamps and vacuum tubes.

Langmuir's method of research depended more on his analytical skills than on the complexity of his experiments. In studying the emission characteristics of thoriated tungsten filaments, for example, he used a simple vacuum tube and portable microammeter to make measurements, then went through a detailed analysis. From this he concluded that the thorium atoms diffused to the filament surface during incandescence, making a single, more or less complete layer. Because Langmuir conducted such simple experiments, his analysis often required the use of elaborate correction factors to offset shortcomings in the apparatus.[77]

Langmuir chose this method because he wanted to use particular types of apparatus – those that would be of interest to GE – and he often employed devices similar to or even identical with company products. His work on electron emissions is an excellent case in point. Here he used two products of commercial importance to GE: the tungsten-filament lamp and the vacuum tube. The results he obtained were applied to improving the products. His understanding of the accumulation of space charge in the vicinity of a filament led him to insert a positively biased, "space-charge" grid near the vacuum-tube filament to enhance emissions. Similarly, his work on heat and particle transfer within an incandescent lamp suggested ways to use inert gases in the envelope space without losing excessive heat. Studying the passage of electricity through gases in 1924, he realized that the standard explanation for the voltage difference between an anode (or "plate") and its surroundings was incorrect. Because he was working with high-voltage rectifiers similar to the ones GE manufactured, his experiments – which demonstrated that a differently shaped anode would be more efficacious in high-voltage operations – led to an improved product.[78]

Langmuir often subjected an apparatus to unusual conditions to see how it reacted. For example, in analyzing the action of lubricants between metals, he used water instead of oil. In studying the tungsten lamp, he introduced all kinds of gases to see what difference they made, even though generally accepted theory suggested improved operation with higher vacuum. When he came to a new understanding of some phenomenon, Langmuir set out the operative characteristics of "ideal" conditions, then worked out corrections to deal with reality, taking into account such factors as the use of finite (rather than infinite) elements or loss of heat through lead-in wires.[79]

Whether dealing with his own research or reviewing that of others, Langmuir always looked for applications. He not only suggested applications to others, but sometimes appropriated ideas from their work to acquire patents of his own.[80] He understood that properly posed questions often yielded results that could lead the researcher beyond the original problem, whether the problem had at first been formulated in terms of science or technology. As Whitney emphasized, chance favored the prepared mind; and Langmuir let few chances to find new explanations or new applications slip by. One excellent example of his concern with application has been related by Kennneth Kingdon, a physicist who joined the Research Laboratory in the early 1920s and initially worked with Langmuir. Kingdon had been making minor structural changes to the elements of GE's magnetically controlled, gas-filled tube. He showed Langmuir results that suggested ions were being trapped within the tube during operation. Kingdon recalled:

> We both went home that evening and wrote in our notebooks about it. I wrote down two or three possible applications to scientific research that occurred to me. Langmuir wrote about 25 or 30 pages about ways in which these trapped ions might be used to produce lower-impedance tubes. Here, then, was the great scientist writing up all the practical applications and the young tyro writing about the scientific applications.[81]

To Langmuir, as well as to other veterans of the laboratory, understanding the principles of the physical world and making improvements to technology were part of the same venture. As industrial researchers they often acquired new knowledge while experimenting with corporate-related technologies. Naturally, they turned first toward ways of using that knowledge to advance GE's commercial aims.

Langmuir's underlying concern with applicability gave considerable direction to his research. At a time when the frontiers of the scientific disciplines were moving beyond the standard concepts of particle interactions – to relativity and quanta, for example – Langmuir chose to retain a worldview based on the existence of discrete electrons, atoms, and molecules.[82] With rare exceptions Langmuir stayed on the proven path, enlightening it, even changing its direction somewhat. Yet he rarely took a new way altogether because he intended to remain a contributing member of the GE Research Laboratory. This meant working within those conceptual structures of science that had regularly yielded technological results in the past and that showed promise of continuing to do so. Such a perspective helped him become a powerful industrial researcher but precluded his making frequent contributions at the frontiers of science – at least as those frontiers were defined by the scientific disciplines. Langmuir had too great a concern with application to step outside the bounds of practicability for long, decidedly limiting the scope of his research work. But as an enthusiastic industrial researcher, that was a price he willingly paid.

In 1932 Langmuir won the Nobel Prize in chemistry for his

Plate 12. Edison's last visit to General Electric, 1923. Front row, from left: Coolidge, Whitney, Edison, Steinmetz, Langmuir. Courtesy of General Electric Research and Development Center.

research on physical processes at the surface of incandescent filaments. This was the first time that an industrial scientist had achieved the honor. More importantly for the GE Research Laboratory, Langmuir acquired sixty-three U.S. patents over the course of his career, many of great importance to the company. During his years at the laboratory, Langmuir showed what first-rate research could be like in an industrial environment. He brought with him the utilitarian outlook of an engineer in addition to the intellectual commitment of a creative scientist. He combined these attributes in his contributions to the broad range of science, technology, and commercial needs while achieving considerable personal satisfaction, measured at least in part in pecuniary terms. Asking probing questions, often using simple apparatus in conjunction with complex analyses, he garnered insights of value to science, to technology, and of course, to General Electric.

Conclusion

Research and development activities in the GE Research Laboratory took many forms during the laboratory's first two decades. This brief consideration of the work of Coolidge and Langmuir by no means exhausts the variety of style and substance in its works. Yet an examination of the two does suggest how Whitney encouraged disparate approaches to research, depending on the problems themselves and the capabilities of the individuals involved. It also shows how Whitney relied on the independent and inventive spirit of his carefully chosen crew in the constant battle to make research pay.

Coolidge and Langmuir used very different research methods, complementing each other in many ways; yet they fully agreed about working to meet company needs. Both took great care to remain involved with the corporate engineering and production functions. Langmuir even made a habit of regularly visiting the manufacturing and engineering departments to offer advice and to learn about problems and opportunities. Coolidge's and Langmuir's interests and methods characterized a laboratory that approached its tasks in varied ways while always remaining in tune with corporate operations. This broadly based style of research, which emerged from the Research Laboratory's difficult early years, served it and GE well in the succeeding decades.

6

The Establishment and Early Growth of Bell Telephone

During the period when the companies which merged to form GE were beginning operations (1879-85), the Bell Telephone System grew out of the technical work of Alexander Graham Bell and the commercial activities of Bell and his backers. Although the GE and Bell companies began at about the same time, their early experiences were very different. Both quickly became dominant in their fields, but only Bell had to fight off numerous attacks in its major market. As late as 1907 the Bell System could count about as many competing telephones in service as its own. Nevertheless, Bell initially took the same approach to the development and control of its all-important commercial technology as did GE: both companies assumed that there would be consistent technical advances in known directions and that they could purchase rights to important inventions. Not until Bell had undergone a significant change in direction would the company recognize the value of following GE's lead in the establishment of industrial research; even then, it did so only because a new technological threat made its entire commercial situation uncertain.

In this chapter I describe the early history of the Bell System in order to illuminate its long-standing corporate approaches to competition, innovation, and growth. This will help explain how changing management attitudes in an unclear commercial situation after 1907 influenced Bell's decision to establish industrial research, and how corporate operations affected the ways its laboratory fit in with the System's increasingly complex operations.

The invention of the telephone

In 1875, three years before he began work on the electric light, Thomas Edison was approached by Western Union to undertake inventive work on the harmonic telegraph. As the era's dominant

American communications company, Western Union intended to control this new type of multiplex telegraphy, which promised to send up to fifteen messages on a single line, reducing capital costs and providing significant commercial advantages. Edison had already made major improvements to the duplex telegraph and invented the quadruplex, so Western Union President Orton was quite pleased when he agreed to a contract.[1]

At a time when telegraphy was a big and profitable business, Edison did not labor alone. Western Union kept several other inventors under contract, while many independent inventors attempted to develop the technology and acquire the patents that would bring hefty compensation from Western Union or from one of its aggressive competitors. Alexander Graham Bell, a Scottish immigrant who started his career in America as an elocutionist and teacher of speech to the deaf, began experimenting with harmonic telegraphs in 1873. At the same time Edison made his agreement with Western Union in 1875, Bell received financial backing from the fathers of two of his deaf students. Thomas Sanders, a wealthy leather merchant, and Gardiner Hubbard, a U.S. Congressman and prominent attorney familiar with the workings of the U.S. Patent Office, invested in Bell because they saw great promise in his work. The three men formed the Bell Patent Association, with each to share equally in profits from Bell's telegraph inventions.

Yet Bell had another, distracting interest. Whereas the surest profit appeared to be in harmonic telegraphy, Bell's life work had focused on speech, and he really wanted to transmit speech, not code, by wire. A discussion in 1875 with Joseph Henry, then secretary of the Smithsonian Institution, firmly established the speaking telegraph (or "telephone") as his primary goal. Bell's partners, who could see little profit in a telephone, pressed him to work on the harmonic telegraph, but Bell continued to work on the telephone despite them.

With the assistance of instrument-maker Thomas Watson, Bell developed the basic concept of telephone transmission by early 1876, though he had not yet made a working instrument. On February 14 of that year – a few hours before Western Union's Elisha Gray arrived at the U.S. Patent Office on a similar mission – Bell filed his application for what would become the first of two controlling telephone patents. Bell submitted the second application on January 15, 1877, after he and Watson had succeeded in transmitting speech. Later, some serious questions arose as to Bell's

Plate 13. Alexander Graham Bell. Reproduced with permission of AT&T Corporate Archive.

priority over Gray. Gray's claim gave Western Union an important stake in the new technology.[2]

Establishing the system

Bell, Sanders, and Hubbard never intended to commercialize Bell's inventions themselves. They approached Western Union with an offer to sell the patent rights for $100,000, but Western Union declined for a number of reasons. The telephone, as far as Bell had developed it, remained crude and weak. Its articulation was poor, and a stentorian voice was required to send signals only as far as twenty miles. Furthermore, the same instrument served as both transmitter and receiver, forcing the user to move the device back and forth between ear and mouth. With its market largely in the transmission of business and journalistic intelligence, Western Union saw no obvious advantages to the telephone. It did not produce a written record – as did the telegraph – which appeared at first to be an insurmountable problem. Another consideration, of course, was that Bell's priority over Gray had not been established. In these circumstances, $100,000 was a very high price for a technology of unclear commercial value.[3]

Rather than accept a lesser amount, Bell and his backers reluctantly decided to commercialize the telephone themselves. They began by offering to lease telephone equipment for communication between two points. In May 1877 they advertised pairs of telephones at an annual rent of $20 for individuals and $40 for businesses, with the lessors responsible for stringing their own wires (though the Bell company would do so for an additional fee). Within three months they had placed 778 telephones.[4]

On July 9, 1877, the partners formally organized the Bell Telephone Company, capitalized at $300,000 under the laws of Massachusetts. They gave one-tenth of the stock to Bell's assistant Watson in order "to associate with them a practical mechanician of sufficient skill and ability, under Mr. Bell, to make these inventions pecuniarily successful."[5] For the next four years, Watson carried out most of the development work necessary to commercialize the telephone as well as superintending all of the company's manufacturing operations.

The Bell Company's success at renting its instruments impressed Western Union with the commercial possibilities of telephony. Consequently, the telegraph company established a subsidiary, named the American Speaking Telephone Company (AST), to enter the market in December 1877. Western Union gave AST rights to Gray's inventions and to those of several other inventors who claimed priority on some aspect of telephony. In addition, Western Union contracted with Thomas Edison to make improvements to the telephone that would circumvent Bell's patent claims. Edison, who was approaching the height of his powers, quickly developed a new concept in telephone transmission based on the variable resistance of carbon granules under pressure, a technique that he had used with the quadruplex telegraph several years before. Edison's "carbon button" transmitter provided far better articulation than Bell's magneto (voice-activated electrical generator), and for the first time permitted outside power to be introduced into the system. This greatly extended the range of telephone communications, giving AST a significant technical advantage.

During 1878 both companies pushed hard to occupy the field. The Bell Telephone Company, without the financial resources of its competitor, franchised its business to help with capitalization. The first "associated company" established was the New England Telephone Company, which ceded Bell 50% of its stock in return for local rights to the telephone patents. New England Telephone soon opened a telephone exchange that enabled all subscribers to connect with each other. This greatly expanded the telephone market, but it also dramatically increased the cost and complexity of providing service. AST responded in kind, and, over the next two years, exchanges were established in most major American cities by one company or the other – sometimes by both.[6]

In mid-1878 the Bell Telephone Company reorganized, issuing additional stock in an attempt to bring in more capital. Because the business was not yet on a firm basis, the original partners had to offer voting rights greater than their own in order to entice investors. As a result, they lost control of the company to a group of Bostonians whose short-term financial perspective would dominate the Bell System for almost thirty years. At the time of reorganization, Gardiner Hubbard convinced Theodore N. Vail, a thirty-two-year-old managerial prodigy with the federal government's Railway Mail Service Commission, to become the company's general manager. Bell's biographer, Robert Bruce, calls this "one of Hubbard's greatest services to the enterprise, if not his greatest." Vail possessed the vision, administrative ability, and technical orientation that the new board of directors lacked.[7] Having cut his managerial teeth on through routing of the mails, Vail quickly determined that the development of long-distance, inter-exchange telephone communications was the best means for Bell to establish and maintain control of a national telephone system.

In September 1878 the Bell Company filed a patent infringement suit against AST, but its hopes of getting an immediate injunction to prevent AST's operations went unrealized. Because of the complexity of the patent issues involved, legal proceedings were likely to consume a number of years. During that time Bell would have to compete with its stronger rival. Good fortune brought Bell patent rights to a carbon transmitter comparable to Edison's, which it purchased from inventor Francis Blake in October 1878. Thus on an equal footing technically if not financially, Bell dug in for a long struggle.

The struggle, however, turned out to be brief. Just as Western Union began to undertake substantial investment in telephone systems, Jay Gould, American financier and stock manipulator *par excellence*, launched an attack on the company. Gould, who already owned the smaller American Union Telegraph, began buying stock in Bell franchises. If he could gain control of Bell, Gould would be able to subject Western Union to competition from a combined telephone–telegraph system. Gould's position would be further enhanced, of course, if the courts decided the patent suit between Bell and Gray in Bell's favor. At this point Western Union's directors decided that it best served their interests to strengthen the Bell Company in order to keep it out of Gould's hands, receiving as much for their beneficence as possible, then retreating to their reasonably secure market in telegraphy. After considerable negotiation – during which Vail convinced his Bell colleagues not to give up rights to long-distance communications – Western Union agreed to sell all of its telephones and transfer its telephone-related patent rights to Bell. It would stay out of the business for the seventeen-year life of the Bell patents. In return, Bell would keep out of telegraphy and give Western Union 20% of its revenues while the contract remained in force. Bell ultimately paid about $7 million, a very high price for peace. Yet, through Vail's insistence, the fledgling telephone company retained the right to develop a long-lines network in competition with Western Union, which really made the deal a bargain. Bell stock rose dramatically in price with signing of the contract in November 1879.[8]

Building the Bell System: From monopoly to competition

While Bell's confrontation with Western Union was still underway in early 1879, the Boston financiers in control of the Bell Telephone Company moved to consolidate their firm's position. They refinanced to an authorized capitalization of $850,000 and absorbed the New England Telephone Company. William H. Forbes, a major investor and scion of a wealthy Boston family, took over as president.[9] Vail remained as general manager. Because the settlement with Western Union required Bell to purchase over 50,000 telephones along with lines and switching equipment, the Massachusetts legislature passed an act enabling the company to capitalize at up to $10 million and to own stock in its licensees and in other companies related to its business. With this reorganization, the American Bell Telephone Company took form on March 20, 1880.

Alone in a wide-open field, the directors of American Bell soon realized that they needed considerably greater manufacturing capacity than that provided by their small installation in Boston and by the few local shops around the country they had permitted to make equipment for their licensees. The Western Electric Company of Chicago (Western Union's telephone-supply subsidiary) had both the capacity and expertise to make Bell's equipment. In 1881 and 1882 Bell purchased first a portion, then the entire company, making it the manufacturing arm of the growing system. An 1882 agreement between Bell and its new subsidiary restricted Bell to buying Western Electric equipment and limited Western Electric to selling only to Bell licensees.[10]

During the early 1880s, with Vail leading the way, the American Bell Telephone Company became firmly established. No longer merely renting telephone instruments, Bell acquired interests in – and sometimes control over – those companies leasing its equipment. The basis of its business was Bell's relationship with numerous regional telephone companies. Typically, Vail or one of his subordinates arranged for local promoters to raise capital, a task made easier by the attractive profits of most Bell licensees. The new company then gave American Bell from 30% to 50% of its stock in exchange for Bell licenses, technical assistance, and contracts to rent equipment. In this way the Bell System's basic framework, which remained intact for 100 years, was built.

The centrally organized Bell Company was run by a line and staff administration. The president, executive committee, board of directors, and various staff officers were complemented by the general manager and his line officers. Through the 1880s, the president and two prominent board members made up the executive committee. Their legal and financial advisors helped them make policy decisions relating to finance, system growth, and relations with other companies. For example, the executive committee handled the protracted negotiations with Western Union in 1879. When many Bell licensees faced competition from independent telephone companies after the controlling Bell patents expired in 1894, the executive committee determined which companies would be given discounts on phone rentals so they could compete more effectively.

The general manager and his line officers handled day-to-day relationships with the licensees, helped establish new local Bell companies, and acquired rights-of-way for the small but growing long-lines system. They wrote contracts, oversaw the collection of fees, and dealt with issues of rental policy and royalties. They also tried to make certain that the local companies received adequate technical assistance and that their operations were run in conformity with Bell System policies. Significantly, before efforts to establish a new local company could come to fruition, the general manager had to receive full approval from the president and board of directors. During the 1880s and 1890s, while the company was still relatively small, this administrative organization remained loosely defined and the number of people involved quite limited.[11]

From the time of his earliest association with the Bell companies, Theodore Vail had strongly believed that expanding to cover the entire continent with Bell telephone service made the most sense from both an economic and technical point of view, even if serving particular areas might prove unprofitable. Vail later expressed this goal in the credo, "One System, One Policy, Universal Service," an objective which come to dominate company thinking. During the 1880s, however, Vail had to fight the conservative business practices of the company's officers, who were mainly concerned about dividends and any threats to their control. In 1887, displeased at not being made president upon the retirement of Forbes, Vail left to go into business on his own.

The Boston financiers who sat on the board of directors saw it as their duty to promote maximum profits for the stockholders, not to expand service along unprofitable lines. And make profits they did! In 1882 American Bell earned about $1 million, paying $600,000 in dividends; in 1883 is earned $1.5 million and paid dividends of $1 million. By 1894, when Bell's patent control expired, the company had expended over $25 million in dividends – an average return on investment of approximately 46%. Yet Bell paid a price in enmity. Its profits came from holding prices high while providing barely adequate service, a combination that understandably provoked hostility among its customers. An attorney and advisor to the company acknowledged this problem when he wrote to the president in 1891: "The Bell Company has had a monopoly more profitable and more controlling – and more generally hated – than any ever given by any patent."[12]

It was not easy to protect such a profitable position. Even after the Western Union settlement, Bell had to work hard to maintain its monopoly. The company's high profits enticed many others to set up exchanges, usually in locales Bell did not serve. Every time it learned of such activity Bell brought suit for patent infringement, usually getting an injunction to halt the new business at once. Bell initiated almost 600 infringement suits during the life of the original patents and in every case succeeded. In 1888, however, it nearly met with disaster when the U.S. Supreme Court ruled by a mere four-to-three majority that the company's controlling patents were valid despite contentions that earlier inventors had anticipated Alexander Graham Bell's ideas and results. By a one-vote margin the court thus saved the company from facing, unprepared, the onslaught of competition that it would confront six years later when the last of its controlling patents expired.[13]

One way in which Bell did prepare for this inevitable competition was to acquire patents on every possible improvement to telephony. In 1881, Forbes and the board of directors approved establishment of the Electrical and Patent Department, which would conduct development work on telephone transmission and switching systems as well as evaluate the importance of outside inventions. In 1884 Bell also put Thomas Edison on retainer and acquired an option on any telephone inventions he might make.[14] During the monopoly period, inventors had no sure way to exploit their patents other than selling rights to Bell; in this way the company collected 900 telephone-related patents by 1894. Vail expressed Bell's position on patent control when he testified in court:

> Just as soon as we started into the district exchange system we found out that it would develop a thousand and one little patents and inventions with which to do the business which was necessary, and that is what we wanted to control and get possession of. . . . We recognized that if we did not control these devices, somebody else would.[15]

But Bell's officers also recognized that the courts were often hesitant to halt the operations of competitors based on "little patents and inventions." Still, these patents had their uses. As the company's patent attorney explained in Bell's 1892 Annual Report,

> The policy of bringing suit for infringement on apparatus patents is an excellent one because it keeps the concerns which attempt opposition in a nervous and excited condition since they never know where the next attack may be made, and since it keeps them all the time changing their machines and causes them ultimately, in order that they may not be sued, to adopt inefficient forms of apparatus.[16]

Between 1894 and 1911 Bell initiated seventy-four infringement suits. The courts, however, were not as cooperative as they had been in the past. Public opinion sided strongly with the independents, and, because of the newly passed antitrust laws, the courts hesitated to sustain monopoly market positions. Time after time they interpreted Bell patents narrowly, opening the way for competitors to use minor variations of Bell-controlled inventions.[17]

The company also hoped to stymie competition through its advantage in long-distance communications. This made Bell's service more desirable because competing systems could rarely make connections beyond their local areas. As its long-lines system grew, Bell would also be able to take business away from its erstwhile antagonist, Western Union. During the 1880s and early 1890s, the company's long-distance capabilities improved considerably. Bell engineer John J. Carty discovered in 1881 that employing a second wire to complete telephone circuits, rather than the customary "ground," reduced interference on the lines and enabled considerably longer-distance transmissions. Using very large copper wires to reduce electrical resistance as well as various techniques developed by company engineers, Bell inaugurated long-distance service between Boston and New York in 1884. By 1893 it had established service as far as from Washington, D.C. to central Maine and from the East Coast to Chicago.[18]

Bell's rate of growth fluctuated dramatically during its first twenty-five years in response first to increasing demand and then to intense competition. The number of Bell telephones in service grew at a high rate in the company's early years, then increased at a considerably slower pace as the business reached a saturation point resulting from Bell's high prices and sometimes-inconsistent service. Although Bell had installed approximately 142,000 phones by 1885, placements decreased to about 6% per year for the remaining nine years of the monopoly, giving it 270,000 telephones in service in 1894. Competition changed this situation. Not only did the independents place telephones at an astonishing rate, but, forced to lower prices and improve service in the suddenly competitive environment, Bell found itself expanding much more rapidly than ever before. By 1900 the company had placed approximately 800,000 telephones in service. Yet even after tripling its units in six years, Bell was losing the race. In actual numbers, the independents placed 600,000 telephones during the same period that Bell placed 530,000, although in 1900 Bell System assets stood at $120 million to the independents' $55 million. The independents enjoyed success at Bell's expense in part because the company shied away from direct confrontation in matters of price, rarely lowering its rates to meet those of its competitors.[19]

In 1885 American Bell established a subsidiary, which it called the American Telephone and Telegraph Company (AT&T). Incorporated under the laws of New York, it would build, own, and operate the long-distance system. AT&T took on a much larger role in 1899, when rapid expansion of the Bell System required additional financing. The incorporation laws of Massachusetts made recapitalization above the authorized $10 million extremely difficult, but New York's laws were much more permissive regarding capitalization and other important matters. Thus the board of directors decided to transfer almost all of the company's assets to AT&T; the long-distance subsidiary took over as parent company of the entire Bell System.

Like its predecessor, AT&T preferred not to compete by rapid expansion, since this brought intense financial pressures and increased the likelihood that the company's large stockholders would lose control. Yet geometric growth proceeded anyway: between the beginning of 1902 and the end of 1904, the number of Bell subscribers doubled; in 1905 the growth rate increased still further![20] The competitive situation, however, meant that each telephone brought in considerably less revenue than it had before 1894, so earnings fell far short of the firm's capital needs. As a result, AT&T's bonded debt tripled to over $200 million between 1902 and 1907, and the power of the Boston capitalists who sat on the board began to wane.

In 1902 a New York banking syndicate headed by financier J. P. Morgan had purchased over $3 million of newly issued AT&T stock, gaining representation on the board of directors. However, the Boston capitalists still maintained tight control of the executive committee. Morgan brought Theodore N. Vail back into the Bell System. As a result of his business activities in Europe and South America, Vail had become involved with the British financial house of Baring Brothers & Company and, through it, with Morgan. Morgan had great confidence in Vail's knowledge, judgment, and personal loyalty, and asked him to sit on the AT&T board. In 1906, again strapped for capital, the Bell directors placed $100 million in convertible bonds with a Morgan syndicate. The syndicate could dispose of only 10% of the issue during the first year because of investor concern over Bell's financial condition and management policies. The Panic of 1907, which brought a severe tightening of the American money market, made further sales impossible. Morgan found himself with $90 million in AT&T bonds; by converting these into stock he finally wrested control of the company from the conservative Bostonians.

AT&T's president and several of its board members resigned as a result, whereupon the newly constituted board elected Vail president. Since his departure from Bell in 1887, Vail had made a fortune of over $3 million in private ventures, both at home and abroad.[21] When he took over the corporate presidency at Morgan's request in 1907, Vail was sixty-two years old but still vigorous and eager to finish what he had begun over thirty years earlier. Working closely with Morgan, Vail set out to implement his deeply felt corporate philosophy: "One Policy, One System, Universal Service."

J. P. Morgan exerted considerable influence on AT&T from 1907 until his death in 1913. A central figure in the mergers and consolidations that had come to dominate much of the American economy, Morgan had been instrumental in the formation of GE. In 1901 he had brought together a number of major steel companies to create the first billion-dollar corporation, United States Steel. Morgan now intended for Bell to gain control of all American telecommunications, including telegraphy. As one element in this general strategy, Bell ultimately had to develop research facilities that would enable it to innovate ahead of competitors, thus protecting it from commercial intrusion. Because they believed that

Plate 14. Theodore N. Vail. Reproduced with permission of AT&T Corporate Archive.

state or federal governments would inevitably regulate telephone service, Morgan and Vail wanted to make regulation as beneficial to Bell as possible. They were willing to trade Bell's acceptance of government regulation for government acceptance of their near-monopoly.

Under the new Morgan–Vail regime, Bell thus set out to outflank and absorb the independents, to acquire Western Union, to change company attitudes toward regulation from strongly negative to cautiously positive, and slowly, as finances permitted, to expand research activities. While Vail's reasons for desiring control of American telecommunications were based more on improvements in efficiency and reliability than on questions of financial return, his vision and Morgan's were compatible, and he unhesitantly carried out the financier's programs. Both men sought a profitable, stable, near-monopoly position for the Bell System in the growing telecommunications field.

Early research and development at Bell

Unlike General Electric, which undertook operations at a time when innovations in electric lighting and power had been going on for more than a decade, Bell began with a rudimentary technology whose only virtue was that it worked – barely. In order to provide satisfactory person-to-person communications, even locally, telephone technology required considerable improvement. Not only did it generate weak, indistinct signals, but interference in the form of crackling sounds ("static") and crosstalk (other conversations on the line) was common. The first telephone systems had no means for interconnecting among subscribers (which required a way to switch between lines), and provided service for a maximum of twenty miles.

From its agreement with Western Union in 1879 to the expiration of the second Bell patent in 1894, the Bell Company had most of the telephone field to itself. Although outside inventors continued to work on telephone-related technologies, the fact that Bell maintained almost all of the telephones in operation meant that its engineers had to perform the complex tasks associated with integrating new equipment into the system and rectifying the operational problems of a growing network.

Thomas Watson first performed these technical functions for Bell. He had been taken into the original company as a partner because he appeared to possess the skills needed to develop a commercial level of telephone technology. In 1878 and 1879 the company hired inventors Emile Berliner and George Anders to join him. Watson soon began to depend on them for development work, while he concentrated on overseeing the company's small manufacturing operation in the shop of Boston instrument-maker Charles Williams. Berliner took the lead in research, working at "general experiments upon the transmitter and magneto telephone," and making "original investigations, in regard to speaking telephones generally."[22]

One of America's first science Ph.D.s came to work for the Bell System in 1880, establishing a connection between Bell and advanced academic research. William Jacques had received his training in Henry Rowland's physics/electrical engineering program at Johns Hopkins. Upon joining the Bell technical staff he quickly lent his in-depth knowledge of electrical phenomena to the solution of vexing problems in interference and crosstalk.[23] When Watson resigned in 1881 to pursue other interests, Jacques became head of the company's first formal laboratory, the Electrical and Patent Department. The department's activities fell under the purview of General Manager Vail, who gave it strong support. Bell's first Annual Report noted:

> A large amount of work has been done in the electrical and experimental department, both in examining new inventions and testing telephones and apparatus . . . and the improvement of telephones and lines, for both short and long distance service. This work is expensive, but it is of the first importance to our company, and must be continued.[24]

In 1883 Vail approved creation of the Experimental Shop to serve as a supplementary research organization. Its name was changed to the Mechanical Department the following year. According to Bell's Annual Report for 1884, the Mechanical Department concentrated on developing long-lines capabilities, protecting the telephone system from strong transient currents like lightning, perfecting apparatus for small exchanges, and testing and standardizing wire. It soon undertook other tasks, such as developing a new type of receiver and better wire for long-distance service, improving insulation, designing underground telephone cables, and examining the quality of instruments produced by Western Electric.[25]

Although self-taught electrician Ezra T. Gilliland served as the Mechanical Department's initial director, within a year he had been replaced by Bell's second Ph.D. scientist, Hammond V. Hayes. With an undergraduate degree from MIT and a Ph.D. in physics from Harvard, Hayes combined the attributes that were beginning to make individuals with advanced training in science and engineering attractive to American industry: theoretically-based understanding of complex physical processes and the ability to apply that understanding to the solution of combined commercial–technological problems. Hayes oversaw Bell's research and development work for the next twenty-five years. Although his own contributions tended to be on the practical side, Hayes at first advocated the pursuit of scientific studies to help solve problems that confronted Bell engineers as the telephone system expanded. After Vail's departure in 1887, however, Hayes was left without a strong advocate at the corporate level, and he soon abandoned his attempt to gain support for such research activities.

Bell did make some major technological improvements in the years of competition, most of them oriented toward lowering costs so that profits would not suffer as income per telephone decreased. Its most important innovation was the telephone cable that carried numerous circuits in close proximity with a limited amount of crosstalk. A great blizzard in March 1888 had demonstrated the vulnerability of overhead wires to environmental factors – New York service, for example, had been wiped out in the storm. The use of cables permitted telephone lines to be laid safely underground. The Annual Report for 1902 noted that 55% of telephone-line mileage within exchange areas had already been converted to buried cables. Used as overhead lines, cables permitted the installation of approximately 600 circuits per pole, compared to about 20 for open wires.[26] Switching to cables significantly decreased conduit and pole costs for the system; it also enabled Bell to establish service in the growing number of communities that did not allow overhead lines.

Yet many of Bell's technical problems were very difficult to solve without recourse to underlying scientific and mathematical principles. Electrically balancing interconnecting lines proved to be extremely difficult in practice, and as telephone switching centers proliferated, problems of circuit balance became acute. Developing more powerful transmitters and more sensitive receivers improved articulation and extended service distance, but also exacerbated the problems of crosstalk and self-induction (which slurred the signal). In addition, the installation of electric power systems by General Electric and Westinghouse introduced a major new source of telephone interference. During the 1870s the great

British physicist James Clerk Maxwell had laid out the theoretical bases for analyzing electromagnetic wave phenomena. This kind of approach was often necessary to solve problems of transmission, circuit balance, self-induction, and interference. Hayes several times requested support for research in directions suggested by Maxwell's work, but AT&T's directors could see no obvious payoffs from such investments and directed Hayes to concentrate on the engineering problems that were always at hand.[27]

Yet the technical problems multiplied, becoming ever more intransigent as Bell's engineers improved telephone instruments and switching systems. It seemed that boosting transmission power and increasing sensitivity opened a Pandora's box of telephone bugs. The Mechanical Department became so involved in solving problems for the associated companies that Hayes completely abandoned his hopes for conducting long-range research. In 1892 he suggested to Bell's new president, John Hudson, that theoretical studies might be carried out for the company by students at MIT or Harvard – but nothing came of the proposal.[28]

In 1893 the Mechanical Department was absorbed into the recently created Engineers Department, which was headed by Bell's first chief engineer, Joseph P. Davis. The Engineers Department designed and constructed installations, developed methods of laying underground cable, and worked to optimize the use of both local and long-lines networks, especially through the design of telephone exchanges. Hayes maintained his autonomy even though he reported to Davis rather than directly to General Manager C. J. French. The Mechanical Department itself retained control of the development of all new apparatus, such as coin-box telephones, improved capacitors, underground cables, and multistation ringing circuits. But Hayes had to be careful not to let work on new apparatus interfere with vital engineering activities. In 1895 he reported:

> I have found it desirable to subdivide the organization still further keeping the experimental work of development as far as possible from the engineering. . . . By thus separating engineers from those who must necessarily be of inventive temprement [*sic*] I hope to enable the former to confine themselves to the thoroughly careful installation and maintenance of properly designed apparatus in accordance with formulated methods.[29]

In the Bell System – as in many American companies of the era – engineering consisted of using "formulated methods" to design, install, and maintain apparatus. Invention was still perceived as a

Plate 15. Hammond V. Hayes. Reproduced with permission of AT&T Corporate Archive.

peculiar activity that required people of "inventive temprement," who used unorthodox methods and were generally incompatible with engineers. Hayes's attitude was similar to, though perhaps more extreme than, that found at GE during the same period.

An 1895 organizational chart of the Mechanical Department

shows it broken down into six sections: Telephone Transmission; Switchboard Engineering; Mechanical Construction and Design; General Engineering; Chemical Laboratory; and Experimental Shop, with the latter under the direction of William Jacques. Nineteen engineers were spread out in these divisions. Two had advanced degrees, and a few, like G. O. Bassett from MIT, had earned bachelor's degrees in engineering, but the majority had begun as technical assistants, then worked their way up to become what the company called "telephone engineers."[30]

In 1890 Hayes hired Ph.D. physicist–engineer John Stone Stone. A family friend of the Hubbards, Stone had studied with Rowland at Johns Hopkins and had represented Bell at the Paris Exposition of 1889. Stone took great interest in the propagation of electric waves and used his theoretical knowledge to attack telephone transmission problems. The solutions he arrived at – such as inducing current leakage to decrease line distortion – often flew in the face of contemporary wisdom. In his ten years with the company, Stone made good use of his scientific and mathematical training. For instance, he demonstrated mathematically that commonly used design parameters for long-distance transmission systems were in error. In 1894 he applied recent research findings in physics to determine the most economical way of constructing open-wire telephone lines.[31]

Yet Stone did not fit well with the mission of the Mechanical Department. Trained under the independent Rowland, Stone thought that he knew better than Hayes how research should be directed. Hayes appreciated Stone's talents, but above all needed help with the urgent technical problems being pressed upon him by the associated companies. He wanted Stone to be more of an "engineer," less of an "inventor." Stone demurred, and Hayes, with the permission of President Hudson, fired him in 1899.[32]

Two years earlier, an engineer who would become one of the company's most important researchers had joined the Mechanical Department's staff. George Campbell took his bachelor's degree in engineering at MIT in 1891, earned a master's in physics from Harvard, then travelled abroad to study with some of Europe's best-known physicists and mathematicians. Campbell's approach to research resembled Stone's at its best. His cogent mathematical analysis of circuit phenomena led to advances that had eluded more practically oriented researchers. Building on British physicist Oliver Heaviside's work, Campbell showed that certain ways of enhancing the inductance of transmission lines significantly reduced signal attenuation, increasing the distance of transmissions. In 1899 he developed the theory of the "loading coil," in which attenuation was reduced by the use of discrete inductances distributed along transmission lines at distances determined by the average wavelength of the signal. Although Hayes and Campbell recognized the importance of this concept, Bell's patent attorneys were familiar only with hardware-based inventions, so they refused to submit a patent application until extensive tests of the loading concept had been completed.[33] Meanwhile, Columbia University physics professor Michael Pupin applied for a patent on the same invention, and Bell ultimately had to pay him handsomely for the right to use it.

During the early years of the 20th century, Bell installed loading coils on its long lines and increased service distance to about 1,500 miles, giving it a substantial advantage in its confrontation with the independents. However, problems in establishing effective communications and lines of authority between the Mechanical Department and the manufacturing divisions of Western Electric made production and installation of loaded lines slow and difficult.[34]

Despite his experience with Stone, Hayes hired more men with advanced training in 1899 and 1904. Canadian Edwin Colpitts had a master's degree in physics from Harvard and spent several additional years studying physics and mathematics. Hayes assigned him to engineering problems like reducing interference caused by electric street railways and developing new methods for measuring alternating currents.[35] Frank Jewett, who had earned an undergraduate degree in engineering from the Throop Institute of Technology, joined the Mechanical Department in 1904 after receiving a Ph.D. under noted experimental physicist Albert Michelson at the University of Chicago, then teaching for two years at MIT. Michelson, unlike the more commercially oriented Rowland, was upset when his former pupil left academia for industrial pursuits.[36] Jewett began his career at Bell with assignments similar to those given Colpitts, but he soon showed his managerial ability and was given charge of various groups within the department.

In 1902, because of Joseph Davis's poor health, the Engineers Department was placed under the administration of a *troika* including Davis and Hayes. When Davis retired in 1905, Hayes became AT&T's chief engineer, assuming control of the entire operation. At that time, the Engineers Department comprised 195 employees, 38 in the Equipment Division, the new name for the Mechanical Department. The Equipment Division was broken down into four departments: Switchboard, Mechanical, Chemical, and Electrical. Campbell, Colpitts, and Jewett were associated with the last. Yet even with all this talent, Hayes remained unwilling or unable to devote much of his engineers' time to the kind of research needed to make major advances.[37] Hayes's 1906 report to the president of the company indicated that he directed work toward solving immediate service problems, that little thought was being given to original research:

> There is one question of policy relative to development work which should be called to your attention. Every effort in the Department is being executed toward perfecting the engineering methods; no one is employed who, as an inventor, is capable of originating new apparatus of novel design. In consequence of this it will be necessary in many cases to depend on the acquisition of inventions of outside men. . . . The very fact that any great invention at the present time must in all probability come from some man of unusual scientific attainments would render a laboratory under the guidance of such men a most expensive and probably unproductive undertaking.[38]

Yet Hayes was a Ph.D. physicist himself and he had shown early inclinations to support ongoing corporate research efforts. His outlook in 1906 clearly reflected the pressures that the conservative group of Boston investors in control of AT&T had long exerted on him to produce a steady flow of practical results in the company's struggle with the burgeoning independents. Historian Lillian Hoddeson concludes that Hayes was "simply too unassertive and reserved a gentleman to defend his conviction of the value of in-house basic research."[39] But based on this report and on the one quoted earlier in this section, Hayes seems to have been uncertain about the differences between scientists, engineers, and inventors in a way that reflected not only his personality but also the immediate needs of the Bell System. Furthermore, his confusion was symptomatic of the lingering 19th-century American ambivalence over both the appropriate place of science in industry, and the changing roles of engineers and independent inventors. The directors and managers to whom Hayes was accountable retained their belief that research belonged in the universities, that inventions were the acts of inspired but unmanageable men, and that engineering necessarily built slowly and carefully upon existing technology. It would take the ascendence of a new group of managers to change the way that the Bell System looked at relationships between science, engineering, and the development of commercial technology.

Hayes noted in his report that as a consequence of his department's methods Bell would have to depend on the often risky policy of acquiring important patent rights from outside inventors. The company was almost always successful in this endeavor because its already-strong patent position assured that inventors would have difficulty exploiting their patents outside the Bell System and because its payment of substantial sums for important patent rights provided most inventors with remuneration higher they could obtain elsewhere. So long as the technical conception of telephone service remained essentially unchanged, AT&T was reasonably secure.

As the Bell System headed into the pivotal year of 1907, when the Boston capitalists who had directed the company almost since its inception surrendered control to the New York bankers headed by J. P. Morgan, a substantial engineering organization had already been established. But although the Engineers Department contained a number of people capable of making significant contributions to the mathematics, science, and technology related to telephony (Hayes's report to the contrary notwithstanding), the company had as yet undertaken very little of the kind of work needed for major advance. Hammond Hayes had seen Bell's research and development processes through their early years. His real contribution, however, came not from the administration of research or the formation of policy but from bringing into the Bell System the small core of individuals with advanced training who would lead the way during the changes that followed 1907. A new era was about to begin.

7

AT&T: The Establishment of Industrial Research

T. N. Vail and the redirection of Bell System policy

J. P. Morgan gained control of AT&T in 1907 because the company had severe financial difficulties. Its stock had declined in value by over 50% since 1902; bonds and new stock were extremely difficult to sell; and income had fallen far short of financing expansion to counter the independents while also meeting current expenses. When Vail took over as president, Morgan expressed concern about the company's solvency, instructing him that "no expenditures should be entered upon in the near future, except such as are absolutely necessary, no matter what the prospective profits . . . may be, – the credit of the Company being of paramount importance."[1]

Vail accordingly ordered the termination of 12,000 employees and cut expenses wherever possible. In line with this policy, he closed the Western Electric Engineering Department branch in Chicago and the AT&T Engineers Department in Boston, consolidating their activities in New York. Because not all of these employees were willing to relocate, the employment of engineers decreased significantly. Of those who came to New York, most went into the Western Electric Engineering Department, located at the subsidiary's manufacturing plant. A few stayed with the parent company, forming the Department of Development and Research, which advised AT&T staff about apparatus specifications and the technical aspects of system needs.[2] Through these efforts Vail hoped to avoid the "excessive and uneconomical diversity of types of apparatus and methods" that still characterized Bell operations. The great majority of engineering staff – and engineering effort – now went to Western Electric, where it could be more fully integrated with manufacturing. Difficulties in coordinating the design and production of loading coils and loaded lines between 1902 and 1907 had forcefully demonstrated the desirability of bringing inventive, design, and manufacturing operations more closely together.[3]

To lead the newly consolidated Bell research and development effort, Vail appointed John J. Carty, a "telephone engineer" who had favorably impressed him during the 1880s. Carty began as a switchboard operator and later developed the two-wire, long-lines concept; he received all of his technical education and experience working in the Bell System. Since 1889 Carty had served as chief engineer for its largest operating company, New York Telephone. There he acquired a reputation for administrative ability and technical vision.

Carty worked to economize in several ways. He cut back on engineering staff, then redirected engineering efforts toward standardizing Bell equipment and operating methods. Standardization promised economies by minimizing supplies and parts needed for repair and by reducing the number of different items Western Electric manufactured. Carty took the opportunity to remove experimental hand-telephone sets from circulation because their adoption would have made older equipment obsolete. Not until 1927 would the "French" phone, with its mouthpiece and earphone combined in a single, hand-held unit, make its appearance in the Bell System. Carty also reviewed the company's consulting contract with Thomas Edison and decided that the great inventor's usefulness to AT&T had long since passed. The arrangement was terminated – an event that symbolized the passing of an era.[4]

Vail, meanwhile, effected fundamental changes in Bell's management structure. He reshaped operating company boundaries, consolidating and grouping them in a more rational manner for pursuit of the business. This brought them more closely under AT&T's control. Within a year they were operating with "Three Column" structures, the columns being "Plant," "Traffic," and "Commercial Activities" – corresponding respectively to equipment, operations and methods, and commercial relations.[5] At AT&T headquarters in New York, Vail established a central administration to evaluate the operating companies' performance and that of the system as a whole, to set policies on relationships within the Bell System as well as between the Bell System and the public, and to provide services to the operating companies such as standardization and help with financing. The eventual effect of Vail's policies was to transform a loosely organized, poorly managed group of semi-independent companies into a truly integrated national system. Whereas his predecessors had seen AT&T (or earlier, American Bell) as their major responsibility, with a number of rather autonomous subsidiaries that paid it dues, Vail thought in terms of the whole System's welfare. He set up AT&T as the central staff organization, with actual operations located in the associated companies – which AT&T, of course, largely owned.[6]

As he assumed control in 1907, Vail retained the outlook he had developed as Bell's chief operating officer during the 1880s. He believed very strongly that the company should expand into all areas of telecommunications. This would provide the most complete, integrated system possible. He saw Bell's greatest strength in its public service role. He was convinced that if the company fulfilled that role efficiently and at reasonable cost, all parties would benefit. Vail conceived of AT&T as much more than a means of making money for its stockholders. Indeed, he saw profit as a secondary consideration whose only importance was that it affected the company's ability to raise the capital needed for expansion. To Vail, the System came first, and all of his actions followed from the desire to build, integrate, and protect the System wherever and however possible.

Vail's motto, "One Policy, One System, Universal Service," dominated his thinking and continued to exert a strong influence on company attitudes through most of the 20th century. This meant that for technological, financial, and even ideological reasons interconnection of Bell plant with equipment controlled by outsiders was anathema. Bell needed to control the entire system – Bell *was* the System. This attitude strongly influenced the company's approach to research and development in the years after 1907, especially with regard to wireless telephony, or radio. The attitude was also consonant with J. P. Morgan's desire to consolidate American telecommunications and led to Bell's acquisition of a 30% share in Western Union during 1909. When Vail assumed the Western Union presidency in 1910, the two companies became fully integrated, and a telecommunications monopoly came within Bell's purview.

Vail took a major step toward the company's goal of "universality of service and connection" when he wrote soon after assuming the presidency that he had "no serious objection" to regulation of telephone service so long as it was "independent, intelligent, considerate, thorough, and just, recognizing . . . that capital is entitled to its fair return, and good management or enterprise to its reward."[7] This statement, of course, represented a complete reversal of long-standing company policy. Vail made it at this time because he and Morgan believed some kind of government interference in Bell System affairs to be inevitable. By anticipating government involvement and taking a statesmanlike position, Vail might avoid catastrophe, and perhaps even legitimize a Bell monopoly under generally favorable conditions. Between 1907 and 1913, while Bell was buying up many of the independents and significantly increasing its share of telephones in service,[8] Vail indicated in his public statements that the company was becoming more and more receptive to regulation. During this period state regulatory commissions proliferated, and the Mann–Elkins Act of 1910 brought the Interstate Commerce Commission into the field of telephone regulation. However, growing regulation rarely caused AT&T great difficulties; in effect, it established a working partnership between the Bell companies and state governments.

The threat of radio

Although the Bell System based all of its operations on electrical communications over wires, the transmission and reception of signals without wires – or "wireless" – was being developed rapidly in the early 20th century. The first wireless communications had used telegraph signals. Drawing on the work of scientists like James Maxwell, Henrich Hertz, and Oliver Lodge, inventor–entrepreneur Guglielmo Marconi had developed a commercial system of wireless telegraphy during the late 1890s in Britain and was soon leasing his services around the world.[9] By the early years of the new century, a number of experimenters both in America and abroad were working on means to transmit voices and music. One of the first to succeed was Reginald Fessenden, an electrical engineer backed by a pair of Pittsburgh investors. Fessenden based his system on the transmission of high-frequency, continuous waves generated by a special alternator designed for him by engineers at GE. As early as 1900 he had sent speech over the distance of a mile; in December 1906 he transmitted a program of music from his experimental station near Plymouth, Massachusetts, to a number of ships at sea.

In early 1907 Fessenden's backers approached AT&T with an offer to sell his radio patent rights. After an investigation by Engineers Department physicist Edwin Colpitts, Chief Engineer

Hayes reported to the AT&T president, "I feel that there is such a reasonable probability of wireless telegraphy and telephony being of commercial value to our company that I would advise taking steps to associate ourselves with Mr. Fessenden if some satisfactory arrangement can be made."[10] Before that arrangement could be completed, however, J. P. Morgan gained control of the company and gave his designated president, T. N. Vail, an explicit mandate to cut expenses. Vail therefore asked the new chief engineer, J. J. Carty, and AT&T's chief patent counsel, Thomas Lockwood, to examine both the patent situation and the state of radio generally to determine whether acquisition of rights from Fessenden was necessary. Lockwood reported:

> If an individual or a corporation is desirous of becoming interested in wireless telephony [radio] for the sake of keeping in touch with progress in electrical transmission work, based on recent scientific research, this would seem to be an excellent opportunity; but for a telephone company, the possibility of substituting a wireless system for a system of toll lines is the most attractive feature of the proposition, and I have a strong conviction that this feature cannot and will not reach any practical realization within the term of years yet remaining to Fessenden's fundamental patents.[11]

Vail declined to buy the Fessenden patents, but Lockwood's report made him aware that the development of radio might eventually have considerable impact on the Bell System. Carty became concerned and began to follow radio activities around the world carefully, even assigning company engineers to attend meetings of radio experimenters and report on progress.[12] Carty and Vail were more open to and concerned about technical advances than their predecessors had been. Because they saw in radio an element of danger to the Bell System's commercial position – one that did not exist in any direct improvement to telephone service itself – they made certain to stay in touch with advances in the new technology.

American inventor Lee de Forest had also been at work on wireless telegraphy and radio since the 1890s. Between 1902 and 1906 his American de Forest Wireless Telegraph Company sold apparatus to the U.S. Army and Navy as well as to the United Fruit Company for its ships and plantations in Central America. In 1906 he erected over ninety stations across the United States to provide long-distance telegraph services in competition with Western Union, but he went bankrupt when technical, financial, and organizational difficulties prevented him from supplying reliable service.[13] That same year, de Forest made one of the most important inventions in electrical communications history. Attempting to develop a better "detector" of wireless telegraph signals, he placed a third element in the vacuum-tube diode (two-element) detector invented several years earlier by British physicist Ambrose Fleming. His triode, or "audion" as de Forest called it, provided far greater sensitivity than Fleming's diode. De Forest used it as the basis for wireless telegraph reception.[14]

In 1907 the inventor established the De Forest Radio Telephone Company (with a capitalization of $2 million) and began to sell primitive radio equipment to the U.S. Navy. Undaunted by his recent failure, he intended ultimately to establish a network of stations whose business would consist of sending long-distance messages, this time in competition with AT&T. During the spring of 1908 de Forest took his equipment to France to gain publicity. There, he succeeded in transmitting voice messages from the Eiffel Tower to receivers as far away as Marseilles.[15]

De Forest was only the best-publicized of numerous inventors working on radio. Many others built systems of transmission and reception based on methods developed in America and abroad. In 1909, for example, inventor–entrepreneur A. Frederick Collins established what he claimed to be the world's first commercial wireless telephone service, between Portland, Maine, and the islands of nearby Casco Bay. The *New York Times* reported:

> Four wireless telephones were used at the same time and each received its designated message. A new tuning apparatus, invented by Mr. Collins was used and the inventor says he has solved the problem of selectivity thus making the wireless telephone even more secret than the present wire telephone systems. Over 600 messages were sent the first day.[16]

This and similar announcements concerning radio led to public speculation that telephone users would soon be able to call up their friends directly over the airwaves, that "each house will have a set of wireless telephone apparatus and then there will be no more trouble with central [operators]."[17] The president of one Bell operating company communicated to headquarters that "the papers throughout this section of the country are filled almost daily with stories about the wireless telephone." He asked what AT&T intended to do about it. Stockholders wrote to AT&T, wanting to know what effect radio might have on the company. Some asked whether they should sell their holdings![18]

The threat of radio to AT&T had become very real by 1909. Radio technology had not progressed far enough to make direct user communication feasible, but systems like the one from Portland to the Maine islands had shown their capabilities as parts of a telecommunications network. Connecting Bell lines to them, however, clearly violated Vail's philosophy of system unity. With the newspapers and magazines full of stories about radio, more inventors and companies were likely to become involved in developing the technology and promoting services. Even if competition between radio and basic Bell services remained illusory, public questions about Bell's position posed a serious threat to the good relations that Vail was trying to build with the company's stockholders and customers.

Radio, the telephone repeater, and research

Carty's study of progress in radio technology made him aware that certain problems in radio and telephony had related solutions. Radio experimenters were searching for ways to amplify signals and to generate and control continuous, high-frequency waves. Many believed that an electronic amplifier could be used to generate these waves when connected to special feedback circuits; other circuits would provide modulation to impress a voice signal on them. As part of AT&T's efforts to extend long-distance service, its engineers had also been at work developing an amplifier (or "repeater" in company parlance) to boost signal levels. Use of the Campbell–Pupin loading coil had extended service as far west as Denver, but without some means of rejuvenating signals, coast-to-coast telephone communications remained impossible. In 1903 AT&T engineer Herbert Shreeve had invented an electromechanical repeater that worked for telephone lines up to several hundred miles in length, but his device introduced excessive distortion when two or more were used in series (which was necessary to transmit for greater distances).[19] The electronic repeater, uninhibited by the inertia of an electromechanical device, promised to reduce distortion, hence permitting further telephone transmissions. It also seemed to be the key to radio.

Vail had always hoped to extend Bell System service all across the country. So, when Carty convinced him that the solution to unlimited long-distance telephony was probably tied to the control of radio through development of an electronic repeater, Vail gave his support for a research program. Carty explained his perception of company needs in an April 1909 memorandum to the board of directors, making a strong case for an expanded effort on the repeater:

> One additional argument making for vigorous work upon the development of a more powerful repeater I call to your particular attention. At the present time scientists in Germany, France, and Italy, and a number of able experimenters in America are at work upon the problem of wireless telephony. While this branch of the art seems at present to be rather remote in its prospects of success, a most powerful impetus would be given to it if a suitable telephone repeater were available. Whoever can supply and control the necessary telephone repeater will exert a dominating influence in the art of wireless telephony and the number of able people at work upon the art create a situation which may result in some of these outsiders developing a telephone repeater before we have obtained one ourselves, unless we adopt vigorous measures from now on. A successful telephone repeater, therefore, would not only react most favorably upon our service where wires are used, but might put us in a position of control with respect to the art of wireless telephony should it turn out to be a factor of importance.[20]

Carty's plea evoked a positive response. The AT&T board of directors authorized pursuit of both the repeater and other related projects that, in Carty's words, "required especially exhaustive and complete laboratory investigation."[21]

On a trip to the West Coast later in 1909, Carty declared publicly that AT&T would demonstrate a transcontinental telephone line at the Panama-Pacific Exposition, scheduled to open in 1914. This promise was a gamble, since the direction of a technical solution to the repeater problem remained unclear. Yet it was also excellent public relations, inspiring confidence in Bell's capabilities and serving notice to the remaining independents – and to their sources of capital – that AT&T intended to gain a formidable advantage in its abilities to offer long-distance service. The commitment meant that Vail and the board of directors had to support Carty's requests for funds to finance research, lest the company break its promise.

After a year's search by the Western Electric Engineering Department failed to make progress toward an acceptable repeater among arc, magnetic, and electromechanical devices, Carty and his assistant, physicist Frank Jewett, decided that their research efforts needed new direction. Jewett then made a study of the most promising areas of research and the types of personnel required. A recent Ph.D.(1902) and former instructor at MIT, Jewett was familiar with contemporary research in the physical sciences, appreciated the technological possibilities of electron discharge, and had excellent contacts in the American physical science community, whose attention had recently been focused on X-rays, radioactivity, and the conduction of electricity in gases. The plan Jewett put forward envisioned scientists and engineers working "with full coordination and under proper direction" while investigating areas of the physical sciences germane to communications technology. He called for a study of "possible repeater ideas, particularly in the domain of molecular physics," and noted that "certain characteristics of discharge of electricity through gases and vapors seem to offer considerable possibility of obtaining a telephone amplifier. . . ." Jewett concluded that it would be necessary "to employ skilled physicists who are familiar with the recent advances in molecular physics and who are capable of appreciating such further advances as are continually being made."[22]

Carty brought this recommendation before the AT&T board of directors, who approved the establishment of a small research laboratory to function within the Western Electric Engineering Department's branch structure. As funds became available between 1909 and 1911, the Engineering Department had grown substantially; by 1911 it was organized into a number of interrelated branches, such as Development, Transmission, Inspection, and Apparatus Design. The new organization was to be known as the Research Branch. It would have to fit in with ongoing Bell System engineering activities. The Engineering Department's annual report for 1911 noted:

> There is an increasing number of problems intimately associated with the development of the telephone business . . . [and] to make adequate progress with this work it was decided to organize a branch of the Engineering Department which should include in its personnel the best talent available and in its equipment the best facilities possible for the highest grade research laboratory work.[23]

Once the case had been made for this approach to research, Vail and the AT&T and Western Electric boards of directors gave the Research Branch their wholehearted support. Both Vail and Harry Thayer, president of Western Electric, were technically oriented and sympathetic to the endeavor. They appreciated the growing complexity of electrical communications and the need to undertake new types of research. Their positive attitude was reflected in the ease with which Carty and Jewett got approval for the new laboratory and in the support the lab received during its early years. By contrast, GE president Charles Coffin, a former shoe-manufacturing executive, did not become involved in his company's technical work, failed to appreciate the need for industrial research, and never gave the GE Research Laboratory his full support. The resulting differences in the two laboratories' origins and early years were striking, as I will show.

At its inception the Research Branch took on two main projects: developing an electronic amplifier and making improvements in duplex telephone cables. As plans to staff the laboratory got under way in 1911, Frank Jewett recruited Harold D. Arnold, former student of well-known experimental physicist Robert Millikan. Jewett, Carty, and Arnold decided that mercury-vapor tubes presented the most promising avenue of advance in electronic amplifiers, so Arnold set to work on them. Although he made several successful patent applications for use of mercury-vapor tubes as amplifiers during the next year, these devices remained unsatisfactory for either telephone or radio service because they introduced considerable distortion and required special start-up procedures as well as frequent maintenance. Other recruits to the Research Branch worked on improving duplex cables, a problem that had engaged the Development Branch for several years. Their contributions led to the determination of "the effect of certain mechanical structures on the electrical characteristics of the finished cable," resulting in the fabrication of better commercial cables in late 1912.[24]

The establishment of the Research Branch clearly represented a change in the approach to research and development in the Bell System. As the Engineering Department annual report for 1911 noted, "In the past, development work has proceeded more or less blindly by cut and try experimental methods. While these methods have given reasonably good results, it is felt that the time is ripe for investigation covering the fundamental principles. . . ."[25] Not only did the Research Branch itself attempt to discover the "fundamental principles," its example soon made other branches within the Engineering Department consider that approach in all their work.

The audion and coast-to-coast service

John Stone Stone, whom Hayes fired in 1899, had continued to serve as a consultant to AT&T. In October 1912 he persuaded

Frank Jewett to take a look at de Forest's audion triode because de Forest and others had recently discovered that it possessed amplifying capabilities. Although the device that Stone and de Forest demonstrated could handle only about a hundredth of a watt before breaking into debilitating "blue-haze" (which made it highly erratic), Arnold, Jewett, and Colpitts quickly recognized that the audion principle of electrostatic grid control held the solution to the electronic repeater problem.[26]

They retained the audion that de Forest and Stone brought so that they could begin studies to understand the tube's operation better. As Arnold started this work, Jewett contacted Carty and the AT&T Patent Department. Jewett placed several laboratory workers at Arnold's disposal, and Arnold assigned them various experimental tasks while he himself considered the physics of the audion. A month after the demonstration, Colpitts provided Jewett with a technical explanation of triode functions, comparing it to the Fleming diode. He noted that Arnold had been working "almost entirely with reference to developing the theory of the device and also in connection with the scientific literature on the subject." Tests had shown the triode to be capable of withstanding "ordinary service conditions." At Carty's request, researchers had also considered the audion for use in radio. Colpitts reported that, "As a repeater for wireless, there would seem to be no doubt of its application to both telegraphy and telephony. Insofar as an amplifying device can assist in the perfection of wireless telephony and telegraphy, this device would seem to be of maximum importance."[27]

Jewett informed the Patent Department of progress while it studied the relationship of de Forest's patents to others in the field. In February 1913 the Patent Department reported that de Forest's patents were important only if it could be shown that the audion would amplify without gas in its envelope space. Carty discussed the report with Jewett, who gave it to Arnold for his comments. Although results at this time remained inconclusive, Arnold's research soon proved that the audion's powers were not gas-dependent. Confident that de Forest's patents controlled the vacuum-tube art, the AT&T Patent Department purchased rights to them in the summer of 1913. The contract excluded all others except de Forest from making triodes for sale.[28] This acquisition of rights to the basic three-element electron tube provided the keystone for AT&T's efforts to develop and control radio as well as telephony. The Research Branch had been instrumental in bringing these rights into the Bell System, and it was also to be re-

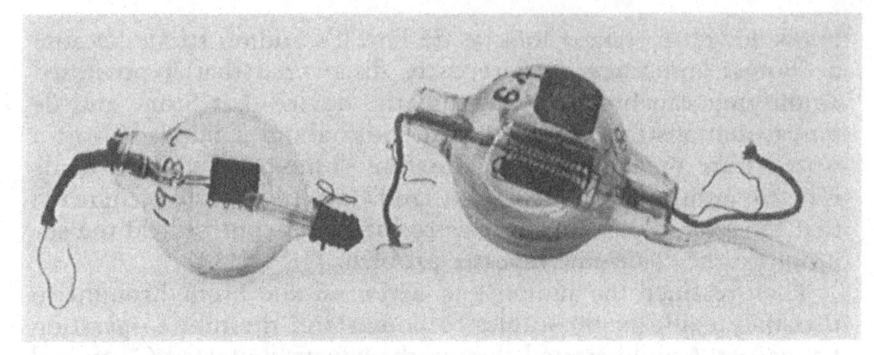

Plate 16. Vacuum tubes: (left) De Forest audion as presented to AT&T, 1912; (right) high vacuum "Type A Telephone Repeater" of the type used in the Washington-to-New York test line, October 1913. Reproduced with permission of AT&T Corporate Archive.

sponsible for transforming the weak, erratic, and little-understood audion into the powerful and reliable triode amplifier that the Bell System needed.

The laboratory's pursuit of the triode as a telephone amplifier lent definition to the task. It was necessary to make the device capable of handling the energy levels in telephone lines and of amplifying the voice's entire frequency range with little distortion. Since one bad tube could disable an entire line, the triode needed to have a long working life, during which it maintained reasonably constant characteristics. The device also had to be susceptible to quantity manufacture at low cost, with a high level of consistency. Finally, its power consumption could not be too great.

The audion, as H. D. Arnold and laboratory had received it, fell far short of these requirements. Although it amplified weak speech currents accurately, normal telephone power levels caused severe distortion, and the life of its tantalum filament was brief. Frequent adjustments of both its filament and plate voltages were necessary to maintain output. The devices were also very fragile, and each one showed markedly different characteristics.[29]

Frank Jewett put H. D. Arnold in charge of a team attack on the physics and engineering of the triode. Arnold launched into a study of its operation; from insights he gained in this manner, he directed other theoretical, experimental, and development work. Jewett, meanwhile, recruited scientists and engineers for the project: within three years Arnold had twenty-five researchers and assistants reporting to him.[30] Arnold worked alone, with assistants, or with other Ph.D.s hired by the Research Branch. He assigned problems and projects, read and wrote reports and papers. He also set up a group of engineers to test the tubes and circuits, providing feedback for the other researchers.

Arnold's studies convinced him that ionizing gas in the tubes caused the "blue-haze" problem. He directed one engineer to operate an audion at high power for several days, which he believed would remove gas molecules from within the tube envelope. He was right; after forty-eight hours of operation, the audion could function at substantially higher power before "blue-haze" occurred. When the newly developed Gaede Molecular Pump arrived at the laboratory from Germany in April 1913, Arnold applied it to an audion and, at a pressure of about 10^{-5}mm of mercury, achieved essentially pure electron discharge.[31]

Because the tantalum filaments that de Forest used consumed a considerable amount of power, burned out rapidly, and were quite fragile, the task of improving them quickly received attention. After considering several different filament materials, including ductile tungsten, Arnold decided that oxide-coated filaments developed in 1904 by German physicist Arthur Wehnelt showed the greatest promise of high emmissivity and long life – and they were free of GE patent control. Arnold set researchers to work on "Wehnelt filaments," and by June 1913 they had fabricated several in the laboratory. This "preliminary standardized form of filament" achieved a life of over 1,000 hours. Vacuum tubes using it were first tested in long-distance telephone lines between New York and Baltimore in October of that year. They operated satisfactorily for 450 hours.[32]

Work on the triode went forward on a number of fronts. In order to determine the importance of element size, shape, configuration, and spacing, Arnold assigned several researchers the job of making a thorough experimental study.[33] He and H. J. van der Bijl, a Leipzig physics Ph.D. and fellow Millikan protégé, undertook theoretical studies of electron emission and transportation in the tubes. Based on this work, van der Bijl developed a methodology of vacuum-tube design, introducing a number of functional constants such as the amplification factor (mu), grid constant (gamma), and energy-level factor. These constants depended on element shape and configuration, filament emmissivity, and plate and grid voltage. As a contemporary noted, "Van der Bijl put the electron tube on a fundamental mathematical basis."[34]

Working with the results of these studies, AT&T researchers designed triodes with significantly improved operating characteristics, often matching tube designs to service requirements. They developed new element configurations and improved the vacuum in the tubes. They also gave attention to operating triodes on alternating current, which was preferable to using batteries or special generators for long-distance telephone service.[35]

The immediate need when the Research Branch took over triode development was to have suitable amplifiers available for the inauguration of coast-to-coast telephone service. Even though triodes had first been successfully tested on telephone lines in late 1913, designing a transcontinental line and implementing service proved to be quite difficult. Several repeaters had to be operated in series along the line, which meant that inductances and capacitances in the tubes, in their related circuits, and in the transcontinental line itself needed to be balanced. Carty had committed Bell to a demonstration at the opening of the Panama-Pacific Exposition, which (after delay) was scheduled for January 1915. To make that deadline, Carty "drove himself and his associates with a force that was untiring and unsparing. Sleep and relaxation in small doses were grudgingly accorded."[36] Research Branch staff members worked with Transmission Branch engineers to design the lines, test them, and oversee their installation in the field.

The effort was a spectacular success. On January 25, 1915, Alexander Graham Bell spoke from New York to his erstwhile assistant Thomas Watson in San Francisco, thus inaugurating coast-to-coast service. Even though extensive work remained to be done, the Research Branch had, in the short span of little more than two years, entered a new area of physical research, developed theory and application together, and created a functional, predictable electronic device along with circuits for its use. As part of the development process, the Research Branch had also devised quantity manufacture methods for the triode. During 1915 it stepped up in-house production, supplying the Bell System with over 3,200 for use in long-distance service.[37]

In an important sense, the technical triumph belonged to J. J. Carty, whose vision and drive had been responsible for the establishment and early growth of the Research Branch. Carty acted as its voice at AT&T's highest levels. When Vail reorganized Bell's management in 1907, he had placed Carty in a staff position with responsibility for apparatus design and innovation as well as research and development. Though Carty's title, "AT&T Chief Engineer," was the same that had been held by Hammond Hayes, Carty's job was very different. He had little concern with day-to-

Plate 17. Alexander Graham Bell (in New York) officially opening transcontinental telephone service, January 1915. J. J. Carty is at left. Note picture of Vail over Bell's head. Courtesy of AT&T Bell Laboratories Archives.

day operations and thus performed no line functions. In advising on the relationship of business to technical problems and in helping to formulate corporate policies on research and engineering, he possessed little authority but wielded great power. To the board of directors, Carty personified Bell research and engineering, although he actually had little direct hand in them. A recent historian of AT&T calls Carty "a man who usually got what he wanted"; and he wanted research that would make sure Bell never had to tie in with other communications systems against its will and never lost its position of control in wired telephony. Carty's military bearing influenced attitudes in the laboratory, while the importance of his voice in management spurred the Research Branch to defer to his wishes whenever possible.[38] The presence of an individual on the AT&T corporate staff whose only responsibility was to oversee research and engineering made a big difference in resources and direction during the laboratory's early years. At GE,

Plate 18. John J. Carty. Reproduced with permission of AT&T Corporate Archive.

Vice-President E. W. Rice split his attention and loyalty between engineering and production. The support that he gave the company's fledgling Research Laboratory reflected this divided responsibility.

Carty improved his sway in the AT&T boardroom by making public display of Research Branch achievements. When the AT&T directors, various notables, and reporters attended the transcontinental line's opening, Carty and Vail made certain to air appropriate encomiums. Carty credited the laboratory researchers; Vail praised their boss:

> Congratulations to the man who, by his personality, initiative, and the practical application of his wonderful mastery of the telephone service in particular and of electrical science in general, has brought about such results. Subordinate to yours, but still large, is the credit due to your staff of scientists and experts who have absorbed your enthusiasm, caught your spirit, and so successfully seconded your efforts. To them and to you, the world and the Bell System owe an appreciation which I am but feebly expressing.[39]

Whereas Vail's remarks would suggest that Carty himself directed research, he actually remained well insulated from it. Because he was not competent to understand most of the lab's work, Carty retained an assistant to advise him on relevant scientific matters.[40]

Work in the Research Branch went through three levels of direction between corporate staff and workers. Carty, with a broad view of research and development policy but with limited scientific capabilities, presented the laboratory's achievements to the president and board of directors, and made its resource requirements known to them. He also brought management's perceptions of corporate needs to the Research Branch, suggesting ways in which they could be met.

Frank Jewett, one of two men who held the title "Western Electric Assistant Chief Engineer," oversaw Research and three other branches.[41] In charge of groups working on transmission problems, chemical analysis, and apparatus design, Jewett helped to integrate the Research Branch's efforts with related activities in the Engineering Department, especially those of the Development and Transmission Branches. Although he had a doctorate in physics and maintained contacts in the scientific community, Jewett published no research papers after joining the Bell System in 1904. One laboratory worker thought very little of his "scientific acumen," believing that Jewett achieved his position solely through his abilities as "a good team player and report writer."[42] Jewett made occasional forays into the laboratory and sometimes even offered advice to researchers, but he acted mainly as a recruiter of personnel, a synthesizer of information, a coordinator with other branches of the Engineering Department, and a conduit to Carty and the AT&T staff.[43] Jewett's line position corresponded rather closely to Hayes's in the years before 1907, though he was responsible for only part of the department.

Plate 19. Frank B. Jewett. Reproduced with permissionof AT&T Corporate Archive.

H. D. Arnold, disciple of Nobel Prize-winning physicist Robert Millikan, actually directed the research process. E. H. Colpitts served as head of the Research Branch until 1915, insulating Arnold from the demands of administration by handling routine matters, preparing reports, and dealing with Jewett. But beginning in 1913, Arnold oversaw most laboratory work. One member of the Research Branch called Arnold "the boss and power house [*sic*] driving the crew." He coordinated the work of physicists, chemists, mathematicians, and their assistants, while carrying on research of his own.[44]

To be certain that the Research Branch received adequate credit and continued to grow, these administrators took every opportunity to demonstrate that it contributed significantly to the Bell System's welfare. Their reports attempted to reinforce such a perception, often making very optimistic evaluations of recent accomplishments. The Western Electric Engineering Department's annual reports were generally used to display the Research Branch in the best possible light to corporate directors. The report for 1914, a year which included much of the work on the transcontinental line, further emphasized that the most important advances had come from new people – that is, from scientists and engineers who had joined the Research Branch in the previous two years:

> To the almost superhuman efforts of this Branch is largely attributable the phenomenal advance in the art of telephone transmission, which culminated in the successful extension of telephone service across the continent. Within the past two years and particularly in 1914, the work of the Branch has largely revolutionized the problem of long distance transmission. The mere work of developing, manufacturing and installing the repeater equipment needed for the Transcontinental service would be a formidable task for a corps of experts, and when it is remembered that practically all of the present members of the Research Branch have had less than two years telephone experience, the feat is indeed remarkable.[45]

The report went on to emphasize the Research Branch's importance in actually putting the line into service by coordinating its work with the Transmission Branch and manufacturing the needed vacuum tubes. This demonstrated the Research Branch's value as a vital resource in the Bell System's total innovative process.

Even though the AT&T and Western Electric boards of directors' commitment to research was never in doubt after 1911, Carty took care to reassure them of the laboratory's accomplishments in order to maintain their confidence and to justify the growing role for research that he and Vail envisioned. The Research Branch had been establshed mainly to develop an electronic repeater and to control long-distance telephony and radio. Its early activities aimed both at accomplishing these missions and at demonstrating the importance of its role. Like the Research Branch, the GE Research

Laboratory had been established to protect corporate interests through the development of vital commercial technology. Yet the AT&T laboratory had a carefully conceived organization and the full support of top management – both of which were lacking at GE. Furthermore, the Research Branch was not an entirely new entity but one of a number of branches in the company's well-established Engineering Department; it did not have to be especially concerned about developing and maintaining relations within a highly diverse company. As a result, the Research Branch could concentrate on a limited number of tasks and pursue them with a relative sense of security from the very beginning. This situation contributed to the ease with which it achieved success as an innovative organization.

Early research on radio

By 1913 the level of radio research activity by independent inventors and a number of American companies had increased significantly. The Institute of Radio Engineers, organized in 1912, provided both a forum for, and a spur to, the interchange of ideas and results. GE had begun radio research, and the Marconi Company let it be known that its engineers were experimenting on radio communication services. Marconi intended to develop a system for transatlantic voice communication – a system into which Bell might be forced to connect. Yet if transatlantic radio telephony were possible (as transatlantic wire telephony then was not), Vail and Carty intended that it become part of the Bell System's "Universal Service."[46] They felt the same way about domestic applications of radio. Flooding in the American Midwest that year had disrupted telephone service, leading to calls for the use of radio as a supplement to the wired system. One of AT&T's engineering managers even expressed concern that the government might begin building radio communication systems or that Marconi could take advantage of the opportunity to go into competition with Bell on domestic long-distance service.[47]

Continuous-wave radio communication was very similar to the wired telephone and telegraph technique of multiplexing, which permitted the simultaneous transmission of several messages over the same line. For transcontinental telephone service, in particular, multiplexing promised great economies. Because it required lower power levels and frequencies than radio, multiplexing was also a logical starting point for radio research, and by late 1913 J. J. Carty had decided that the laboratory should put significant efforts into radio.

Carty thus suggested to E. H. Colpitts that the Research Branch mount a concerted effort to develop multiplex telephony and to work toward achieving long-distance radio communications. Somewhat hesitant, Colpitts responded that it would take an expenditure of $15,000 for one year's work before "we would have sufficient data to enable us to estimate pretty closely our chances of ultimate success and consequently what expenditures might be warranted." But Carty was not to be dissuaded. After laboratory researchers succeeded in designing important radio-related circuits in the spring of 1914, he assured Vail that transatlantic radio was within reach. On July 30, based on Carty's recommendation, the board of directors issued a formal work authorization.[48]

Arnold, in charge of the multiplex and radio research effort, periodically reported progress to Carty via Colpitts and Jewett. During the summer and early fall of 1914, he, Colpitts, and van der Bijl worked together to establish a multiplex system concept. Because their capabilities in circuit analysis had not yet progressed far enough to deal with multifunction circuits, they decided to use three independent circuit modules: an oscillator, a modulating tube, and a single-stage, high-frequency amplifier. Arnold brought a laboratory engineer closely under his direction to construct the apparatus and make tests. Within a few months they had a crude multiplex telephone system working in the laboratory.[49] Though this was quite promising, problems of crosstalk and selectivity ("tuning") required considerable refinements in technique. As a result, AT&T was not actually able to use multiplexing in telephone service until after the First World War.

These difficulties made Arnold and the laboratory researchers realize that a good deal of mathematical analysis of circuit phenomena would be necessary to understand subtle but highly important circuit intra- and interactions. Accordingly, Arnold assigned several people to work on developing the necessary analytical techniques. During 1914 and 1915, they produced treatises on circuit operations, with an emphasis on the role of the triode as a circuit element.[50] By the time the Research Branch undertook extensive radio systems design in 1915, a significant groundwork of mathematics and operations theory had been established and efforts were continuing. It is interesting to note how sharply this pursuit of theory and mathematics contrasted with the company's approach to development under Hayes. Jewett, Arnold, and the new laboratory researchers recognized the importance of taking a step "back" from the technology to a level of understanding based on theoretical and mathematical considerations. Moreover, they were given adequate resources to pursue this important part of their task.

In early 1915 Arnold formed a radio development group to test and modify circuits designed in the laboratory. Equipped with the feedback that this provided, and with an expanding core of theory and mathematics to use, Arnold, van der Bijl, Colpitts, and several other researchers undertook an extensive exercise in circuit design. Because high-power, high-frequency amplification was necessary for radio transmission, Arnold worked on multistage and parallel-tube amplifiers while collaborating with others on methods of neutralizing internal tube capacitance (a problem that became acute at radio frequencies). Other researchers worked on modulators, oscillators, and amplifiers, developing and patenting numerous schemes for each function.[51]

Research in the laboratory soon focused on transatlantic radio. Engineer Lloyd Espenschied, who was involved in the project, saw progress this way:

> The low-power-level grid modulation devised by van der Bijl required that the modulated high-frequency carrier be amplified to material power preparatory to radiation. Both he and Arnold recognized this – what became the master-oscillator power-amplifier type of transmitter, and the combination was patented in Arnold's name. The first step toward realizing a power amplifier was taken by Arnold by paralleling low power tubes. . . . Meanwhile the construction of bigger and more powerful tubes, presenting the problem of degassing, was undertaken. Progress was made that winter and by the spring [1915] there was coming to hand in rude bread-board fashion, a power-amplifier radio telephone transmitter ready to be tested in the field.[52]

"Tested in the field" does not convey the difficulties that had to be surmounted. Operating the system components together often led to unexpected results, for the complexities of their interactions were not yet completely understood. Members of the radio development group spent several months constructing, testing, and modifying equipment before long-distance transmission tests could begin.[53]

The Research Branch paid little attention to radio receivers com-

Plate 20. Visiting dignitaries and staff at the Montauk, Long Island, (AT&T) radio transmission tests, April 1915. From left: (second) H. D. Arnold, (fourth) John Mills, (fifth) Frank Jewett, (sixth) John Carson, (seventh) Robert Millikan, (eighth) Lloyd Espenschied, (ninth) J. J. Carty. Photograph courtesy of the Smithsonian Institution.

pared to its efforts with transmitters because transmitters were generally perceived as the limiting factor, so work naturally concentrated on them. In addition, design of receivers held great allure for independent inventors and smaller laboratories: the technical – and not so technical – literature contained information on a number of innovative circuits. Under Arnold's direction, the Research Branch concentrated its receiver work on limiting atmospheric interference ("static"), in which it was quite successful.[54]

Laboratory researchers began preliminary long-distance transmission tests from Montauk, Long Island, to Wilmington, Delaware, in April 1915; soon they were able to demonstrate one-way radio communications to company officials. The radio development group conducted further tests the following month between Montauk and the coast of Georgia, a distance of about 800 miles. That summer they readied equipment for a transatlantic trial. The final test transmitter comprised a low-power grid modulator designed by van der Bijl and a single-stage, 300-tube parallel amplifier developed by Arnold. Each amplifier tube produced 25 watts, giving the device a total power of about 7,500 watts. But

Plate 21. Theodore N. Vail (in New York) officially opening the AT&T transcontinental radio-telephone hook-up, October 1915. The signal travelled from New York to Arlington, Virginia, by wire, then by airwave to San Francisco. Reproduced with permission of AT&T Corporate Archive.

the amplifier caused considerable difficulties because its 300 separate circuits interacted in unforeseen and often uncontrollable ways. Making it work required significant modifications to circuit design as well as constant adjustments.[55]

Early that fall, radio contact was established between the East Coast and AT&T receiving stations in California, Hawaii, and the Panama Canal Zone. Telephone lines connected company headquarters in New York to AT&T transmission equipment at the U.S. Navy's radio tower in Arlington, Virginia. Signals went partially by landline and partially by airwave, demonstrating the possibilities of interconnecting the two media. On October 21, after several unsuccessful attempts, AT&T equipment on the Eiffel Tower received voice broadcasts sent from Arlington. This ended the early, highly organized phase of Bell radio research.[56]

The transmission quality and reliability of this first transatlantic broadcast were not adequate for commercial purposes, but the Research Branch's efforts had not been aimed at preparing Bell's entry into transatlantic radio-telephone service. Rather, Vail and Carty wanted to acquire patents in advance of all others and gain the technical capabilities that would keep the company in the forefront – both in fact and in the public view. They realized, of course, that technical success brought with it the possibility of commercial difficulties. AT&T's accomplishments might increase public demand for radio-telephone services, possibly drawing new entrants into the field. Members of some regulatory commissions began to suggest that Bell itself should provide domestic radio communication service, which the company resisted because it would have upset established and profitable operations. In order to avoid such consequences, AT&T management attempted to shape the public image of laboratory accomplishments so as to fit corporate interests. Thus, when the Research Branch established long-distance radio communications in the fall of 1915, J. J. Carty told the press, "The results of the long distance tests show clearly that the function of the wireless telephone is primarily to reach inaccessible places where wires cannot be strung. It will function mainly as an extension of the wire system and a feeder to it."[57] For the occasion, Vail sent Carty the following telegram, reported in the *New York Evening Post* of September 30, 1915:

> Carty, I want to congratulate you. . . . To throw your voice directly without aid of wires from Washington to Hawaii. . . . was wonderful, but to send the recognized voice part way over wire and part through the air was still more wonderful and was the demonstration of the chiefest [*sic*] use that will probably attach to the wireless, as amplifying and supplementing, not substituting, the wire system. . . . Your work has indeed brought us one long step nearer our ideal – a "universal system."

AT&T mixed news of success with comments about the inapplicability of radio to regular telephone service. Statements to the press noted that there were inherent problems with interference as well as limits to the number of stations that could operate simultaneously. AT&T spokesmen also suggested that radio communications could not be kept secret – even though laboratory researchers had at the time submitted patent applications on several complete secret signalling systems. One participant in the long-distance tests later recalled that "the company was fearful its own success would lead the public to believe that wires were about to be supplanted by radio, whereby they might sell their telephone stock."[58] AT&T management wanted to make certain that they would not.

By taking this approach, AT&T demonstrated both its inexperience in industrial research and its peculiar position as a private corporation in control of a public-service market. The protection of AT&T's wired telephone interests had been foremost in the minds of Carty, Vail, and the board of directors when they established a research laboratory. The Research Branch helped them expand and protect those interests through development of the triode vacuum tube and establishment of coast-to-coast telephone service. Still, the basic service concept of telephony remained unchanged. Radio presented entirely different types of commercial possibilities; yet Bell management thought first of protecting its wired-telephone position. Only later, after commercial success in radio by GE and others, would AT&T attempt to profit from the laboratory's radio research. The company required more experience with the inventive and innovative powers of industrial research before it would reach out beyond telephone and telegraph service to new market possibilities. In this way AT&T differed significantly from GE, which had long competed in a number of market areas and was better attuned to commercial opportunities.

During the years when the Research Branch pursued its early vacuum-tube and radio research, the size of both its staff and its research budget grew considerably. J. J. Carty had Vail's strong backing as well as the confidence of the board, so resources flowed into the laboratory. Beginning in 1911 with H. D. Arnold and a few assistants, the number of personnel increased rapidly to 23 in 1913, 45 in 1914, 73 in 1915, and 106 in 1916. Laboratory expenditures rose during the same years from $71,000 to $137,000, $231,000, and $249,000. Moreover, the buildup occurred at a time when business conditions forced the company to cut both expenditures and personnel in several other Engineering Department branches. This new type of research was considered so important that the Research Branch and the two other Engineering Department branches that worked closely with it – Development and Transmission – received increased support even as cutbacks were being made almost everywhere else in the company.[59] The situation had been far different at GE in 1907, when economic difficulties, combined with perceived Research Laboratory inadequacies and a lack of management commitment to research, led to a budget reduction of over 40%. Only after the GE Research Laboratory had proved itself through the development of ductile tungsten did it receive the level and consistency of support that marked the Research Branch from its inception.

Research and corporate needs

The establishment of a laboratory at Bell staffed with scientists and research-oriented engineers signified a major departure from earlier approaches to the development of technology. This move stemmed in part from the company's desire to achieve coast-to-coast telephone service and in part from its intention to protect itself from a potentially disruptive new technology, radio. When the more usual corporate methods of development failed to produce a telephone repeater for long-distance service after several years' effort, it became apparent that the situation called for a new type of research effort. J. J. Carty appreciated the possibilities of an electronic repeater and pushed for the creation of a laboratory that could deal with its complexities – a laboratory that approached technology in conjunction with the kinds of studies usually associated with the pursuit of science. The decision to employ scientists and engineers to consider "fundamental principles" was a major change of direction. As late as 1907 Bell's policy had been to do no original research because management had not yet recognized that support of a research program which looked beyond immediate needs served the System's best interests.

In fact, Bell's commercial situation in the years before establishment of the Research Branch militated against such a step. Resources were always scarce, and other investments appeared more attractive. With the expiration of the controlling Bell patents in the 1890s, the company had found itself in fierce competition with numerous independents, requiring considerable capital to expand its wired facilities. During the early years of the 20th century, AT&T experienced a chronic shortage of capital, overextended itself financially, and proved to be a ripe plum for J. P. Morgan's banking interests when 1907 brought a tightening of the money market.

One important reason that research received little emphasis in Bell's early years was that management had not fully recognized the potential impact of new technologies. The company's long-entrenched directors believed that telephone technology would progress at a moderate pace in established directions. If AT&T could maintain its position by acquiring "a thousand and one little patents and inventions,"[60] most of them from inventors outside the Bell System, there was little reason to invest in a research program. At this point the telephone industry had developed what historian Reese Jenkins calls a "business-technology mind-set" – conceptions, assumptions, attitudes, and values that dominated the thinking of its leaders. Jenkins has shown that unexpected, exogenous developments could wreck an industrial structure rigidly built on such a mind-set.[61] AT&T was especially vulnerable because it depended on a single form of technology.

The change in Bell's business-technology mind-set took place between 1907 and 1910, apparently for three reasons. First, other large companies had recently demonstrated that research provided much-needed corporate insurance. GE established its laboratory in 1900 and expanded it during the following decade. In late 1909 GE announced its development of ductile tungsten, thus forcefully demonstrating the commercial value of industrial research. And, of course, the German chemical, pharmaceutical, and dye industries had supported research laboratories staffed with scientists since the 1880s; much of their worldwide commercial success rested on the laboratories' results.

Second, the new management that took over AT&T in 1907 was determined to change the company's conservative policies. The presidency had changed hands several times between 1880 and 1907, but the corporation had been controlled throughout by the Boston capitalists who owned a large share of its stock, dominated its board of directors, and showed great concern with short-term profits. The ascendency of the Morgan–Vail–Carty regime broke this continuity and opened the door to change. Vail had been a strong advocate of Bell System innovation since the early 1880s; he welcomed the opportunity to support the greater research and development activity that Carty – the first AT&T chief engineer with the perspective of a staff position – recommended.

Finally, the company saw in radio telephony an as-yet unperfected but potentially disruptive technology that might require it to connect into others' long-distance communications systems or even circumvent its carefully assembled patent protection for telephone service.

Bringing scientists and engineers together in a concerted effort to achieve long-distance telephony and then transatlantic radio communications, the Research Branch succeeded in achieving its technical and commercial goals. It grew quickly because it had a well-thought-out, carefully administered research program and because it received strong support at all corporate levels. Under the administrative guidance of J. J. Carty, Frank Jewett, and H. D. Arnold, the Research Branch quickly established its position by displaying its importance in many ways, from overseeing installation of the transcontinental telephone line to placing the company in the forefront of radio development. This demonstration of the power of research led to a general reorientation within the Western Electric Engineering Department; other branches began to give greater attention to "fundamental studies," often in cooperation with Research Branch scientists and engineers. The skills that Carty, Jewett, and Arnold together possessed assured that the Research Branch would receive the resources, direction, and corporate appreciation that it needed during its crucial early years.

By comparison, the GE Research Laboratory's early fortunes depended largely on the perceptions and directions of Willis Whitney, with some guidance from the Research Laboratory Advisory Council. Whitney's fumbling efforts to develop an administrative strategy during the laboratory's first decade did not demonstrate his inadequacies as a research director so much as the lab's lack of support and outside direction. As a diversified company operating in a number of market areas, GE had neither a coherent commercial–technological strategy nor an individual manager whose major responsibility was the formulation of corporate research and development policy.

After Morgan and Vail took over AT&T, they worked to gain control of American telecommunications through purchase of independent telephone companies and acquisition of Western Union, acts that engendered hostility and opposition. By 1913 the Department of Justice and the Interstate Commerce Commission had begun investigations to determine whether Bell's activities violated the Sherman Antitrust Act. In contention were the company's control of Western Union, its often-questionable tactics in acquiring independents, and its refusal to allow other telephone companies to tie into its long-distance lines. With antitrust cases having recently led to the dismemberment of Standard Oil and American Tobacco, Vail decided to defuse the controversy, even at high cost. Accordingly, he agreed in December 1913 to relinquish control of Western Union, to seek the approval of the Interstate Commerce Commission before acquiring more independents, and to allow other companies access to Bell's long-distance lines.[62] With this compromise Vail saved the Bell System in its integrated form, tying it even more closely to government regulation, and legitimizing its hegemony in – but not its monopoly of – the American telephone network.

As a result, research became more attractive as a corporate investment. AT&T's growth was limited either to increased telephone service in geographic areas it already controlled or to entrance into nontelephonic fields. Research held the promise of expanded service and reduced costs through technological innovation. The company's desire to maintain its wired-telephone position cast research in the roles played in part by competitive and financial tactics in the past. Furthermore, research actually became less expensive to the company at this time. Support for it came to AT&T from the associated companies, which, as a result of growing regulation, could usually include research expenses in their rate bases. Thus, telephone subscribers paid directly into the Bell System to support research and development – activities that lowered costs and increased capabilities to consumers' benefit but also helped protect the System from competition.

Research for the World War and after

Within a few months of the Arlington-to-Paris tests, the laboratory turned its attention to preparing the American military for war. Both Carty and Jewett accepted commissions in the Army Signal Corps. After the United States declared war in 1917, company personnel joined the Signal Corps *en masse*. Research Branch scientists and engineers generally remained in the employ of AT&T, developing radio and communications technology for the war effort, or they spent time instructing the military in the use of radio equipment.[63]

With J. J. Carty deeply involved in wartime Washington, Frank Jewett took over as AT&T chief engineer, and H. D. Arnold became director of research. When Carty returned in 1919, he was made AT&T vice-president in charge of development and research. Carty spent the next decade promoting the value of the company's scientific and technical activities and proselytizing for industrial research. The creation of this special vice-presidency was a further indication of the great importance that Bell had given to research in the years since 1907.

During the war, activities in the Research Branch continued with little attention from Carty and Jewett. Work took place in many areas, from the design of light, portable transmitters and receivers for the military (with vacuum tubes that could withstand battle conditions) to the development of advanced modulators and transmission systems, including secret-signalling methods. Concerted research on high-power tubes also began, since the transatlantic tests had shown "paralleling" large numbers of low-power tubes to be unsatisfactory. The laboratory now dealt with problems of large-scale production as it was called upon to deliver more than a half-million vacuum tubes for the U.S. military during the short course of the war. The number of its patent applications in 1917 dropped considerably below the level of the previous two years, even as the state of radio technology available in the field – as opposed to in the laboratory – improved considerably.[64]

At the end of the war AT&T reconsidered its position in radio. A group from the Research Branch met with Jewett, George Folk of the Patent Department, and Bancroft Gherardi, a staff assistant to Harry B. Thayer, the former Western Electric president and Vail disciple who had taken over the AT&T presidency upon Vail's retirement in early 1919. Together they drew up a "comprehensive wireless program" that included construction of marine stations as well as expanded research efforts. The laboratory calculated that if the company should choose to enter transoceanic wireless-telegraph service, it could expect to make over $2 million per year in profits.[65] Based on these discussions, Gherardi sent the following report to Thayer for presentation to the board of directors:

> The Bell System has at the present time a better status in wireless telephony, both physically and from a patent standpoint, than any other company or organization. In order, however, that large practical results may develop with reference to wireless telephony, it is necessary that much additional work be done and if we do not do this work promptly, others will undertake it and we will lose the favorable situation which we now occupy. We would soon be met by demands to connect with wireless systems controlled and operated by others, and we would be confronted by an increasingly difficult patent situation in any radio operation that we might wish to undertake ourselves. The position of this company with reference to the communication field . . . is such that we cannot afford to leave the development of the art to others.[66]

With the war over and radio technology on a sure footing, AT&T actually increased the number of people and the amount of resources devoted to radio-related research. On Thayer's recommendation, the board of directors authorized a $500,000 expenditure for radio research. Company accounting figures indicate that the effort actually received funding of $263,000 in 1919 and $901,000 in 1920.[67] This period was characterized by expanding research on many fronts, some of it to extend earlier efforts and capitalize on knowledge gained during the transatlantic tests and the war, other parts going off in entirely new directions. Although commercial possibilities remained unclear, AT&T intended to maintain its position at the technological forefront, especially in terms of patent protection.

In addition to continuing their work on oscillators, modulators, and amplifiers, Bell researchers undertook projects on secret signalling, on multistation communications systems, and on vacuum-tube design and fabrication methods. Research covered the entire spectrum of radio-related technologies. AT&T's successful radio and vacuum-tube patent applications, which had fallen to twenty-five in 1917, more than doubled in 1918, and rose considerably thereafter.[68]

Even though the laboratory had lost the highly specific goal orientation of the prewar period, Arnold remained firm in his administration of research. When the company became embroiled in several important patent suits, he directed projects to supply corroborating research results and courtroom demonstrations. In 1919 he formed a colloquium for the laboratory's scientists, using this means, as well as regular conferences, to help coordinate research.

In 1919 there was also a large-scale reorganization of the rapidly growing Engineering Department. Several new divisions were created, and the Research Branch became the Department of Physical Research Engineering. By 1921 it had 234 employees, with Arnold at its head. Arnold also supervised the Departments of Chemical Research Engineering and Transmission Engineering, with 48 and 131 employees, respectively.[69]

In the early postwar years the laboratory's activities broadened significantly. In addition to research on radio and vacuum tubes, it became involved in studies of microphonic actions of carbon, design and composition of metallic contacts for telephone switching apparatus, structure of enamel and phenol-fiber insulation, properties of magnetic materials, and determination of telephone and telegraph transmission parameters.[70] Like GE, Bell had determined that once its new industrial research laboratory fulfilled the initial mission of preserving vital corporate markets, the lab then served company interests best through diverse activities that advanced and protected the company's business on many fronts.

As research efforts grew during the early 1920s, AT&T decided to make research itself into a corporate entity, in part to enhance

Plate 22. Harold D. Arnold. Reprinted with permission of AT&T Corporate Archive.

the company's public image. Management believed that "benefits for the Bell System" would come from "deliberately continuing to promote the public recognition of these laboratories as the greatest scientific organization in the country."[71] The Bell Telephone Laboratories, incorporated on January 1, 1925, as a wholly owned subsidiary of AT&T and Western Electric, certainly gained high visibility. The company actively promoted it as a kind of national research laboratory, where the fruits of pure research benefited science, technology, and American economic interests. AT&T believed that support of such research helped distinguish it as one of the "good" trusts – and hence one that should not be dismantled – a point that company management stressed in the Federal Communications Commission's investigation of the telephone industry during the 1930s.

A large portion of the Western Electric Engineering Department was incorporated into Bell Labs, along with members of the AT&T and Western Electric corporate staffs in areas such as personnel, sales, legal matters, and commercial and public relations. Frank Jewett was made president, and H. D. Arnold became director of research. In its first year, Bell Laboratories employed approximately 3,600 people, with 2,000 on the technical staff, and had a budget of over $12 million. Researchers worked in the areas of radio, electronics, chemistry, magnetics, optics, applied mathematics, speech and hearing, conversion of energy between electrical and acoustical systems, generation and modification of electric currents, instruments of all kinds, paints and varnishes, and problems relating to the aging and preservation of wood (for telephone poles, of course).[72] The size and complexity of this operation provides a measure of the extent to which the relatively new function of industrial research had, by 1925, become an established and highly significant part of the American industrial economy.

8

AT&T: The Research Process

The Research Branch's position within the Western Electric Engineering Department, combined with its missions relating to vacuum tubes and radio, influenced its structure, goals, and methods of research. The branch's establishment signalled an important change in corporate attitudes toward the development of technology, and subsequent demonstration of its power to contribute to AT&T's technical needs helped transform research methods throughout the Engineering Department.

As the central development group for the Bell System, the Engineering Department had a management structure that reflected Vail's and Carty's concerns about overall System rationalization. Each department function tied in with needs of the growing telephone network, from efficiency studies and standardization to cable development and the design of automatic apparatus.[1] Because it was part of the Engineering Department, the Research Branch inherited this managerial approach to research. Its administrators knew that their results had to function harmoniously within a system environment, so they carefully organized and controlled laboratory activities for both technical and business reasons. They made certain that researchers maintained close working relationships with their counterparts in the Development and Transmission Branches to be sure that all resulting techniques and devices fit in with Bell System practices and could be readily adapted to manufacture and implementation.

Under the decentralized management structure of GE, by contrast, the Research Laboratory functioned as a semiautonomous organization and was managed according to Willis Whitney's perceptions of appropriate directions and methods. Although it lacked the Bell System's thoroughness, this approach did ultimately bring GE important advances in a number of disparate fields.

Research at Bell went through a period of close direction and organization, then broadened in scope as the laboratory worked to cover a number of communications-related fields. During the first stage of research on vacuum tubes, multiplex, and radio, J. J. Carty's drive to meet technological goals and the almost military atmosphere he inspired resulted in well coordinated, tightly controlled operations. After the First World War, two important changes took place: the scope of research widened because of AT&T's decision to diversify research and accumulate patents in many areas germane to telecommunications; and Frank Jewett replaced Carty as chief engineer, giving the Research Branch a guiding spirit more in tune with the ethos of the larger scientific community. These two events served to relax some restrictions on researchers' interactions with scientists and engineers outside the Bell System and to provide more individual latitude within the lab itself. By the early 1920s, areas of research had broadened considerably. Staff members were then encouraged to make themselves part of the growing American scientific and technical communities in order to maintain contact with contemporary developments in science and engineering and to build good will for the Bell System.

Constraints and pressures

During the first stage of AT&T electronics research, the intense group effort to design and implement coast-to-coast telephone service and then transatlantic radio resulted in a highly structured research organization. H. D. Arnold and H. J. van der Bijl worked on the theoretical aspects of vacuum-tube and circuit operations, while other researchers provided the experimental results needed to test and extend their theories, then to begin developing tubes and circuits. Still others worked on such problems as the fabrication of oxide filaments, tasks that called for both scientific analysis and engineering design. This team approach to research and development produced impressive results quickly, while the strict enforcement of secrecy prevented those outside the laboratory from benefiting. The Research Branch progressed, both in its understanding and in its capabilities, far more quickly than those in the outside scientific and technical communities.

AT&T wanted no one to know the direction or extent of its research before completion of the transatlantic tests and enforced complete secrecy. Even on recruiting missions, Jewett could give prospective researchers only a hint of the type of work going on.

One new employee who was familiar with contemporary electronics research noted that upon reporting to Bell in July 1914 he "found the vacuum tube developed far beyond anything published." Another researcher, commenting on his first days at the laboratory in the summer of 1914, remarked:

> There was for example an air of secrecy which, perhaps not evident to the natives, was quite noticeable to a new comer [*sic*]. . . . Later, when the radio tests began, we were ordered to complete secrecy, not even our wives were to be told of our jobs. The penthouse on the Hotel Dupont [the receiving end of the Montauk-to-Wilmington tests] was not occupied until heavy window shutters had been installed and woe to us if we didn't keep them closed. Even at [the laboratory] things were under lock and key.[2]

Similar precautions were taken during preparation for the transatlantic tests. As one AT&T engineer recalled, "All the work at Arlington was carried on very quietly and, when the time came to start tests, the vacuum tubes required were shipped from New York with a great deal of secrecy. When the tubes arrived Dr. Arnold and Mills under the cover of night obtained the tubes from the express company. . . ."[3] To preclude outside knowledge of the tests, the AT&T experimenters composed their radio signals of musical tones interrupted to form telegraph code letters so that anyone picking them up would assume they were telegraph signals and not realize that someone was engaged in radiotelephone experiments.[4]

The very important theory of sidebands, worked out in the Research Branch during 1914 and 1915, remained almost entirely unknown outside the company for several years. One AT&T researcher noted:

> The knowledge of sidebands seems to have been generally confined to our engineers for some time. As much as two years after my introduction to sidebands their presence was not known by all prominent outside radio engineers. . . . When this country entered the war and we helped educate army and navy men in radio we had to point out the sidebands even in the case of their expert radio aides.[5]

Without an understanding of sidebands, outside radio experimenters could not have competed on an equal basis with Bell's researchers.

Secrecy regarding vacuum tubes and radio was practiced within the Western Electric Engineering Department as well. A year and a half after the beginning of research on the triode, Jewett wanted to be sure that only those directly concerned with it have access to the device. In a memorandum to the head of the Development Branch, Jewett suggested that all vacuum tubes be kept in a "locked box" because he did not "care to have knwoledge of the audion characteristics or structure too generally circulated."[6]

Arnold and Colpitts exercised control over the flow of information within the Research Branch itself. Although they tried to make certain that each staff member learned everything he needed to know about internal developments, they limited distribution of reports to those concerned with similar types of research, perhaps to guard against someone "defecting" to a competitor, bringing along an overview of AT&T work.[7] Arnold very carefully directed and controlled both research and the information that resulted from it. This left a number of people discontented, since his methods violated the norms of science they had assimilated during graduate training. One AT&T engineer commented that "Arnold kept things to himself," adding, "Probably that was one reason why van der Bijl left the company."[8]

Within the GE Research Laboratory, by contrast, information flowed as freely and completely as Whitney could manage. Even when the laboratory was striving to develop a metallic filament, Whitney believed that the need to share ideas and the importance of high morale outweighed any risk that outside researchers or competitive concerns might learn about GE results.

Although the publication of scientific and technical materials from the Research Branch began haltingly in 1914, a number of papers had already been written by that time – but for in-house distribution only. These papers served two purposes. First, they presented research findings in a digestible form for other laboratory workers and for researcher–administrators like Arnold and Colpitts. Kept in a central file, they made the latest information on various important topics readily available to designated lab members.[9] Second, writing (and reading) these papers helped to simulate the large scientific environment, where research normally was published or presented at meetings and thus became "public knowledge." Within the Research Branch the "public" was, of course, rather limited, but it often included some of the most advanced researchers in related fields. During the course of its multiplex, radio, and vacuum-tube research, the laboratory actually sustained substantial scientific and technical communities of its own. People like R. A. Heising, R. V. L. Hartley, Carl Englund, John Carson, George Campbell, and E. H. Colpitts in electronic circuitry, or H. D. Arnold, H. J. van der Bijl, O. E. Buckley, H. W. Nichols, William Wilson, and C. J. Davisson in electron physics made up highly respectable subsets of these two communities. Because the types of problems pursued tended to be concentrated in a few areas, and because dissemination of research results was restricted, the laboratory community itself often contained the most knowledgeable and sympathetic audience possible. Thus, the Research Branch gave its professional staff a scientific environment in which to function – a community of substance that could effectively extend or withhold its approval.

In one case, while Carty was still chief engineer, a laboratory researcher was permitted to publish a paper concerning his work. Jewett promoted this activity because he felt that it helped in recruiting good people. He believed in the value of publication if it could be done in such a way as to reveal no important information. To gain Carty's permission, Jewett wrote to him:

> You may remember that two or three weeks ago I spoke to you about the publication of an article which [J. W. Woodrow] had prepared, descriptive of a new and rather ingenious method of determining extremely low vacuum pressures. The article describes a vacuum gauge for such measurements. It is the type of article which I think it would be well for us to publish, both for its effect on the Research men and also because it would, I think, tend to enhance the standing of our Research Department in the scientific world and make it easier for us to locate and secure A-1 research men. I cannot see that its publication would give away any material advantage we now possess.[10]

Jewett sent the article to physicist Robert Millikan for his assessment. With Millikan's endorsement and then with Carty's approval, he forwarded it to the journal *Physical Review*, where it was printed within a few months. This, however, was the only paper from the Research Branch published during Carty's tenure as chief engineer.[11]

Because they could not usually publish their results during the laboratory's early years, Bell researchers often got no public recognition for important discoveries in radio and electronics. Others, often years behind them have been credited with advances initially made in the Research Branch. For example, E. Howard Armstrong, a highly original thinker who worked at Columbia University, received awards and acclamations for advances that were actually first accomplished at Bell. A 1963 article in *Electrical Engineering* is suggestive:

> [Armstrong's 1915 paper] did a good deal more than present a new circuit concept. It gave the radio engineering fraternity the first correct explanation of how the "mysterious" audion really worked. . . . Without resort to a single equation Armstrong was able to provide a simple, clear, and complete technical description of the action of an audion when used as a detector, an amplifier, an oscillator, and a heterodyne receiver, with additional embellishments such as a static elimination scheme. While he was at it, he introduced the use of oscillograms to analyze radio circuit waveforms and drew the first useful vacuum-tube characteristic curve.[12]

When Armstrong published his paper in 1915, illustrating the operation of some simple circuits and explaining the functions of the triode (all, it should be noted, without benefit of mathematics), the AT&T researchers were about to establish radio contact between America and Europe. Their knowledge of vacuum tubes and circuitry was considerably in advance of Armstrong's. Numerous treatises written within the laboratory – but never seen outside – had already dealt with the physics and mathematics of vacuum tubes and the electrodynamics of circuits. The "first useful vacuum-tube characteristic curve," which Armstrong described in mid-1915, had actually been worked out in the Research Branch during February 1913.[13] Workers outside of Bell had to duplicate research already accomplished there, which meant that the pace of advance in electronics and radio was retarded. Other scientists and engineers consistently received credit for discoveries made in the laboratory because the Bell researchers usually could not publish, nor were the details of their accomplishments ever brought to public attention.

Similarly, GE's William Coolidge had been unable to publish results of his metallic-filament research while it was underway, so that he dispaired of ever gaining a scientific reputation. Yet once the patent applications on ductile tungsten had been filed, Whitney encouraged Coolidge and other researchers involved in the work to publish fully. They did and received due credit. In the early years at AT&T, by contrast, laboratory management was deeply concerned that revelation of results beyond what was absolutely necessary to acquire patents would aid the competition or bring new people into the field. Neither research papers nor full statements of accomplishments were made public.

Up through the First World War, Bell researchers were permitted – even encouraged – to attend meetings of scientific and technical societies. But they went to listen rather than to contribute. Under instructions not even to disclose the type of work in which they were engaged, they could not fully take part, so they remained on the fringes of the growing scientific and engineering communities.[14] During the early years of the GE Research Laboratory researchers had also been restricted in what they could present and discuss at professional meetings. Even so, Whitney realized the importance of the interchange of ideas for the laboratory. He therefore encouraged his people to take part in these meetings to the greatest extent possible without divulging proprietary information.

The control of research and development

Between 1912 and 1915 the Research Branch slowly began to move away from the rigid task allocation system that had marked engineering activities in the Bell System. Its scientists and engineers gained a modicum of freedom in their pursuit of research. In dealing with such people, Jewett understood – and Carty came to realize – that stimulating internal motivation could be more important than imbuing the sense of corporate purpose that drove managers and most other employees. George Campbell, the Harvard physics Ph.D. who had joined the company in 1897, noted that to Hammond Hayes "the idea was 'working unselfishly for the good of the business.' With Carty it became 'enlightened self-interest'."[15] Under such a regime each researcher had to make his own way, in a sense; he was judged on the quality and originality of his work, on the extent to which it answered the laboratory's needs, and on his contributions to the work of others. Whitney ran his GE operation the same way.

J. J. Carty believed that researchers should be strongly encouraged in the matter of patents. In a 1912 memorandum he emphasized the importance of patents, urging that applications be made for all possible patents relating to the audion: "I think that the patenting of alternatives is a very important feature of our work and I suggest that the routine covering such matters be looked carefully over and strengthened, if necessary, the idea being that as far as possible on all new developments of substantial importance, we patent the alternative methods."[16] The Western Electric chief engineer agreed, noting that such a plan had been discussed and would soon be implemented. Thereafter, researchers often pursued work even after it became apparent that the results would be minor variations of devices already patented.[17] Because the company wanted patents on alternatives, "enlightened self-interest" strongly suggested that they do so.

Until the radio transmission tests of October 1915, most Research Branch effort had been directed at specific technical goals. Patents, although important, generally followed from, rather than led to, research. After the success of transatlantic radio, Jewett and Carty reassessed their research policies. The capabilities of laboratory scientists and engineers had been clearly demonstrated – but the company had also discovered that its own technical success could pose a threat to its telephone interests. An *intensive* research-and-development effort of the type made on transatlantic radio could lead to too much change, too quickly. As a result AT&T might be forced to modify its service at great expense, or even face new competitors. Thus, the decision was made to broaden research activity, to adopt an *extensive* research policy that would give the company patent coverage and a wide range of technical capabilities in several important communications-related areas. Researchers who wanted to pursue in-depth development of a particular technology were often discouraged from doing so if that meant removing resources from patent-gathering activities. When several engineers requested permission to continue the concerted radio research effort after the 1915 tests, with work directed toward perfecting a long-distance communications system, they were rebuffed. Raymond Heising, one of the most productive of the radio researchers, later recalled that "after the 1915 transatlantic tests, no steps such as we advocated were taken . . . but the radio work we were allowed to do was government requests [for the World War], and . . . tests which I was informed were to gather more information, *especially patents.*"[18] After 1915 company policy encouraged research projects that yielded patents on diverse aspects of radio and telephone technology, especially those not yet exploited by Bell. The Western Electric Engineering Department's annual report for 1916 noted: "Three hundred ninety-two inventions made by members of the department during the year were presented to our patent department for consideration. Approximately one-third of these inventions related to apparatus which we are producing or intend to manufacture; the remainder cover features of the art which are thought to be of future value."[19]

From the record of patents issued to workers in the Research Branch, it appears that groups occasionally made organized attacks on particular problems in areas management deemed especially important for commercial reasons. Perhaps the best example of this is the 1915 effort to develop modulating circuits to control the output of high-speed, high-power alternators like GE's Alexanderson alternator. Alexanderson himself was working on modulators of this type at the same time. Even though AT&T held no rights to the alternator, modulator research might provide secondary, possibly controlling patents. A few months after one lab staff member wrote a report on the coverage of Alexanderson's patents and an explanation of alternator operations, three others applied for a total of four patents on modulators. They filed all the applications within a period of one month, which strongly suggests a group project.[19] These patents, it should be noted, were not likely to be of use to AT&T except as bargaining chips in a commercial confrontation with GE.

The influence of administration

Frank Jewett became the head of Bell System engineering a year after completion of the transatlantic tests, and this change of administration influenced the tenor of research throughout the laboratory. Carty's military bearing and his pragmatic attitude toward research – that is, his belief that one should first state the problem, then solve it – had strongly affected the style of work in the Research Branch. Carty understood that the route from statement to solution could not always be direct, but he wanted the aim of all research to be visibly practical. In describing his perceptions of the place of research in the Bell System, Carty made this quite clear:

> These laboratories are . . . organized on a strictly business basis, and the work conducted in them is directed to no other purpose than improving and extending and conducting in a more economical manner the service which we render to the public. . . . The criterion which we apply to the work conducted in these labs is that of practical utility. Unless the work promises practical results it is not undertaken, and unless as a whole the work yields practical results it cannot and should not be continued. The practical question is "Does this kind of scientific research pay?"[21]

Carty, a Bell employee since 1879, gave his first loyalties to the System. Even though he recognized that members of the Research Branch responded to somewhat different stimuli than most engineers or company managers, Carty could not allow them to act as if other values took precedence over Bell's welfare. Although his imposition of specific technological goals and enforcement of strict secrecy did prove effective in the short run, over a longer period of time Carty would probably have had difficulty maintaining the sense of purpose that contributed to the cohesiveness of the laboratory in its early years. It is difficult to say what would have happened had Carty's tenure as chief engineer continued past 1916, but it is reasonable to suggest that the timing of his departure was fortunate.

Frank Jewett's assumption of the position of AT&T chief engineer, the First World War, and then the 1919 corporate decision to diversify research all affected the laboratory. The structure of its administration changed, as did the relationship of its researchers to the rest of the Engineering Department and to the larger scientific and technical communities. Radio systems development for the war effort once more provided technical goals. And as a result of the international situation, secrecy took on a patriotic hue. Yet Jewett's liberalizing attitude could be felt almost immediately. In fact the first presentation of a laboratory member's paper at a scientific meeting took place shortly after Jewett assumed the duties of chief engineer.[22]

Jewett had been a Bell employee since 1904, but his doctoral studies at the University of Chicago, his continued close association with Robert Millikan, and his experience as a professor at MIT gave him a perspective on research very different from Carty's. Under Jewett's influence the Research Branch took on several attributes of a university research environment. Rather than operate with a few well-organized teams, the laboratory staff broke up into a number of groups, each of which maintained a certain level of autonomy in its work. Of course Arnold and Jewett coordinated and directed research, moving staff members from group to group as needs changed. The style of laboratory administration that emerged under this regime permitted individual scientists and engineers considerable freedom in the pursuit of research and the publication of results – but not necessarily in the choice of problems. Jewett also made certain that Research Branch staff members coordinated their work with the Development Branch. This became especially important after 1919, when AT&T gave Western Electric permission to produce advanced instruments for commercial markets, and members of the Research Branch were called upon to help with development and design.[23]

Although Jewett permitted researchers to publish, restrictions on content were strictly enforced. All articles first went to the Patent Department, where attorneys decided whether they compromised Bell's position. That could happen if the publications revealed ideas for as-yet unfiled patent applications or if "the information . . . might come to the attention of outside inventors or competing companies and enable them to anticipate our lines of development, to investigate the various fields before we have had time to do so and to obtain patent claims which might embarrass us." The articles that appeared in scientific and technical journals beginning in 1917 usually discussed research concluded several years earlier or took the form of general explanations of circuit and tube phenomena. Few papers dealt with current research or new technologies.[24] In one particular area – study of the thermoelectric activity of oxide-coated filaments – Jewett encouraged prompt publication of results, but this was because the AT&T patent attorneys believed that new evidence would bolster Arnold's case against Irving Langmuir in their pending high-vacuum patent interference suit. General policies on publishing continued to be restrictive until the early 1920s. At least one researcher lost credit for his discoveries because he could not publish them "except," as a colleague noted, "in the form of patents"; but the patents were not granted until many years later.[25]

By 1922 management attitudes toward publication began to change further. Still unable to make disclosures that might compromise Bell's position, researchers were nevertheless encouraged to publish other results. As the Engineering Department's report for 1922 explained: "During the year our [scientists and] engineers have prepared for publication about seventy-five technical papers. . . . This activity is of very great importance in creating in the minds of a very influential group of the public a favorable attitude toward the Bell System."[26] Research was valuable for a number of reasons, and by the early 1920s management had learned that improved public perceptions of Bell System operations was one of them. The publication and promotion of some of its researchers' work served the company's long-term interests, more than compensating for the assistance that these publications might give competitors.

Accommodations

Even the restricted publication policies of Jewett's first years as chief engineer amounted to an important change in laboratory management's attitude toward its researchers and toward the laboratory's place in the scientific and technical communities. Carty would scarcely have countenanced the requisite expenditure of time and resources to publish a paper in one of the journals unless this served Bell's interests directly, whereas Jewett clearly realized the importance of indirect benefits. Shortly after he took over, Jewett noted that "the principal difficulty has been the securing of a sufficient number of trained workers" to meet staffing needs.[27] Because he sought the best possible scientists and research-oriented engineers, Jewett had to offer them the chance to publish at least some of their work and to remain active in their chosen fields. In addition, the diversification of the laboratory's research after 1915 (and especially after the World War) meant that in some areas the lab was no longer so far in advance of work elsewhere as to make an interchange of ideas unproductive. As part of his efforts on behalf of the National Research Council of the National Academy of Sciences after the war, Jewett was attempting to promote the national value of industrial research, so an insular, secretive stance would have been untenable.[28] He therefore urged laboratory workers to take their places in scientific and technical organizations and to contribute to publications in their fields.

Interchange and dissemination of information within the laboratory played important roles, both in coordinating research and in accommodating workers to the industrial environment. This took place by way of three media: in-house scientific and technical papers; the research library; and (beginning in 1919) colloquia. I have already discussed the preparation of in-house papers, which made research findings available to selected staff members and served as a "public" forum for ideas and results. This enabled researchers to maintain one of the strongest traditions of science, albeit in a modified form.

The Engineering Department established a scientific and technical library for the use of researchers in 1913. The library staff of one librarian and six assistants (in 1914) indexed and abstracted relevant articles, prepared bibliographies, translated articles from the important foreign journals, and, upon request, researched topics at libraries in New York City. In 1914 the library contained 1,050 volumes; by 1915 it held 2,300; and by 1916 the number had grown to 2,800, with subscriptions to 112 journals. In both 1915 and 1916 its staff translated over 1,500 journal pages.[29] The library provided researchers with a support service better than they could expect to find almost anywhere else. The abstract and distribution services assured that news from outside scientific and technical communities reached them quickly and systematically. The indexing, translation, and bibliographic services provided organized literature sources for their work. The library served to accommodate scientists in the industrial environment; it also became an important research tool in its own right.

In the years before the World War, Colpitts and Arnold had called special meetings to discuss in-house papers and other topics of interest, and in 1919 the laboratory established a regular colloquium. Not intended as a general meeting, the colloquium included those workers who were "in actual touch with research work" and who had been elected to membership in the American Physical Society, American Chemical Society, or American Mathematical Society. The colloquium's function, in the words of a member, was "to follow and report competently on scientific progress, either through one of its own speakers, or, on special occasions, through addresses given by some invited guest."[30] The colloquium spread ideas, helped laboratory administrators keep in touch with research, and brought attributes of the university to the industrial environment. In addition, it helped create a sense of community. Its restrictive membership policy encouraged researchers to become active in scientific societies, a practice that the company had decided served Bell's interests. Because Jewett and Arnold believed that researchers should keep abreast of advances in their fields – whereas the laboratory environment tended to create an insular atmosphere – they encouraged workers to report on the current literature to their colleagues. In fact, in 1917 Jewett hired a physicist specifically to analyze and report on recent scientific presentations and publications.[31]

Research for industry

Because its leaders were determined to make the Research Branch serve Bell's needs, projects had to be carefully chosen and results marshalled to produce a product or service of value to the System. Researchers were thus assigned, often in groups, to work on specific undertakings or in areas of special interest. One group of this type was made up of Arnold, van der Bijl, and Heising when they were developing vacuum-tube modulators for high-power, high-frequency alternators in 1915. Ralph Bown, Carl Englund, H. T. Friis, D. K. Martin, and R. K. Potter, assigned by Arnold in 1920 to study the propagation of radio waves in the atmosphere, comprised another.[32] C. J. Davisson's group experimented with filaments similar to those used in GE's vacuum tubes; as he wrote to a colleague: "At other times the results [from the tungsten filaments] were erratic. These were . . . side issues to the main problem which was to find if G.E. had anything on us in the matter of an efficient source of electron emission."[33]

The Arnold–Langmuir patent interference case on the use of high vacuum, at issue since 1915, engendered a considerable amount of research in the laboratory during the succeeding five years. The most important question was whether oxide-coated (Wehnelt) filaments emitted electrons as a result of positive-ion bombardment from surrounding gases – as Langmuir had suggested – or whether, thermionically active, they "boiled" off electrons like GE's pure-metal filaments and could thus function in a perfect vacuum.[34] Between 1916 and 1920 Bell researchers published a number of papers that suggested ionization played little or no part in the operation of oxide-coated filaments. Arnold summed it all up in a 1920 article, concluding that the results "negatives [*sic*] the idea, which a few people have held, that positive ion bombardment is a controlling factor in electron emission from oxide-coated filaments."[35] Laboratory researchers spent time bolstering Arnold's high-vacuum case in a number of ways. H. J. van der Bijl designed and built several types of amplifier tubes for courtroom demonstrations. Other researchers worked closely with the AT&T Patent Department, making extensive searches of the relevant scientific and technical literature and conducting experiments to determine the validity of Langmuir's claims.[36] These were some of the new roles for science in industrial research.

Research for patents

Another important role, of course, was aiding in the procurement of patents. Direction of this work was a very important matter for the Research Branch. The burden of planning it and otherwise attending to patent matters fell to Colpitts, Jewett, Arnold, and C. E. Scribner, the Western Electric chief engineer. These administrators studied patent situations in areas of interest to the company, kept workers informed, and directed them toward the areas of research they believed likely to result in patentable inventions.

The relationship of the laboratory to the AT&T Patent Department was rather complex and strongly resembled that at GE. Most commonly, researchers submitted memoranda describing their inventions, then Colpitts or Scribner sent the memos to the Patent Department, along with brief evaluations of the importance to Bell of the technologies involved. In at least one case, however, Scribner indicated to the Patent Department that little in a memo seemed "of immediate importance" and that it was "unnecessary at the present time to consider any of these schemes from a patent standpoint," but the Patent Department went ahead and processed several applications based on the disclosures it contained.[37]

The Patent Department often asked for laboratory notes relating to inventions, and in some cases, researchers spent time with company attorneys explaining their methods and results. Once the Patent Department drew up an application, it was sent to the Research Branch for comments, suggestions, and approval. The designated inventor met with one of the laboratory administrators; together they decided whether the application adequately represented his work.[38]

Patent Department attorneys were in close contact with research. They often came to the laboratory to speak with the staff and help decide what work should be submitted for patent coverage. The attorneys sometimes suggested further research that would be likely to yield valuable patents and also proposed follow-up work to substantiate submitted patent claims. Memos from Scribner and Colpitts kept the attorneys informed of progress as well as alerting them to projects that, though still in their preliminary stages, appeared to be leading toward significant results – and therefore should be carefully monitored for patent applications.[39]

Thus, the patenting process was fully integrated into the laboratory's research efforts. Patent attorneys kept abreast of the situation in fields related to telephony, vacuum tubes, and radio. They also kept track of the company's needs through conferences between Carty, Jewett, Scribner, and George Folk of the Patent Department.[40] Intimate contact between members of the Research Branch and the AT&T patent attorneys assured that research not only met corporate needs directly, but that it was conducted in a way likely to result in patentable inventions. It is indeed striking how similar the GE and AT&T patent departments were in their approach to monitoring and directing work done in their respective laboratories.

Relations within the engineering department

From its inception the new laboratory's interactions with other parts of the Western Electric Engineering Department were close. Some of its work – for example, developing amplifiers for the transcontinental telephone line – tied in directly with the responsibilities of other branches and had substantial impact on them. Because the Development Branch maintained close contact with the company's major manufacturing facility at Hawthorne, Illinois, Research Branch personnel often worked with members of the Development Branch to assure that designs for large-scale manufacture were appropriate. The Engineering Department's Committee on Design and Manufacture of New Apparatus helped coordinate the work of the Research and Development Branches with other engineering organizations in the Bell System and with Western Electric's manufacturing, sales, and merchandising operations.

Developing special manufacturing processes involved the Research Branch with other parts of the Engineering Department and with Western Electric manufacturing engineers. For example, fabrication of vacuum tubes was undertaken in the laboratory to overcome "difficulties of production in large quantities." Only after considerable improvement in the process had taken place did the operation go to a manufacturing division, and "a number of engineers were transferred from the Research Branch" to aid in establishing it.[41] The GE Research Laboratory worked much the same way.

When J. J. Carty became AT&T's chief engineer in 1907, he initiated a transformation of the Western Electric Engineering Department that accelerated under Research Branch influence. Carty inherited a diffuse engineering organization that was ineffective in dealing with the numerous technical difficulties confronting AT&T and its associated companies.[42] He reorganized it and began to consider new approaches to long-standing problems. Establishment of a research laboratory was a major step in that direction, signifying a new way of thinking about technical advance in the Bell System. The laboratory's use of scientists and its concern with what Carty called "fundamental principles" spread within the Engineering Department as lab research programs proved their effectiveness.

The Engineering Department's annual report for 1914 commented:

> Perhaps the most striking change in the work of the Development Branch during the past year has been in the direction of concentrating more on fundamental studies and spending relatively less time on individual cases. . . . As in the case of the Development Branch, the work of the Transmission Branch has tended to run largely to fundamental studies. . . . Many of these studies are borderline cases which have to be handled in part by the Research Branch and in part by the Transmission Branch. The two branches are working in close harmony.[43]

As the Engineering Department expanded during the decade after establishment of the Research Branch, "fundamental studies" became an important component of much of its work. Thus, although often farthest afield from AT&T's immediate business concerns, the Research Branch was not alone in the methods it used. When discussing the development of industrial research in the Bell System, then, it is important to realize that the ideas and methods fully manifested in the establishment of the Bell Telephone Laboratories in 1925 had spread beyond the Research Branch soon after it was founded. In this important process of change, it was energizing all of Bell System engineering. The Research Branch retained its position as central research laboratory for the Engineering Department even after the department's major reorganization in 1919. Lessons learned in coordinating its work with that of other branches in the Western Electric Engineering Department were used in devising the complex administrative structure that determined Bell Labs' relationship with the engineering and commercial acitivities of the System as a whole.[44]

Researchers for the laboratory

As Bell's research efforts in radio, vacuum tubes, and telephone transmission grew after 1912, Frank Jewett recruited many new workers for the laboratory. His close relationship with Robert Millikan at the University of Chicago proved fruitful in obtaining Ph.D. scientists. In addition to Arnold, Millikan sent van der Bijl,

H. W. Nichols, K. K. Darrow, M. J. Kelly, and J. Mills to the lab.[45] Jewett recruited four physics Ph.D.s from Cornell: R. Bown, O. E. Buckley, R. W. King, and P. I. Wold. All of them joined the Research Branch upon receiving their degrees except King, who had stayed on to teach at Cornell for two years. Jewett took the chemists J. E. Harris and C. Hocker from the University of Michigan; from the University of Wisconsin he acquired the physicists T. C. Fry and E. Stoekle.

Jewett looked for accomplished researchers to staff the laboratory. Kelly, Bown, King, Wold, Harris, and Stoekle had all published papers in the leading American journal of physics, *Physical Review*, before being hired. R. A. Heising, an electrical engineer with a master's degree from the University of Wisconsin, had done so as well. Several other new researchers had also published before coming to work for Bell. C. J. Davisson authored several papers while teaching at the Carnegie Institute of Technology. William Wilson, who earned his Ph.D. at Victoria University in England, had spent several years with the well-known physicists Ernest Rutherford and J. J. Thomson; his publications dealt with electron emissions.[46] When Jewett spoke of a shortage of qualified researchers, these were the kinds of people he meant. In order to entice them into Bell's ranks, Jewett had to offer an opportunity to publish some of their work and permit their participation in professional organizations.

Given the laboratory's emphasis on the team approach to research, Carty and Jewett avoided hiring people of unusual imagination and creativity who would not be likely to fit in. They sought instead bright, motivated researchers trained at the highest levels of contemporary science and engineering who were willing to work under close direction on team projects. Bell needed people who would be content with making incremental advances in their areas of expertise.[47] Although research might lead to significant breakthroughs – in radio or in electron physics, for example – project goals always remained clearly defined and, hence, inherently limited. Bell researchers' work had to fit in with the complex, integrated activities of the Engineering Department. During the laboratory's first decade, at least, that work remained closely tied to the System's technical needs.

Many scientists did not fit into the laboratory under such circumstances. Obviously, a technological orientation and a readiness to deal with the engineering aspects of research were necessary. But not all graduate scientific training prepared people for this kind of work. Even though a knowledge of, and interest in, the latest developments in physics and chemistry provided valuable insights for such research, the industrial scientist needed to have a thorough grounding in "classical" physics and chemistry. Frank Jewett was quite explicit about this:

> The universities are producing physicists who apparently are well qualified to publish worth while [*sic*] researches in spectroscopy and atomic structure, but who have almost no training in basic mechanics, hydrodynamics, electrical theory and thermodynamics, such as taught thirty years ago. We believe that in an industrial laboratory, the physicist or engineer who has the fundamental classical background is of greater value than a physicist who has almost exclusively specialized in the modern physical developments.[48]

Because Carty and Jewett believed that the route to solution of the repeater and other problems lay in electron physics and electrochemistry, they sought researchers who combined thorough grounding in the basics with advanced training in these new fields. With the help of such people, they expected to be able to solve the growing number of technical problems plaguing the expanding System. As Jewett noted:

> At the time when . . . this great research organization was started . . . the industry had outgrown its ability to progress wholly on the basis of random invention. . . . It had outgrown the second stage in which inventive ability and genius was [*sic*] teamed up with engineering skills. . . . It had reached a stage in which it was clear that some other kind of attack on many problems had to be made. . . . In other words, we had to bring somehow into the picture . . . the trained mind, and the same type of techniques which had developed the fundamental knowledge.[49]

These new industrial researchers, often working in teams that included scientists, engineers, mathematicians, and technicians, proved to be the powerful force Bell needed. They brought to its research efforts both the knowledge and the technique of which Jewett spoke. High-level studies had made them familiar with current scientific thought; graduate research training enabled them to plan and execute theoretical and experimental attacks on scientific and technical problems. By hiring such people, organizing their efforts, and providing them with assistants and equipment, Carty and Jewett changed long-standing methods of communications research and development in the Bell System, pursuing it in a manner that few others could afford to emulate.

New recruits at AT&T, just as at GE, usually abandoned academia for two reasons: to find more time and better resources for research, and to receive better pay. Opportunities to conduct research in an academic setting remained quite limited during this period. In all except the most highly research-oriented universities, faculty members found themselves with little time or resources for such activity. C. J. Davisson, for instance, while teaching at Carnegie Tech in 1914, lamented that "I will have a little more time for [research] after the middle of the year – At least I don't see how they can continue to find as many classes for me next semester as this."[50] Irving Langmuir had encountered a similar situation at the Stevens Institute of Technology in 1909 and left to join GE. In addition to making available large amounts of time for research, the AT&T laboratory provided its professional staff with support in the form of technicians and laboratory assistants. These workers usually had bachelor's degrees and high mechanical aptitudes. Lester Germer, who worked under Davisson, began in such a position.[51]

Research Branch salaries were considerably higher than those for academic positions – even higher than at GE. One AT&T researcher noted that he left his teaching position at Yale shortly after the First World War because he could not live comfortably on his academic salary; Bell offered him twice as much. Returning to academia, of course, became considerably more difficult as families grew accustomed to the higher standard of living. Though no records can be obtained, it is certain that salaries for the better researchers rose considerably during their tenure. Frank Jewett stated that, "Having a monetary motive, success in industrial research is measured largely by a monetary reward."[52]

What constituted "success in industrial research"? Surely, acquiring patents for the company was an important part – but only a part. A Bell industrial researcher succeeded by contributing to the overall laboratory effort, whether in formulation of theory, defense of patents, correlation and dissemination of knowledge, administration of research, or design of tubes, circuits, cables, or metallic telephone-switching contacts. Those researchers succeeded who cooperated and became part of the team because in the Bell System the team approach was all-important. Most advances from the Research Branch had to fit in with the carefully engineered telephone network. Because they were fully involved in all the complex functions of that network, administrators of the Engineering Department and the laboratory tended to see their own operations as an interactive network as well. The people who resonated within that network truly succeeded in industrial research.

The pursuit of science and technology

Even though the development of scientific theory in the laboratory did not provide the Bell System with any direct commercial benefit, theoretical constructs formulated in ways that related physical properties and processes to the behavior of man-made devices could promote corporate interests through the advance and control of communications technology. Within Bell's research laboratory environment, science did not lead a life apart; from the beginning, it was cultivated together with technology. Staff investigators for the Federal Communications Commission, evaluating the laboratory's history from the perspective of the mid-1930s, recognized this. Their report concluded:

> The research group appears to have been merely a more scientific kind of development department. Far from indulging in basic research of a nature which should prove useful over a broad field of essentially unpredictable practical matters, they conducted inquiries into specific and commercially useful apparatus, broadening their basis of research sufficiently to apply scientific knowledge to the greatest possible extent of its usefulness in the project under consideration. In short, it seems that *practical apparatus was the primary objective and fundamental knowledge the byproduct.*[53]

Few of those who participated in early Bell research efforts would have disagreed with this evaluation, and few would have thought that it should be otherwise. This type of research program met laboratory and company needs very well. It is important to realize that "fundamental" knowledge has to be fundamental *to* something – at AT&T it was fundamental to technology.

The importance of science to the laboratory lay in its ability to suggest and direct application. Scientific knowledge that led to application in a straightforward way had obvious value; knowledge that suggested further research or that pointed the way toward new theoretical constructs could be quite useful as well. Theory might be formulated on many levels, from the most abstract type of conceptualization to the analysis of simple mechanisms. Bell researchers worked to develop what might be called "technological theories" – analyses of man-made devices, often based on idealizations of their structures and functions. In doing so the researchers usually discarded the programs and even the conceptual bases of the scientific disciplines, but they did so on practical rather than on metaphysical grounds. Like Willis Whitney, the Bell research managers realized that, whereas building disciplinary thought in the sciences led to fuller understandings and explanations of the workings of nature, it usually failed to help them answer the questions that were of greatest interest to industry. A different but no less "scientific" type of research program was needed.

In the Research Branch, scientific theories, when combined with the (often mathematical) analysis of specific cases, led to the formulation of technological theories – conceptual and mathematical constructs that described the behavior of particular types of technology. Technological theories could be used directly or, with experience, codified for further development and design. Scientific theory was valuable insofar as it contributed to the formulation of technological theories that could be used to design new and useful processes or devices. In such a model of research and development, invention was actually inherent in theory: as researchers worked to delineate critical factors and describe their relationships to each other, their formulations evolved into technological theories, which, in appropriate cases and when properly formulated, became design methodologies – technologies in themselves.[54] In examining this research methodology, it is difficult to distinguish activities called "science" from those identified as "technology." Thus, even though we can attempt to classify various undertakings as "fundamental" or "basic" research (as did Carty and Jewett), "pure science," "applied science," or "technology," the designations we arrive at tell us more about our own ideologies and prejudices than they do about the research itself.[55] The strength of Bell's effort, in fact, resided in its ability to defy such singular classifications of its methods and results.

Technological theories were extremely important to the laboratory even though they could not be patented. (Only concepts that had been "reduced to practice" qualified as invention under the patent laws.) Nonetheless, to an organization concerned with advancing its technical capabilities and acquiring as many patents as possible in a few select areas, technological theories were sometimes the most valuable of all "inventions" because they suggested how to deal with complex systems. Furthermore, they sometimes led to numerous patentable inventions. One radio researcher, looking back over the development of signal modulation theory in the laboratory betwen 1913 and 1915, noted: "Perhaps no piece of apparatus was ever built for the Bell System that was more practical or useful than this theory. . . . Latent in this theory were many, many inventions."[56] Not surprisingly, pursuit of technological theories of this sort occupied many of the laboratory's best researchers.

Early research and development of the triode

To understand more precisely when and how researchers pursued science, how general theories were transformed into technological theories, and how technological theories helped in the development of technology, it is instructive to consider the laboratory's early electronics research. The effort on the triode provides a good illustration of the research and development methodologies characteristic of much Research Branch work.

After the October 1912 decision to pursue the audion as a telephone repeater, Frank Jewett removed H. D. Arnold from other projects, setting him to work exclusively on triode development. Jewett placed several of the new research workers at Arnold's disposal. While Arnold himself conducted an initial literature survey, he directed electrical engineer Paul Pierce to try several simple experiments with the triode, taking measurements and plotting voltage–current graphs. From Pierce's work and from his own studies Arnold gained a rudimentary qualitative and quantitative understanding of triode functions. He then undertook further experiments, reconciling important theories he had encountered in the scientific literature with his own results.[57]

Reassured that triode operations could be understood in terms of the emission and transportation of electrons, Arnold assigned a number of mathematical and experimental tasks to other researchers. Because he had come to believe that the triode functioned independently of residual gases, he was particularly concerned with the emission and transportation of electrons in a vacuum. Arnold realized that to design suitable audions he would have to calculate the currents passing from filament to plate as a function of their voltage difference, orientation, and distance. This set of relationships had been worked out in 1911 by American physicist C. D. Child, but Child had assumed that the tube's filament and plate were infinitely large, parallel, equipotential surfaces.[58] His equations yielded only approximate results in practice, so Arnold directed lab physicist William Wilson to develop the mathematics needed to deal with actual tube elements. In effect, Wilson transposed Child's equations into technological theories – they now described the operation of a real, man-made device.

Subsequent experimental work in the Research Branch centered on finding the effects of variations in the size, shape, and position of vacuum-tube elements. Laboratory engineers working under van der Bijl's direction built a vacuum tube with moveable and removeable elements.[59] Their results laid a foundation for continuing experimentation in vacuum-tube design and provided van der Bijl with the data he needed to establish a system of tube description and a methodology of design.

While this work was in progress, Arnold and van der Bijl attempted to develop a comprehensive technological theory of triode operations. In November 1913 they wrote an in-house paper titled "Theory of the Audion," which presented largely qualitative conclusions. In reviewing this work, Carty, Jewett, and Colpitts emphasized the importance of carefully controlling the direction of research to make it effective in meeting Bell's immediate needs. Colpitts informed Arnold:

> As to actual procedure, I understand that in perhaps ten days time you think that Mr. van der Bijl and yourself can outline a statement of your ideas . . . when we can then consider what factors should be made the subject of development work. It is my feeling that when such a statement as we had in mind has been prepared, and when the matters for investigation have been selected, we should consult with Professor Millikan. I think we both feel that the further investigation of the audion is a matter for very serious consideration, if we are to avoid being led into possibly interesting but rather fruitless bypaths.[60]

At GE, of course, such "bypaths" were seen as the road to serendipity.

After Arnold and van der Bijl had conferred with Millikan, and as more experimental results became available, van der Bijl extended the paper, submitting a more comprehensive work entitled "Audion Development" in April 1914. This report dealt with electron emissions, functions of the grid, and element parameters with respect to design. It was the first real design treatise written on the triode. Like the earlier paper, it circulated only to designated individuals within the laboratory.[61]

Plate 23. Evolution of the AT&T line amplifier (L) telephone repeater, 1915–27. Improvements included new forms and configurations of elements and better internal connections and supports. Reproduced with permission of AT&T Corporate Archive.

Over the next five years, van der Bijl directed experiments on vacuum-tube element configurations, concomitantly developing technological theories that he expressed as systems of equations useful for tube design. In 1918 he published a paper on functions of the triode; in 1920 he brought out a book on the subject.[62] By this time AT&T's laboratory researchers had long been using van der Bijl's design methodologies for building vacuum tubes to meet various service conditions and to create new (and often patentable) element designs and configurations.

This early triode research exemplifies the method of vacuum-tube and electronics work in the laboratory. Once the decision had been made to explore a new area of technology, researchers took a step "back" to underlying principles. They supplemented an extensive literature search with the empirical work needed to make measurements and verify important theories. This gave them a qualitative and quantitative basis for further analysis. Theoretical and experimental work then went hand in hand as the researchers sought to develop their own ideas. They tried to relate theories to particular technologies, expressing relationships mathematically wherever possible in their attempts to formulate technological theory. Laboratory administrators carefully circumscribed these efforts with work orders and review of regular reports so that only research directly related to specific problems would be continued. Such work often produced technological theories (usually expressed in equations) along with the charts and graphs useful for design. With this preliminary stage completed, laboratory engineers could design devices to meet particular needs or develop patentable variations. Of course, further background research usually continued in order to refine and extend the earlier work. Van der Bijl, for example, spent much of his time over a five-year period attending to the theory and design of the basic triode.

The Research Branch's orientation is exemplified by the thorough and systematic literature review undertaken at the onset of most new projects. The Engineering Department's library staff usually provided aid, taking the search to other libraries in New York City if necessary. The literature review always included scientific as well as technical subjects because it was recognized that the development of technological theory, and hence of technology itself, often depended on a thorough understanding of underlying scientific principles.[63]

Sometimes this technology-to-science relationship was not immediately apparent, so that the crucial aspect of research became an attempt to formulate the problem in appropriate scientific terms. Arnold's early success in understanding the triode, in fact, rested on his conception of its operation in terms of the more general phenomenon of the conduction of electricity through gases and vacuum. He therefore studied the audion using direct current and constant voltage rather than the fluctuating currents and voltages normally encountered during use. Many other researchers had attempted to formulate a technological theory of the audion based on normal operations and had failed. Arnold's breakthrough came when, taking account of the more general theory, he achieved an understanding of the emission and transportation of electrons between a negatively charged filament and a positively charged plate. His assumption that this process could take place in a vacuum – by no means the commonly held scientific opinion of the day – proved crucial in the analysis and greatly accelerated AT&T's development of the device.

Other laboratory researchers, whether working on filament materials, glass-to-metal seals, modulating circuits, or the propagation of radio waves, carefully analyzed general problems before they tackled the tasks at hand. For example, Davisson and Germer undertook an extensive study of the conditions governing electron emission from incandescent filaments before entering into filament design and fabrication. Experimental research of this type sometimes revealed serious conceptual problems, forcing workers to re-evaluate the related science. For example, an unexpected success in sealing glass to metal caused William Houskeeper to reconsider the chemistry of adhesion and to make a mathematical analysis of seal stresses.[64]

Knowledge shared within the laboratory concerning ongoing projects, whether through in-house papers, colloquia, or informal contacts, was often very important in furthering research. Davisson and Germer learned about the chemical properties of coated filaments from J. E. Harris's studies. Harris had discovered and analyzed the diffusion of the filament coating into the core. This phenomenon, if unrecognized, would have ruined Davisson and Germer's delicate electron emission experiments.[65]

The development of design methodologies

To go from a statement of theory to the design of technology required reformulation of the theory in appropriate terms. With electron tubes, for example, the general laws governing electron emission and transportation had to be transposed to deal with finite elements of particular shapes arranged in various configurations. Such work, usually mathematical in character, involved consideration of the physical effects of size and of shape irregularities. Since it was not always possible to accomplish such analysis directly, more roundabout routes had to be taken, often involving the correlation of several equations with one or more common variables. C. J. Davisson employed this method in devising his "power emission chart," which became standard for filament design. Davisson went from theory to design by replacing several independent variables with constants. This made it possible for the designer to determine the values of remaining variables under specified conditions.[66]

Mathematically based analyses often required certain assumptions and simplifications that limited their value in practice, so laboratory researchers frequently resorted to empirical means to describe and analyze circuit behavior. R. A. Heising's work on oscillating circuits is illustrative. Taking up the mathematical treatment of the triode oscillator circuit begun by van der Bijl and H. W. Nichols, Heising carried analysis far enough to use a system of equations to describe circuit behavior. In 1920 he published an article on this work in *Physical Review.* Yet Heising knew that his mathematical approach did not deal adequately with all parameters in oscillator design; so he made measurements of circuit operations – qualifying, limiting, or extending the equations as necessary, graphing and charting the results where possible. In another article, published in the *American Institute of Electrical Engineers Journal*, Heising acknowledged the shortcomings of his mathematical methods and, based on the empirical research, offered graphical representations of vacuum-tube oscillator circuit functions.[67]

In a 1921 companion article on the vacuum-tube modulator, Heising discussed design in terms of circuit parameters such as efficiency and introduced standard circuits like the "proper" and "improper" amplifier on which to base his analysis. This reduction to standard circuits played an important role in the analytical process and in the development of design methodologies. Laboratory researchers broke down complex circuits into standard networks of simple elements. One such very useful construct was the "equivalent circuit of the triode amplifier," described by John Carson in a patent specification; it consisted of a resistance and load impedance in series.[68]

Because the equations that researchers developed to represent vacuum-tube and circuit operations often failed to deal fully with their complex behavior, the equations had to be modified in practice. Even empirical work in conjunction with mathematical analysis sometimes failed to produce fully representative equations. In these cases, researchers and designers made the best use of the information available. After noting that one of his equations remained valid only during certain operating conditions that were frequently breached in practice, van der Bijl added that he had "generally found this equation to hold sufficiently well, to a first approximation at least, and [had] been using it in connection with work on the amplifier tube." Similarly, at the conclusion of an article on analysis of the triode as a circuit element – a procedure of great importance in Research Branch circuit design – H. W. Nichols noted that his "methods of treating the audion in a circuit are approximate only, because of the limiting assumptions made, but considerable use of them in connection with experimental circuit work has shown that they are useful." Sometimes a mathematical analysis had to be dispensed with entirely when no way could be found to apply general equations to specific cases. Van der Bijl remarked that such situations "are frequently met with in the study of discharge through vacuum tubes, and the problems involved become so difficult that the desired result [must be] determined empirically." As late as mid-1917, one researcher noted that the laboratory's method for improving vacuum tubes involved "wholesale experimenting." He concluded: "Every conceivable variable is varied and as much as possible is found out about details of the action."[69]

Mathematics was not always useful, but it did make important contributions to electronics research. The engineers used mathematical techniques in their vacuum-tube work to determine strains and stresses on elements and support structures, tempering their designs accordingly. T. C. Fry worked with William Houskeeper on the glass-to-metal seal and made an extended mathematical analysis of strains and stresses in a seal whose metal took the shape of a "ribbon." In attempting to attain the largest cross-section of the ribbon for a given width (to carry maximum current), Fry described a curve that lay "between the cosine curve of the glass considered as a column in compression and the curve of the deflection of a beam rigidly fixed at both ends such that maximum fiber stress is nowhere exceeded." His equation was subsequently employed in all ribbon-seal designs.[70]

For circuit analysis Bell researchers often used mathematical systems as circuit analogues, a method in which a term or set of terms performed the functions of a circuit element. By solving the equations, an engineer could design new circuits.[71] In some cases the transposition of general equations to specific cases led directly to patentable inventions. Bell's electronics-related patent applications after 1915 frequently set out mathematical derivations, then went on to show that the proposed circuits or tube-element configurations behaved in certain ways based on their congruence to the equations. These new designs actually emerged from the equations; moreover, the equations themselves often justified claims to invention.[72]

The realization that mathematics could play this central role in the invention process was itself a discovery of great importance which came about largely through the efforts of John Carson. Carson joined the AT&T Patent Department temporarily in 1914 to write an application on George Campbell's wave filter. Campbell had put forward his invention about five years earlier, and it had already been the subject of an unsuccessful patent application. Campbell's work fared poorly in this matter because he presented it solely in mathematical terms, and neither the AT&T attorneys nor the government patent examiners understood the equations or saw how they could justify granting a patent. Carson, who had been using the equations for his own work, understood their importance and presented them so as to clarify the claim for invention. His success brought the realization that theoretical-mathematical analysis could lead to inventions directly as well as indirectly, thus giving added impetus to the pursuit of mathematical formulations.[73]

The period from 1915 to the end of World War I – the time when Frank Jewett became the dominant force in the laboratory – brought a transition in researchers' attitudes toward the usefulness of mathematics and the development of technological theories. One researcher noted that in 1914 van der Bijl had proposed a mathematically based theory of modulator operation, one that "was straightforward enough," yet "did not stir up enthusiasm," even though it soon proved to be quite effective for modulator design.[74] By 1917 such theories received far more attention because Carson had shown that they might be turned rather directly into patents and because the Research Branch was shifting from the technological goal orientation of the Carty years toward the broader research and patent-gathering orientation of the Jewett regime. Development of related theory and mathematics proved very effective for the latter type of work.

Engineering and science

When theory not only led to, but, in a sense, became invention itself, the traditional distinction between science and technology was difficult to maintain, and the roles of scientists and engineers merged. No attempt was made to distinguish between scientists and engineers in the Research Branch, either in status or in terms of appropriate types of work. Of course, every professional member of the Engineering Department was considered an "engineer." Ph.D. physicist H. D. Arnold, for example, listed himself as a "Research Engineer" in the biographical dictionary *American Men of Science*. The tasks assigned to laboratory staff involved a broad range of theoretical and experimental science, mathematical analysis, and the design, testing, and implementation of technology. Several Ph.D. scientists recruited by Jewett had undergraduate degrees in engineering; for them, the merging of roles and mixture of tasks came naturally.[75]

In the union of science and engineering lay both the laboratory's strength and its weakness. Strength came from the ability to transform Bell's approach to development and control of technology.

The Research Branch brought to the Engineering Department a new method based on consideration of underlying principles, followed by the pursuit of mathematical formulations to describe and apply them. The concerted development of technological theories and their exploitation in advancing technology provided AT&T with the most extensive and comprehensive patent coverage in the electrical communications field.

Tying science so closely to engineering did, however, tend to shackle the science, much as American physicist Henry Rowland had feared it would, thirty years earlier. The Research Branch surely did not advance the scientific disciplines as much as it could have, had it been run differently – a ramification of no particular concern to AT&T. But restriction of research had technological consequences as well. Rarely able to take uncertain steps in unlikely directions (at least before 1925), Bell researchers usually arrived at relatively conventional solutions to both scientific and technical problems. As late as 1923 Willis Whitney believed the main difference between GE's lab and that of Bell was the extent to which the latter limited its work to pursuit of engineering-related problems.[76] In addition, the AT&T laboratory initiated very little research that was not concerned with some type of technology already under development. This greatly limited the scope of its research efforts and often stood in the way of those conceptual leaps that led to major breakthroughs in technology. Lloyd Espenschied, looking back on his years as an AT&T engineer, related this perception of the problem in a letter to George Campbell: "For some years now I have been so critical of our own conduct of research, what we call research but what is really development to my mind. . . . We unduly absorbed our more creative talent in the application and perfection of things that were known without having left enough such talent free for origination."[77]

The result of such a research program was that AT&T covered the telecommunications and vacuum-tube fields well but, in a surprisingly large number of cases, did not actually lead them. In 1940 one Bell patent attorney chose fifty-four patents that he believed to be most important in the history of the vacuum-tube art, yet only nine had come from within the Bell System.[78] What the laboratory gained as a result of its orientation was, of course, the ability to solve particular technological problems of crucial importance to AT&T. Instead of helping to effect innovation across a broad front, the Research Branch protected Bell's interests by promoting efficiency and progress in developing an integrated

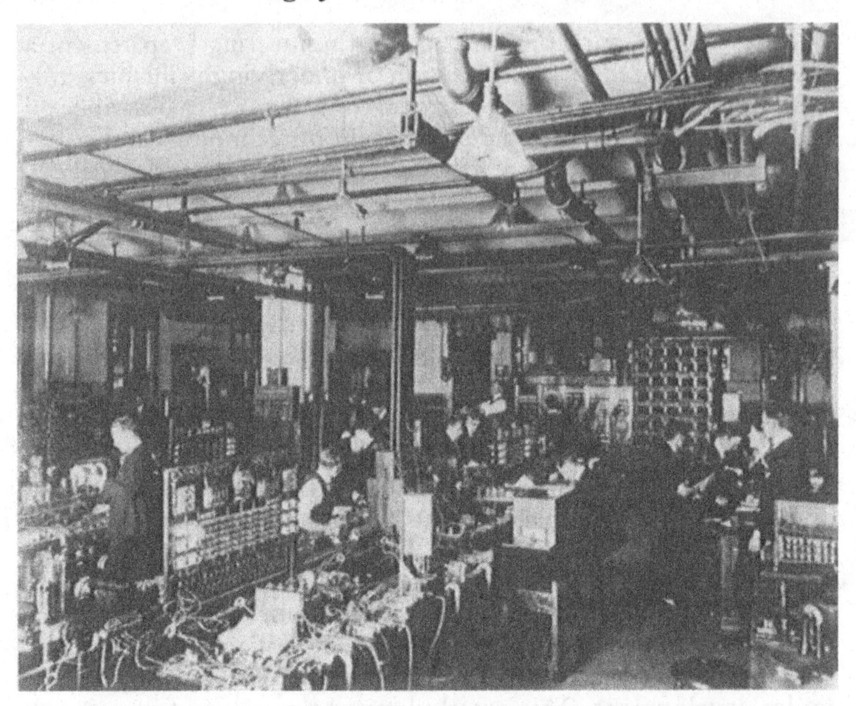

Plate 24. Western Electric Engineering Department laboratory, New York, 1920. Reproduced with permission of AT&T Corporate Archive.

national network. That success in turn ensured that the Research Branch – and related research and development activities – would have a secure claim to substantial resources in the Bell System. At GE, research operations were in a more precarious position for many years.

GE and Bell developed quite different approaches to the use of science and the direction of industrial research, especially in the period after the GE Research Laboratory's difficult early years and before establishment of the Bell Telephone Laboratories in 1925. Engineering held great sway at GE, but the Research Laboratory had purposefully been set apart from the engineering and production divisions. Its most important roles were to pursue science in conjunction with the development of new products and processes and to aid in the conduct of GE's business, wherever and however possible. Both companies intended their research laboratories to bring science into their arsenals of technological development and market control, but in the Bell System science was harnessed to an ongoing engineering program. The new researchers' use of the methods and content of contemporary science helped to transform the Engineering Department's approach to its work, but their goal of developing new technology within the context of Bell System operations almost always remained the same. The GE Research Laboratory's position outside the company's engineering establishment enabled it to take a more peripatetic approach to research – an approach based on its director's perception of the state of science and technology, and their relationship to the needs of GE. The GE laboratory's effort did not cover any fields nearly so well as did Bell's (although it came close in incandescent lighting), but its contributions were considerably more diverse and far-ranging as a result of its higher level of autonomy.

At the AT&T laboratory, science and technology were often indistinguishable in practice. Scientists became engineers, engineers became scientists, and their work usually contained elements of the very broad science–technology spectrum. Pursuing more general scientific theories when necessary and employing mathematics where possible, Research Branch members analyzed operations of the complex communications network of wired and wireless telephony. By making use of technological theories and the design methodologies developed from them, Bell researchers were able to acquire numerous patents on every phase of the telephone, radio, and vacuum-tube arts. That these methods limited the breadth of their research activities and, ultimately, circumscribed the scope of their development of technology, was a price that the laboratory and the company willingly paid. As Frank Jewett said, "Our research and development organization is a truly scientific body, but one in which the results of science are designed to be of utility to fit into the orderly progress of electrical communications."[79] At AT&T maintenance and control of that "orderly progress" always remained of paramount importance.

9

Research, Patents, and the Struggle to Control Radio

During the 1920s GE and Bell, the two leading innovators in industrial research, locked horns in a struggle over radio and broadcasting. As I have shown, GE's domination of the market in electric lighting and Bell's control of wired telephony had both been accomplished largely through their research and development activities. However, radio was not an important established market that needed to be protected by research; instead, in this case several companies engaged in a struggle to control emerging, potentially profitable new markets. I will look in particular at how the companies that had established industrial research laboratories made use of their results, as several firms attempted to dominate new markets in broadcasting and the sale of radio receivers.

Early developments in radio

Both GE and Bell had been concerned with radio since early in this century. GE became involved in 1903 when inventor Reginald Fessenden approached the company, requesting that its engineers build him a high-frequency alternator for use as a source of transmission waves in radio experiments. Steinmetz designed the first alternator, and engineer E. F. W. Alexanderson continued to develop the device. By the time of the First World War, GE possessed a radio-wave generator capable of producing 100 kilowatts of power at a frequency of over 100,000 cycles per second. Vacuum-tube research at GE began as a result of Alexanderson's search for an efficient means of modulating the alternator's output. Because of Alexanderson's interest in the de Forest audion, Irving Langmuir and a number of his laboratory colleagues became involved. They improved the tube significantly and designed numerous circuits for its use.

By 1916 GE was capable of building radio transmission and

reception systems based both on the alternator and on the high-vacuum triode. Although AT&T had acquired de Forest's audion patent, GE hoped to control vacuum-tube technology through Langmuir's claim to the use of low pressure. Langmuir's and Arnold's patent applications on the high-vacuum triode were placed in interference by the U.S. Patent Office in 1915.[1] The resolution of this conflict seemed likely to alter the balance of power significantly in the fight to control emerging radio markets.

As Chapter 7 has shown, AT&T had been concerned about the commercial implications of radio since 1907. Its researchers undertook their first extensive radio work in 1914, when a program began to build an apparatus for bridging the Atlantic with continuous-wave, voice-carrying signals. First tested between Montauk, Long Island and Wilmington, Delaware, Bell's radio systems were successfully transmitting to Paris by October 1915, though great problems of fidelity (especially "static") remained to be solved.

During American participation in the First World War, the U.S. government wanted to promote production of wireless telephone and telegraph apparatus for military purposes, so it removed patent restrictions on all devices and methods. The U.S. Navy assumed financial responsibility for any patent infringements which might arise. As a result, several companies, including GE and Bell, were able to devote the war years to further development of radio systems. One commentator observed:

> The United States Government undertook to develop two-way radio-telephone sets on a large scale. . . . In the short space of a year or so hundreds of thousands of tubes and thousands of sets were developed and manufactured. . . . The apparatus was featured technically by . . . the attempt to make the operation of the sets simple and foolproof, as by the elimination of filament rheostats and the standardizing of tubes and circuits to permit of ready interchangeability.[2]

Although the laboratories made substantial improvements in circuit and tube design, the advance of greatest consequence during the war was that they achieved mass production of standardized tubes, transmitters, and receivers. Previously radios had been made one at a time and often were one of a kind (at least in their characteristics, if not their designs). Now the manufacturers produced thousands of identical sets, all with similar operating characteristics. Just as importantly for the industry, large numbers of military-trained radio operators were disseminated around the country after the war. These two factors – an advanced technology of mass production and a pool of potential employees, customers, and servicemen – would provide an important spur to the commercial development of radio.

When the war brought the nascent industry to life, GE and AT&T supplied the government with radios and radio parts. Westinghouse did so as well, though it had developed no patent position of its own. The apparatus these companies produced in such quantity during the course of scarcely two years demonstrated the capabilities of the high-vacuum triode as the heart of radio systems. As an oscillating source of broadcast waves, it proved far more versatile than the Alexanderson alternator, which was not easily portable nor able to generate short wavelengths. It thus became apparent to GE, Bell, Westinghouse, American Marconi, and other companies considering the manufacture of radio systems that in order to do so they would first have to acquire rights to the triode.

An episode that occurred before America entered the war serves as an excellent introduction to the maneuverings that followed. The British Marconi Company, which held the patent rights to the Fleming diode for use in radio, brought suit in 1915 against de Forest, claiming that the audion infringed upon the diode patent. De Forest brought countersuit based on the Marconi Company's violation of *his* patent rights by its use of a third element in its tubes. In September 1916 the court ruled in favor of – and against – both parties. Upholding Marconi, it declared the audion to be an infringement on the diode when used in radio; and, that ruling notwithstanding, it decided that Marconi had, in fact, infringed upon the audion patent. Neither of them could use the triode in radio![3] Some time after the decision, the two companies tried to work out a scheme whereby de Forest produced the tubes and Marconi distributed them, but that arrangement was faltering when the exigencies of war made it unnecessary.

As the war drew to a close and patent rights were about to be reinstated, the situation threatened to become legally and economically chaotic. Besides the question of who could build the basic triode, there were many other conflicts over tubes and circuits. Each manufacturer had pushed its research as far as possible, only to encounter some device or circuit that was already patented by another.

Post-World War developments

At war's end the Marconi Company approached GE with an offer to buy exclusive rights to the Alexanderson alternator. Possession of the alternator would greatly improve Marconi's wireless telegraph capabilities and finally lead it into wireless telephony. However, the Marconi policy of leasing, but refusing to sell, patented equipment aroused great antagonism in the U.S. Navy, which found itself dependent on a British-controlled company for vital ship-to-shore communications. Not surprisingly, there was strong sentiment at higher navy staff levels against the consummation of a GE–Marconi agreement. Using the assurance of a lucrative navy contract as one incentive, a high-ranking officer proposed to the GE directors that rather than selling alternator rights to Marconi, they instead purchase the American Marconi Company, acquiring all Marconi patent rights for the United States.

British Marconi was aware both of the U.S. government's opposition to its control of American radio and of the way the government could hinder its operations. It soon agreed to terms. In October 1919 GE purchased the British company's stock in American Marconi (over one-half the total). The American stockholders accepted a conversion of their holdings to the new Radio Corporation of America (RCA), which GE formed to take over the Marconi assets. GE contributed over $3 million to the venture, receiving RCA stock in return. The plan was for RCA to be the distribution and sales arm of GE in radio; GE was to supply the apparatus, RCA to market it. RCA would additionally engage in long-distance radio telecommunications on a fee-for-services basis. The two companies exchanged all patent rights for radio-related inventions made up to 1945.

At the time of the contract these collective patent rights were themselves not sufficient to permit production of an effective vacuum-tube radio transmitter or receiver. So, as one of its first acts, RCA management negotiated a cross-licensing agreement with the other major holder of radio patents, AT&T. As part of this agreement, signed in July 1920, AT&T purchased RCA stock valued at $2.5 million and became a partner in the venture.

The companies wrote into their contract certain important restrictions concerning patent rights. These restrictions did not cover particular patents; rather, they defined the areas of exploitation open to each party. AT&T received exclusive licenses under everyone's patents in wired telephony and telegraphy as well as certain specified rights to the use of radio in conjunction with the telephone network. This assured that it would never have to tie into domestic radio-telephone systems controlled by others. RCA and GE acquired rights to use all of the parties' patents in wireless telegraphy and in international two-way radio communications.

They were also given the right to "make, use, lease, and sell all wireless telephone apparatus for amateur purposes."[4]

Not intending to be left out of radio, Westinghouse had been building a formidable patent position since the end of the war. The company concentrated on circuits, both through purchase of patent rights and through developments in its new research laboratory, established under the direction of electrical engineer Charles Skinner in 1917. By October 1920 Westinghouse controlled two of the most sophisticated detection circuits, the heterodyne and superheterodyne. Even though there is some question as to what use Westinghouse would have been able to make of them – GE, for example, immediately contested the superheterodyne patent when Westinghouse acquired it, claiming that it infringed on an earlier GE patent – these and other Westinghouse patent rights were quite important for producing a receiver of advanced design. Consequently GE invited its electrical-industry rival to join the cross-licensing agreement. On June 30, 1921, the GE–RCA agreement was amended so that RCA would purchase 60% of its radio apparatus from GE and 40% from Westinghouse. When complete, the RCA–GE–Westinghouse–Bell System agreements covered about 1,200 patents.[5]

By the middle of 1921 a formal cooperative structure was built in an industry that had been competitive and chaotic less than two years before. Primarily responsible for this was Owen D. Young. As legal counsel for GE he had handled the purchase of American Marconi and the establishment of RCA; as head of the new Radio Corporation he had enticed AT&T into the crucial cross-licensing agreement. To Young goes the credit for bringing these different companies with disparate interests into an arrangement that, had the market not significantly changed, would probably have survived for some years.

Based on its goals and its assets, each party to the agreement got what it desired and what it thought it deserved. The group of companies made up of GE, RCA, and Westinghouse (the "GE group") intended to concentrate on wireless communication, whereas Bell was much more concerned with wired (and with wireless–wired interconnections). Although the original commercial goals of RCA were rather modest, they did cover most areas of radio then expected to be profitable. At the time it took over from American Marconi, RCA engaged in wireless-telegraph service, both transoceanic and ship-to-shore. Almost immediately it began to sell apparatus to "amateurs" – those who experimented with radio and those who broadcast or received as a hobby. When Westinghouse entered the agreement in 1921, it was to take a portion of this market. Because sales of amateur apparatus had grown considerably since the war and showed good prospects of continuing to do so, GE could afford to concede 40% of RCA's sales to Westinghouse in order to avoid entanglement in a tricky legal situation.

One other advantage the agreement brought to the GE group was protection from the most potent of its competitors. Indeed, AT&T had been seriously considering a foray into transoceanic and ship-to-shore communications.[6] Although it lacked certain important patent rights held by the others, especially in receiver circuits, there was no assurance that the rapid pace of scientific and technological advance would not soon bring it other rights of equal or greater value. AT&T was a particularly powerful rival because its research and development techniques were likely to give it an edge in any area of the new technology where the company decided to focus its considerable resources. By keeping Bell out of wireless communications, the GE group protected itself from what in 1920 and 1921 appeared to be its most substantial competitor.

Expansion into the radio apparatus market was natural for companies like GE and Westinghouse. Capable of manufacturing products of great technological sophistication, they were already diverse; adding new product lines usually proved to be relatively easy. Furthermore, the companies were committed to this type of expansion. To maintain corporate integrity in the long term they needed to secure new markets to compensate for others that would ultimately deteriorate for technological or competitive reasons. Industrial research had been established at least in part for this purpose, and its success promoted the corporate strategy of entering entirely new commercial fields, using products that emerged from the laboratories.[7] With already-established research, development, production, distribution, and sales organizations, GE and (to a lesser extent) Westinghouse had substantial advantages. With long-term corporate security at stake, they had good reason to enter and then try to dominate the market in radio.

For its part, Bell gained protection in pursuit of its outstanding corporate goal – continued control of American telephone communications. In obtaining an exclusive license under all parties' patents to "make, use, lease and sell wireless telephone apparatus connected to or operated as part of a public service communication system, whether wire or wireless,"[8] AT&T was able to stymie the competition of two-way radio with its extensive wired network. It also made certain that wherever radio was used as an adjunct to Bell wires, Bell itself would control the radio systems. By conceding certain profits to the GE group in the form of ship-to-shore and transoceanic revenues, Bell blocked the "perennial gale" of competition before it reached the carefully integrated, nationwide telephone network.

It should be emphasized that research leading to patents in radio helped the company gain the protection it sought. In a memorandum after the 1920 agreement, Frank Jewett commented to J. J. Carty:

> As I look back on it, it seems to me that this enlarged and enhanced position [in radio research] played no small part in enabling us to reach our present satisfactory understanding with the General Electric Company and the Radio Corporation of America and that if we never derive any other benefit from our work than that which follows the safe-guarding of our wire interests we can look upon the time and money as having been returned to us many times over.[9]

The market – Destruction and reformation

The careful work that had gone into building this new industrial structure came to naught within a few years. As quickly as it had been created, it was destroyed by developments unforeseen as late as mid-1921. Technological advances contributed to the crisis, but did not directly precipitate it. Rather, new technology brought new commercial possibilities; the sudden realization of those possibilities brought on the collapse.

These developments started in November 1920 when Westinghouse began operating the first radio "station." The company expected this operation in Pittsburgh (named KDKA) to stimulate sales of Westinghouse apparatus, and intended to subsidize the evening-only broadcasts out of profits from radio-related sales. With sales growing rapidly in Pittsburgh, Westinghouse opened two more stations in the fall of 1921: WBZ (Boston) went into operation in September, and WJZ (Northern New Jersey–New York) began broadcasting the following month. RCA actually operated a station in competition with WJZ in the winter of 1921–2, but decided very shortly to join forces with Westinghouse when the directors of both companies perceived that their interests coincided. RCA paid one-half of WJZ's expenses.[10]

GE and its partners found themselves ill prepared for the surge of orders that followed the opening of these stations. There were two types: (1) for receiver sets and parts, and (2) for transmitters, so that others could establish broadcasting operations of their own. Under the generally accepted definition of the post-war period, the newfound radio audience consisted of "amateurs," so according to the agreement, the GE group could "make, use, lease, and sell" radio apparatus for and to them. Thus, GE and Westinghouse geared up manufacture of radio equipment and speeded up development of improved receivers, intending to get them into production as quickly as possible. A contemporary account gives some idea of the market conditions that prevailed:

> The immediate result of the work of the past few months is shown in the creation of a new array of buyers. Radio-supply stores have sprung up by the hundreds all over the United States, and the manufacturers are finding it impossible to keep up with the demand for equipment. At the moment the retail dealer finds himself short of stock owing to the demand on him. To the disgusted buyer this seems to be a chronic condition, though the difficulty will soon be remedied by the further development of manufacturing facilities.[11]

Although the GE group was free to expand into the receiver market as quickly as possible, the agreement prohibited it from selling broadcast apparatus. It could produce that equipment for its own use – providing its members with a strong incentive to go into broadcasting – but could not "sell, lease, or otherwise dispose of transmitting apparatus" to outsiders.[12] GE, Westinghouse, and RCA initially referred all requests for broadcast equipment to AT&T.

So long as the quantity of apparatus to be sold remained relatively small and broadcasting appeared to be an expense rather than a source of profit, the industrial structure set up in 1919–20 remained intact. But by late 1921 it had become apparent that such was no longer the case, and Bell had the most reason for concern. Bell had secured its wired-telephone position, but had passed up a share in new profits from the manufacture and sale of radio sets. True, it held sole right under the contract to sell broadcast equipment, but the number of transmitters that could be sold seemed to number at best in the thousands, whereas the potential market for receivers was in the millions. If it wanted to realize substantial profits, Bell had two choices: either to make broadcasting pay or to force its way into the receiver market. Company management decided to try the first tactic, though it kept its options open on the second by continuing to support internal research and development work on all facets of radio.

AT&T's attempt to dominate broadcasting presents the case of a company using its very strong market position in one field as leverage to force others out of another. Because commercial broadcasting had not been anticipated at the time of the 1920 agreement, that agreement contained no provision granting specific rights for the manufacture and sale of broadcasting equipment to any party, though the GE group was expressly prohibited from doing so. This was an unusual arrangement; the prohibition had been inserted "for the protection of the Telephone Company," perhaps without full consideration of the consequences. Under the circumstances, AT&T held the right to lease or sell broadcasting apparatus only under its own patents. Fortunately, these were sufficient for the purpose.

By late 1921 the AT&T directors had realized the importance of halting the proliferation of stations established by rivals, especially those of the GE group. Their first act was defensive in nature. Using patent rights granted by the agreement to a monopoly on all activity related to wired telephony, they prohibited members of the GE group from using telephone lines to send signals from remote pickups (e.g., sporting events, public lectures) to their broadcasting studios.[13] Since most new stations considered this type of remote transmission to be an important aspect of broadcasting, the prohibition represented a substantial threat. AT&T continued this practice, usually denying pickups to the GE group and even to those who bought Bell equipment if they were competing with an AT&T station in their vicinity.

Although GE, Westinghouse, and RCA could build transmitters for their own use, others had to rely on AT&T for equipment. None too anxious to outfit a troop of competitors, Bell refused most requests for transmitters. Those it did supply were granted only under a license that stipulated they could not be operated for hire – no advertising! As further dissuasion, AT&T set the cost of a transmitter very high: $9,000 for a low-power model (100 watts), $12,500 for a more powerful one (500 watts).[14]

By mid-1922 AT&T had decided on a course of action that would make broadcasting pay. Beginning in August the company opened its own stations, intending ultimately to link them together as a network. Revenues were to be generated by selling air time, or broadcasting for toll, much like long-distance telephone service. When station WEAF was about to open in New York, AT&T made the following announcement:

> Anyone desiring to use these facilities for radio broadcasting should make arrangements with Mr. Drake, general commercial manager. . . . Mr. Drake can advise fully with reference to all particulars concerning the use of the station including information as to the periods of operation and charges thereof. He is also in a position to give helpful suggestions with reference to the arrangement of programs and the kind of subject matter which it is thought will be most acceptable to the radio audience.[15]

But no one applied!

The company expected to produce its own broadcasts for a few days, until, it believed, others would pay to take over. Finally, twelve days after opening, WEAF sold its first air time, but only for an advertisement, not an entire show.[16] This misconception of the commercial demand for broadcasting time put the company in the same position that it had condemned as undignified and inappropriate when it refused to let others broadcast advertisements with Bell equipment.

That winter the company decided to pursue a policy based on a system of commercial relationships similar to those of the telephone business. The announcement sent out to Bell's associated companies explained:

> In each locality an important group of people will get together and form a broadcasting association. . . . For that association we would erect, own, and operate a broadcasting station; they to provide all the programs; they to give the public what the public desires but we to have the latest facilities known to the art and all of the things that go with them including remote-control lines and speech-input equipment. That station is to be operated by the Bell System under definite guarantees from the association as to expenses plus a reasonable return.[17]

By May 1924 AT&T had opened two other stations, one in Philadelphia and one in Washington, D.C., operating them occasionally as a network. But the idea of community stations never caught on. Bell was unable to organize the local broadcasting associations.

It was uncertain about how to operate a broadcasting network at a profit, but Bell management harbored no doubts that such a

Plate 25. Interior of AT&T radio broadcast control room, Washinton, D.C., 1923. Reprinted with permission of AT&T Corporate Archive.

monopoly was appropriate. In the same bulletin to the associated companies an assistant vice-president wrote:

> We have been very careful, up to the present time, not to state to the public in any way, through the press or in any of our talks, the idea that the Bell System desires to monopolize broadcasting: but the fact remains that it is a telephone job, that we are telephone people, that we can do it better than anyone else, and it seems to me that the clear, logical conclusion that must be reached is that, sooner or later, in one form or another, we have got to do the job. . . . I may state to you that I have talked this over with Messrs. Thayer, Gifford [vice-president], and Bloom [vice-president] and each of them think [*sic*] it is a proper set-up.[18]

But AT&T's aggressive tactics engendered strong opposition. Newspaper and magazine editorials condemned the nascent monopoly. Concern was expressed even at the highest levels of government. Secretary of Commerce Herbert Hoover was clearly referring to Bell when he wrote in 1924, "I can state emphatically that it would be most unfortunate for the people of this country to whom broadcasting has become an important incident of life if its control should come into the hands of any single corporation, individual, or combination."[19]

Such opposition to a broadcasting monopoly posed a further threat. It could create poor relations with Bell customers and with government regulators, perhaps even leading to opposition to the company's control of wired telephony. This was cause for serious concern.[20]

Had AT&T succeeded in its early schemes to organize and finance broadcasting, the public would have been presented with a *fait accompli*. The company failed, however, to consolidate its position before a ground swell of opinion made that impossible. By 1924 it was apparent that broadcasting could not be dominated by any one concern. Bell had lost the opportunity to profit from its market of first choice, so it turned to the sale of radio receiving sets to the public.[21] The 1920 agreement gave this market segment to the GE group, stating that AT&T had "no license under this agreement to make, lease or sell wireless telephone apparatus *except* as part of or for direct use in connection with transmitting apparatus made by it." (This exception was intended to provide for two-way radio as an adjunct to the wired-telephone system.) Nevertheless, Bell had built up a momentum in radio and vacuum-tube research and development that by early 1924 placed a superior receiver in the company's commercial arsenal.[22] Seizing on the exception, Bell began to sell receivers with fixed frequencies of reception tuned to AT&T broadcasting stations. It even went so far as to install one in the White House, an action that caused great consternation at RCA. In addition, Bell spokesmen began to claim that once a radio signal had come in the antenna and passed through the detector (or "tuner") it was no longer wireless but wired telephony and therefore open to them under the contract. The company began to sell what an RCA internal memorandum called "radio devices or parts which constitute about 80% to 90% of a complete broadcast receiver."[23] Because such a situation was intolerable to the GE group, it initiated official arbitration as provided by the 1920 agreement.

Meanwhile the GE group faced competition from still other quarters in its drive to control the receiver market. Several other companies had placed sets on the market as early as 1922, many with components free of the cartel's patent control. This was possible because at the time de Forest sold the audion patent rights to AT&T in 1913, he had insisted on retaining a license for himself. When the diode patent held by RCA expired in 1922, de Forest became free to produce triodes for sale. Though the GE group controlled most of the important circuit patents for receivers, some others were functional. One in particular – the neutrodyne – worked quite well. The De Forest Company's tubes, used in the neutrodyne circuit, produced excellent receivers. The first of these appeared in the spring of 1923; soon fourteen companies in all were manufacturing neutrodyne-equipped radio receivers.

Despite the impressive research laboratories at GE and Westinghouse, the GE group had difficulty getting up-to-date sets on the market. The problem generally occurred in the final development stage, when engineers designed the receivers and prepared them for full production. Since two different companies produced apparatus for sale under a common label, it was necessary to standardize products and, in certain instances, to coordinate production. As one historian of radio remarked, "RCA . . . found itself under the necessity of harmonizing the views of three research and engineering departments for design and construction and, at the same time, of harmonizing those views with the public demand as determined by the sales department." A GE radio engineer noted that "RCA required that the two companies standardize their designs so that the casual purchaser could not tell the difference. Sometimes this 'standardization' took as long and cost as much as the original development."[24] The system worked so slowly that even after RCA approved final designs, several months usually passed before the first product deliveries.

Because the research needed to produce a commercial, battery-powered receiver had been accomplished by 1922, the competition that developed in the first few years involved limited advances in product design. Science-oriented research laboratories like those at GE, Bell, and Westinghouse could produce breakthroughs that destroyed the structure of an industry; they could establish and improve complex manufacturing processes; but for competition on styling and features in a temporarily stable technology and market structure, the far less sophisticated engineering staffs of any number of manufacturing enterprises proved just as effective.

Consequently the GE group faced stiff competition from companies capable of usurping its lead in product design during the early 1920s. Unable to launch an effective offensive, the group decided to fall back on its research-generated patent protection. It challenged the neutrodyne patent, claiming in 1924 that certain aspects of the neutrodyne were anticipated by GE and Bell researchers as early as 1913. RCA, the company pressing the suit, did not contend that the neutrodyne patent was invalid. Rather, it claimed that (like the triode as an enhancement of the diode) the neutrodyne was based on RCA-controlled circuits, so that anyone wishing to use the neutrodyne had to procure a license from RCA as well. RCA lost the initial decision in district court but pressed its case, winning in the Court of Appeals in 1927. Thereafter the GE group controlled all major circuit patents for radio receivers; any company producing them needed an RCA license. RCA patent licensing royalties increased from $136,000 in 1926 to $3.3 million in 1927 as a result of the decision. Some smaller companies went out of business because the 7.5% royalty rate forced up their prices and took away their competitive edge. Others did not even get a chance, for RCA restricted the granting of licenses to "$100,000 customers."[25] To maintain its dominant position in the field, the GE group further required that all licensees give RCA an option to acquire any of their radio-related patents. There was no choice but to comply.

The new agreement

During the early 1920s, as the GE group faced market harassment from a number of smaller competitors, AT&T was trying to gain a major share of the market for itself. Although the way to do so had not become clear by 1923, both GE and Bell were aware of the power of patent rights and knew that their laboratories would continue to supply them with patents and technical expertise. The arbitration first begun in 1923 aimed merely at interpreting the 1920 license agreement and clarifying the signatories' rights, but AT&T soon decided to seek an entirely new contract that would redefine the market and restructure the industry.

It should be pointed out that AT&T was not alone in undermining the original agreement. In the years since 1920 the GE group had continued to expand its broadcasting interests, violating the spirit if not the letter of the contract. GE, RCA, and Westinghouse claimed that the provisions permitting them to operate their own stations implicitly conferred the right to do so for profit, whereas Bell believed that the agreement envisioned a more restricted role for them. The GE group maintained extensive research and development programs in radio transmission as well, taking out patents that did not revert to AT&T under the contract. There is no question that these efforts were a threat to Bell's position.

RCA initiated proceedings because it was perturbed by Bell refusals to supply pickup lines or to meet its other demands concerning broadcasting. In mid-1922 it hired an outside attorney to make an "impartial interpretation" of the agreement. The attorney's reading of the often ambiguous document left neither side satisfied. In fact, it led to the realization by both that areas they had assumed closed off might be open under one or another interpretation of the contract. This led to emboldened thrusts into the market, such as Bell's sale of pre-tuned receivers, described earlier in this chapter.

The 1920 agreement stated that either side could call for formal arbitration if "any difference . . . shall arise which the parties are unable to adjust between themselves."[26] In May 1924, by mutual consent, they undertook binding arbitration. The main points in dispute were (1) whether the GE group could use AT&T pickup lines in its broadcasting operations (that is, were these lines "wired telephony" and thus strictly in the Bell province, or were they an adjunct to the GE group's right to maintain its own stations?) and (2) whether AT&T could manufacture radio receivers pretuned to its own stations. Since AT&T hoped to eventually control much of broadcasting – in which case most receivers would need only to be set for the Bell stations in their vicinities – a favorable decision on the latter question would open the way into a large segment of the market.

In a preliminary "Draft Decision" dated November 13, 1924, the arbitration referee found in favor of RCA on almost all disputed points. AT&T management made a highly effective response in March 1925, however, when it produced a legal opinion that obviated putting the draft into final form. The crux of this argument was that, as construed by the referee, the agreement violated the Sherman Antitrust Act because it constrained Bell from producing and selling radio receivers, even though it could do so entirely under its own patents. Much to its dismay, the GE group could find no effective response, so negotiations entered a new stage. Through the summer of 1925, AT&T held the upper hand in bargaining. The dispute no longer concerned whether Bell could enter the radio market, but what share of that market it could take.[27]

Then, in the fall, a stunning reversal occurred. The Arnold–Langmuir interference suit on the use of high vacuum in electron tubes, which had been in litigation since before the World War, was decided by the U.S. Court of Appeals in favor of Langmuir and GE. Since all phases of the contemporary radio art required these tubes, an entirely new situation developed: blocked in the use of high vacuum, Bell could no longer produce receivers completely under its own patents, nullifying the antitrust argument. Nor could it any longer sell broadcast equipment. The Bell attorneys made an appeal to the U.S. Supreme Court as a matter of course, but the likelihood of a final decision in favor of GE now loomed large in the dispute.[28]

In the summer of 1926 the two groups came to terms. Repulsed in its battle to enter radio sales and unsuccessful for a number of reasons in its attempts to monopolize broadcasting, AT&T retreated to its main line of defense – control of the wired-telephone network. Under the new license agreement the Bell System received a telephone monopoly reassurance. Within the purview of the companies' combined patent rights, it also acquired control of all two-way communications systems, including ship-to-shore and transoceanic radio telephony, a market area that had gone to GE in 1920. The agreement gave members of the GE group the right to use telephone lines for station pickup and for network transmissions. In fact, it obligated them to do so (as opposed to using telegraph lines), thus ensuring AT&T of a substantial source of revenue.[29] For its part, the GE group accomplished what it had wanted all along: domination of the radio receiver market and the right to use telephone lines as an adjunct to profit-seeking broadcasting. Bell sold its stations to RCA and agreed to stay out of broadcasting. The groups decided to compete in the least financially rewarding radio market area, the sale of broadcast equipment. They also gave each other nonexclusive licenses for developments in motion pictures with sound; Bell was limited to sound and pictures transmitted together by wire and the GE group to sound and pictures transmitted by radio waves – what later became known as television. RCA and AT&T did compete very strongly during the late 1920s in one related area, sound equipment for motion pictures.[30]

By mid-1926 a new structure had been established in the radio industry. The new agreement's preamble stated that because "the art in certain fields dealt with in said [1920] agreement had not progressed to a point at which it was possible fully to comprehend the problems involved, disputes have arisen between the parties as to the meaning of various provisions of said agreement." As a result, "certain provisions of said agreement are not, as a practical matter, workable in the present state of the art." Unless the parties settled these disputes and made the agreement workable in practice, "progress in the fields . . . will be greatly hampered and delayed."[31] This really meant that the companies were making a new attempt to define more clearly the boundaries of each other's domain so that all would profit and none would be able to overstep its territory.

The new agreement remained in force for six years, when it was officially dissolved by a consent decree. The Justice Department instituted antitrust procedures in 1930, alleging that this method of market control violated the Sherman Antitrust Act. In the consent decree signed in November 1932, GE and Westinghouse agreed to divest themselves of their RCA holdings (AT&T having done so previously), thus finally making RCA an independent company. In addition, the exclusivity of the exchange of patent rights – whereby the company owning rights to a particular patent could not itself use them in market areas designated for others – was rescinded. This appeared to open up competition in all telecommunications areas. But the appearance was deceptive. As Frank Jewett explained in 1932:

> Broadly speaking, the practical effect of the [consent decree] is to limit the field of possible development of each party to its present major activities. . . . It is clearly impossible for the granting party to contemplate successful competition when confronted with an adversary who has both its own and the other person's [*sic*] patents. . . . Thus, while a casual reading

> of the [consent decree] by one not thoroughly conversant with all the factors may appear to establish the basis for an enlarged free development in most of the fields, this is not actually the case.[32]

As a result, this still very powerful set of companies continued to exert effective control over their respective markets – including those related to radio – throughout the economically depressed 1930s.

Patents, Research, and Competition

What roles, then, did patents and industrial research play in the struggle to control radio? Clearly, there were several ways in which patents could be of use. The first was the most obvious: to prevent competition. All of the companies involved sought market control of some sort and used patents to keep would-be competitors at bay. Control of important patent rights could also be used to prevent competitors from acquiring strong patent positions of their own. RCA accomplished this by inserting in its license contracts an option to acquire rights to all radio-related patents developed by its licensees. Together with the wide patent coverage of the GE group, this destroyed licensees' incentive to do original research.[33]

Other ways of using patent rights to stymie competitors were more subtle but no less important. Sometimes inventions that originally appeared to have no strategic value became quite useful later. An excellent example was the GE group's use of pre–World War patents – which had been of no consequence for ten years – in a successful move to regulate use of the neutrodyne circuit in 1924. Frank Jewett discussed this type of strategy in 1932:

> While it is obvious that the basic inventions which control a large new field are not made very often, one can never tell where or when they will crop up. . . . When [they] do, possession of a strong and unmortgaged patent position on the part of an industry needing rights is frequently the most powerful and sometimes the only available weapon for securing those rights. Ability to stop the owner of a fundamental and controlling patent from realizing the full fruits of his patent by the ownership of necessary secondary patents may easily put one in the position to trade where money alone might be of little value.[34]

This statement brings out the third strategic use of patents: trading. The story of the creation and re-creation of structures in the radio industry has essentially been one of trading, with companies exchanging market-area rights to all patents rather than all rights to particular patents. Jewett made clear how worthwhile he believed Bell's research in radio to have been – even though much of it eventually wound up under the control of the GE group through trading – when he testified before the Temporary National Economic Committee in 1936:

> I told you earlier . . . that I considered this expenditure in radio one of the most profitable expenditures [AT&T] had ever made, and I still do. . . . It has created a patent situation that has protected the Associated Companies, either directly or through [AT&T], from the attacks of people who would have otherwise obtained patents or inventions which relate not only to wireless and radio, but to all the wire plant.[35]

Perhaps nowhere have corporate attitudes toward industrial research, patents, and the trading of patent rights been more fully or forcefully expressed than in a Bell System internal memorandum written in 1927 and uncovered in the Federal Communications Commission's investigation of the telephone industry. Although AT&T has disavowed the memo, claiming that it in no way represented corporate policy, the perspective expressed in it does reflect the sort of managerial attitudes that informed and directed corporate policies relating to research, development, and market control. In fact, the memo writer's perceptions are based on Jewett's ideas set forth in the two quotes immediately above. The memo is explicit:

> The regulation of the relationship between two such large interests as the American Telephone and Telegraph Company and the General Electric Company and the prevention of invasion of their respective fields is accomplished by mutual adjustment within "no man's land" where the offensive of the parties is recognized as a natural defense against invasion of the major fields. Licenses, rights, opportunities, and privileges in connection with these competitive activities are traded off against each other and interchanged in such a manner as to create a proper balance and satisfactory relationship between the parties in the major fields. . . .
>
> It seems obvious that the best defense is to continue activities in "no man's land" and to maintain such strong engineering, patent and commercial situations in connection with

> these competitive activities as to always have something to trade against the accomplishment of other parties.
>
> If [Bell] abandons its activities in the commercial competitive field and other potentially competitive interests continue their activities, it means that they will carry their offensive right to the wall of our defense and our trading must be in our major field against activities in their outlying commercial fields. The nearer the trading can be carried to the major field of our competitors the more advantageous trading position we are in.[36]

Thus, based on the philosophy that the best defense was a strong offense, the rational course of action lay in developing a formidable patent position as close as possible to a competitor's field of interest that threatened Bell. This is exactly what Bell did in the six years between license agreements. It failed to acquire a share of the receiver market and control of broadcasting only because of an adverse legal decision on crucial patent rights in the former case and inept handling of a poorly understood market in the latter. Yet, although Bell lost these battles, it had only to retreat as far as the lines of its telephone service, and to extended lines at that. The GE group, for its part, maintained strong research and patent positions relating to broadcasting even while the first agreement was in force – a time when it had few rights to exploit broadcasting commercially. The effect of this policy was to keep pressure on Bell and to provide materiel should trading have became necessary or desirable.

These uses of patent-related research must be added to the more straightforward ones of improved products and new markets that have been the central themes of most historical scholarship on industrial research.[37] The development of laboratories like those at GE and Bell marks the emergence of a new science-based industrial strategy of expansion and control. The companies which supported large, multifaceted research laboratories soon found that they were able to exert considerable influence over many new and potentially profitable (or disruptive) commercial technologies. A number of competitors' engineering laboratories might gain the upper hand in temporarily stable market situations, but the power of industrial research to cover a field or to make breakthrough advances almost always brought ultimate market control to those companies supporting appropriately conceived and directed industrial research efforts.

When several of these companies vied for control of new commercial technologies, industrial research helped each protect its own vital interests. At Bell, where those interests were defined as "One Policy, One System, Universal Service," radio research paid for itself many times over simply by securing all services that interconnected with the wired-telephone network. The company's "Universal Service" remained unbreached. Bell incidently realized substantial profits as well from point-to-point radio communications and from the fees broadcasters paid to use its telephone lines.

GE's vital interests were more closely tied to developing new products and new markets in order to compensate for those that it lost for technological or competitive reasons. GE's temporary control of the lucrative radio receiver market thus fit well with its overall business strategy. That strategy had evolved in response to the power of research to create new products and processes; it was based on the new reality of the American economic environment – a reality that presumed the development, maturation, and probable eventual loss of major market areas.[38]

With the help of their industrial research laboratories, GE, Bell, and many other companies gained economic security of the sort that Willis Whitney had in mind when he stated: "Our research laboratory was a development of the idea that large industrial organizations have both an opportunity and a responsibility for their own life insurance. New discovery can provide it."[39] Of course, that security was not complete, as the radio episode reveals. But as a vital component of a carefully conceived and executed commercial strategy, industrial research clearly helped assure prosperity in the long term.

10

Conclusion: The Impact of Industrial Research

As the previous chapters have shown, industrial research laboratories were first established in the United States primarily to help protect large corporations from competition. Changes in the contents, methods, and institutions of science and technology during the 19th century had created situations in which the development of increasingly sophisticated products posed serious threats to the market positions of a number of well-established, technology-based corporations. Their creative response to these threats in the early 20th century took the form of laboratories that not only protected their established markets, but brought competitive advantages in other ways. Although GE and Bell established research laboratories with a traditional competitive strategy designed to maintain control of existing markets, the two laboratories soon demonstrated that their usefulness went far beyond defense, encompassing the improvement and rationalization of manufacturing techniques, promotion and control of innovation, and – perhaps most importantly – creation of new products. This brought the companies important commercial opportunities.

Both laboratories were established with specific missions: GE's to advance the technology that would maintain the company's hegemony over the American electric lighting market; Bell's to develop an electronic repeater for telephone service and to control radio technology. Because of these initial missions, research in both laboratories was carefully coordinated during their early years. Successes in electric lighting, long-distance telephony, and radio gained the two labs an important measure of security, allowing them to move beyond the rather tightly controlled administration of research and development that characterized their early efforts.

Only as research activity diversified in this way could the laboratories' full potential for innovation and growth be realized. Industrial research then helped to reshape fundamental corporate attitudes toward changing technology. Whereas most 19th-century managers had been cautious about the development of advanced technology – preferring to make careful moves in known directions – the institution of industrial research began to change managerial outlooks by making possible technological leaps in capability and direction, while simultaneously providing legal barriers to entry with a phalanx of research-generated patents. Corporate leaders soon realized that industrial research could give them the power to upset old markets or to create entirely new ones. If one company could effect major innovation in this way, then others who wished to compete with it had to do likewise. This created a new dynamic of technological change and competition based on the abilities of a number of companies to innovate, often while preventing competitors from doing so as well.

The structure and needs of the companies that supported industrial research strongly influenced their labs' research strategies. At GE, where product lines – and potential product lines – varied considerably, a diversity of research topics and methods was encouraged under the watchful eye of the director. A carefully constructed system of liaisons with other parts of the company assured that researchers always knew about corporate needs. Because GE was essentially a manufacturing company, calls for help from the manufacturing divisions received priority. Bell had a limited number of commercial interests, so it carefully structured and directed research activities, even after the diversification of research following Frank Jewett's assumption of the chief engineer's duties in 1916. The two laboratories' organizational structures and the way they were managed thus reflected the basic nature of the companies and their markets.

Industrial research served as a new format for pursuit of science and development of technology, opening up career opportunities for the scientists and engineers who were being graduated in increasing numbers from America's higher education system. It also changed the way that researchers approached their tasks. Because of corporate needs, neither entirely "pure" nor strictly "applied" work had a secure place in industrial research methodology. Rather, science and technology together became a complex, integrated activity that defied the usual characterizations. The roles of scientists and engineers in industrial research laboratories merged, and significant advances in both science and technology resulted. Industrial research was in this sense more in tune with the American conception of science as "useful knowledge" than with the "pure science" ideal or with academic science generally. Industrial research grew so rapidly in the United States because it was in many ways an affirmation of long-standing beliefs about science and technology.

The industrial research laboratories at GE and Bell were two of the earliest and most important, so they had a strong influence on those that followed. Though rarely copied directly, their operations inspired and instructed managers at hundreds of companies establishing labs in the following decades. Through both personal contact and institutional suasion, Whitney, Jewett, and other early industrial research directors influenced a generation of corporate executives and leaders of science. Yet perhaps the most forceful arguments in favor of industrial research were GE and AT&T successes in electric lighting and electronics – and the corporate benefits that followed from them.

Establishing industrial research

GE and Bell instituted industrial research for one basic reason: to control technologies of immediate commercial concern. The companies found themselves threatened in two ways; industrial research provided a defense against both. The first menace came from smaller competitors who were able to undercut prices, making it possible for them to take away substantial market shares. GE initially fought such competition in electric lighting by continued innovation in lamp fabrication techniques (to decrease manufacturing costs) and by using its strong patent position to force small producers into agreements that relegated them to minor roles in the market. Bell used its patents to prevent the independent telephone companies from offering competitive long-distance service.

Yet neither company had real security, because their engineering approach to research and development was only larger in scale – not different in kind – from the effort smaller companies could mount. GE's and Bell's highly fortified patent positions notwithstanding, it was quite possible that less well-endowed competitors might gain technical and market advantages, especially because of judicial interpretations of the Sherman Antitrust Act that limited acceptable methods of patent control. Taking the step to ongoing, science-based research presented an opportunity to use methods and achieve results that their competitors would find difficult to match. This promised to lift them above the fray, to put their products and processes so far in advance of smaller companies that they would usually be able to maintain market control.

The realization that they could block smaller competitors in this manner was not, however, sufficient in itself to make GE and Bell decide to mount science-based research efforts. They took that step because of the challenge that advances in science and technology posed to their commercial interests. This was the second threat. It came to GE from electrochemistry and European research on metallic incandescent filaments, and to AT&T from electron physics and recent advances in radio. This threat to vital corporate markets resided not only in the ideas and devices themselves, but in the thousands of people being prepared for careers in science and engineering. Their increasing availability made industrial research both possible and necessary.

GE and Bell responded to these twin problems with the establishment of their research laboratories. In so doing they acknowledged that long-standing methods of dealing with changing technology had become inadequate. By undertaking industrial research they began to pursue a continuous means of creating and controlling technological discontinuity – for discontinuity presented them with both their greatest threats and opportunities.

Industrial research fit well with evolving corporate strategies of centralized management, vertical integration, and diversification. As arms of the corporate central staff, industrial research laboratories helped perform such essential management functions as rationalizing operations and setting corporate directions. They assisted centralized management in maintaining control of far-flung, diverse operations and made administration more efficient. As part of a vertical integration strategy, industrial research provided important sources of supply, not of ores and other raw materials, but of products, processes, patents, and technical expertise. Because of the financial and market strength of technology-based corporations created by merger in the late 19th and early 20th centuries, maintaining and controlling this kind of supply was crucial to a company's ability to dominate an industry in the face of strenuous competition. Product diversification became an attractive strategy for large corporations as growth leveled off in their original markets; it also spread their risks. An industrial research laboratory helped create market diversity by protecting established markets and creating opportunities in new ones.

The organization and administration of research

Companies like GE and Bell established industrial research in order to achieve commercial objectives through the control of technology. Isolated laboratories did them little good. To achieve full potential, industrial research had to be thoroughly integrated into a company's production, sales, and innovation processes. This required the nurturing of relationships between groups in the laboratory and other parts of the company. For a laboratory to be fully effective, corporate managers, both in the central administration and in divisional offices, had to be aware of its needs and capabilities. They also had to be sensitive to its relationship with the corporate engineering and production organizations. For their part, laboratory administrators like Whitney and Jewett needed to be well informed on business concerns and to make certain that their researchers were too. A somewhat delicate balance was struck: the normally parallel (and hence separate) cultures of business and science were brought together in several places. Neither scientific–technical considerations nor business concerns could be primary, at least not for long.

The uses – and therefore the value – of industrial research lay in its role within the complex interactive system of innovation that involved a corporation's sales, service, accounting, legal, engineering, and manufacturing departments. This integration was obvious at GE, where the Research Laboratory had an official advisory council and maintained numerous formal and informal liaison relationships. The integration of Bell's Research Branch into corporate operations through the efforts of Vail, Carty, Jewett, Colpitts, and others was less obvious but perhaps even more effective. AT&T actually established a Systems Engineering group specifically to serve these liaison functions after it consolidated research in the Bell Telephone Laboratories in 1925.[1]

As I have shown, the early research laboratories at GE and Bell were run in very different ways, yet both succeeded in meeting corporate needs. Two distinct styles of laboratory organization and administration proved effective because the companies' management structures and commercial situations differed markedly. Each required a particular type of lab to fit its operations and meet its needs. There were, nonetheless, similarities as well as differences in the two companies' approaches to research. Examining both should suggest the extent to which research style and organization were functions of the problems at hand, the expectations and influences of corporate management, or the commercial situation of the parent company.

When GE and Bell established their research laboratories, both were expected to meet corporate needs in defending primary markets. The companies saw these tasks as extensions of their engineering practices. Technology had changed; to advance it now required new methods and a knowledge of contemporary science. Management believed that, with a well-conceived and carefully administered program, results would soon be forthcoming. Willis Whitney, who had achieved results quickly in his consulting project for American Aristotype before joining GE, undertook the work on electric lighting in the belief that his staff would make good progress using the knowledge and techniques of chemistry, physics, and electrochemistry. Early frustration in this work drove him to providing services for the GE engineering and production departments in order to demonstrate the Research Laboratory's usefulness. Then, taking his cues from the business and engineering environment in which he found himself, Whitney carefully directed research on metallic filaments. His approach was inherently conservative because it depended almost entirely on Whitney's preconceptions about materials and methods. Finally, as the result of William Coolidge's inspiration and the dogged work of his colleagues and assistants, the laboratory produced the breakthrough that GE had sought.

Learning from this rather painful experience, Whitney came to believe that as long as advances in technology did not have to be in a single, well-defined direction, significant progress could be made far more readily if researchers were given greater latitude in the problems they chose and the methods they used. Once GE's immediate needs in incandescent lighting had been met and some pressure for results had been removed from the laboratory, Whitney decided that he could be more effective in his use of resources by relaxing direction and control. This was true because the areas of possible application were so great in this already diverse corporation, which, from the now-secure financial base of incandescent lighting, had interest in diversifying even more.[2]

Much the same happened at Bell, and for similar reasons. When Vail, Carty, and Jewett established the laboratory as a new branch of the Engineering Department they expected it to develop an electronic repeater and radio in order to give Bell a major advantage over the smaller telephone companies in long-distance service and to keep radio out of the hands of competitors. Until the electronic vacuum-tube amplifier had been fully developed, and until AT&T felt secure in its control of radio, corporate needs dictated that the laboratory be very tightly organized and administered. With success came diversification, as at GE; but because Bell's potential market areas were considerably more restricted than GE's – based on its experience, resources, and relations with the government – its scope of research diversification was considerably smaller.

The laboratories at GE and AT&T had remarkably similar procedures for directing research toward company patent needs. In both cases there was close cooperation between corporate patent departments and laboratory researchers. Because patents were among the most important fruits of the researchers' labors, they expended considerable effort in development and defense of company patent positions.

The two laboratories were thus similar in a number of ways. They were established under threatening commercial circumstances, with like preconceptions and expectations. They went through periods of closely administered research directed at vital business ends, but ultimately relaxed control while diversifying research. The importance of patents and the way in which the patenting process influenced their work was also quite similar.

Differences of approach to research in the GE and Bell laboratories during their early years were manifold, usually resulting from responses to differing conditions within the two companies. Whereas GE had begun with limited product scope and a technical tradition based on engineering, the new Research Laboratory was expected to bring science into the company's arsenal of invention and innovation, thereby changing both the methods and results of its development processes. In addition to GE's strong desire to protect its electric lighting market, the circumstances most strongly influencing laboratory operations were that GE was primarily a manufacturing company and placed great importance on improving manufacturing efficiency; that President Coffin and the board of directors wanted to diversify product lines; and that the existence of well-established engineering organizations with long-standing relationships to manufacturing meant that the new laboratory had to find a niche for itself beside an already functioning system of design, development, and production. Whitney was careful to complement rather than compete with company engineers. Indeed, entire new fields beyond the purview of other company organizations lay open to him. Even when the Research Laboratory worked in areas already under development by the engineering or production departments, the complementary aspect of its role left it free – in fact, really required it – to try entirely new methods of solving problems and developing technology.

Whitney's style of management evolved within this complex of constraints and opportunities. His perceptions of corporate needs led him to seek out researchers with an independent turn of mind, people who came up with fresh approaches to knotty problems but who sometimes had difficulty fitting into organized laboratory structures. Whitney met the challenge of keeping them informed of, concerned about, and working on corporate-related projects by using the laboratory's various liaison relationships and its interactions with the GE Patent Department. Because the Research Laboratory often worked in areas that were outside immediate company interests, Whitney could permit considerable latitude in the choice of both problems and methods, although he was careful to keep them within the bounds of commercial applicability, at least in the long run. Because he wanted his researchers to deviate from the well-trodden paths of science and engineering, Whitney tried to make them rely more on their own ideas and observations than on the published results of their predecessors; hence his prescription that researchers experiment and reason before looking into the pertinent scientific and technical literature. Within this context of needs, opportunities, and rather unorthodox methods, serendipity often brought new insights and important results.

Bell established its laboratory for much the same reasons as did GE, but because of its greater involvement in services than in products, and because diversification always remained secondary to gaining and maintaining control of American telephony, Bell's approach to research differed. The major motives behind its management policies included protecting investment in existing plant, so innovation had to come at a carefully measured pace; maintaining corporate credit, which required that individuals and institutions have continuing confidence in the company's operations and its prospects;[3] and keeping competitors at bay, so that Bell never lost its central market position or had to violate the concept of "One Policy, One System, Universal Service" by tying into others' systems. The role of the research laboratory within this context was rather closely circumscribed; it usually involved "covering the field" to make steady progress in chosen directions so that the corporation could maintain the control and confidence Bell directors considered crucial.

As part of the Engineering Department, the Research Branch was strongly influenced by Bell System engineering needs and methods. AT&T's chief engineer, J. J. Carty, had come up through the company's technical ranks, and his understanding of science was closely tied to engineering practice. Carty thus perceived the laboratory as an advanced engineering organization. Lab physicists such as H. D. Arnold listed themselves as "Research Engineer" in biographical dictionaries because they worked as engineers in building and maintaining a communications system. Although the laboratory later branched into radio broadcast technology and even motion picture sound tracks, the great majority of its work was oriented toward improvements in the Bell telecommunications system. This involved dealing with a highly complex, interactive service network (rather than with various product lines, as at GE). Laboratory researchers had to function within the structure of Bell System engineering, which strongly encouraged thoroughness rather than flights of imagination. Unlike Whitney at GE, AT&T lab administrators wanted their researchers to review all of the pertinent scientific and technical literature carefully before beginning work in new areas because they were more concerned with building on a functioning system than in making leaps of understanding and practice. At least until incorporation of the Bell Telephone Laboratories in 1925 – when research activities diversified considerably – this approach severely limited the types of results that came from the laboratory. Its advantage, however, was that it produced outstanding results on a narrow research front – results that could quickly be translated into practice.

Market control, innovation, and growth

The advent of industrial research changed corporate attitudes toward market control, innovation, and growth. Although industrial research was not a panacea for corporate competitive difficulties, it enhanced the ability of companies to innovate in both old and new market areas, providing them with the means to protect vital markets as well as to enter new ones. It also changed attitudes toward innovation and stimulated corporate growth, both through increased sales and through productivity gains.

After the institution of ongoing research programs, companies like GE and Bell no longer had to depend on outside inventors for technical advances to help them maintain important market positions. Such dependence on extracorporate technology was becoming more risky at the turn of the 20th century because recent advances in physics, chemistry, and electrochemistry were leading to rapid and essentially unforeseeable changes in commercial technologies. Industrial research brought science to the aid of established industry, enabling GE, Bell, and other companies with similar laboratories to advance and, to a limited extent, control science in their pursuit of commercial ends. It is important to realize, however, that control of science and technology could not be complete because social and professional attitudes, as well as the vagaries of scientific research and technological development, precluded total domination by any one concern.

The advent of industrial research changed the direction and increased the rate of corporate innovation. Of course, American and European industry had been undergoing rapid change since the early 19th century, when manufactures entered a fast-paced series of process and product innovations. This happened first in textiles, then in areas such as firearms, clocks and watches, farm equipment, telegraphy, and steel. Independent inventors and small companies were often able to make significant advances in these and other areas of industrial technology during the 19th century. However, increasing complexities in both technology and science meant that only those with advanced training were likely to continue doing so in the 20th, at least in some of the more technologically sophisticated areas such as chemicals, rubber, electronics, photography, and petroleum refining. When, in 1907, AT&T decided it should no longer retain the services of America's greatest inventor, Thomas Edison, its action signified the changes that had taken place.

Since only big, profitable companies like GE and Bell could support large-scale research efforts, they gained substantial advantages over smaller, less well-endowed, or less farsighted competitors. Because of these advantages, companies which supported industrial research more readily innovated as a corporate strategy for expansion and market control. They knew that they had technological advantages over competitors which could be maintained through their advancing patent positions. When several companies that supported industrial research attempted to enter the same new market area, as in radio, their research laboratories provided powerful weapons to use against each other. They also provided defense: one way or another, industrial research protected the interests of all the major parties competing to control radio, enabling them to advance their strategies for security. At the same time, they were able to keep most smaller competitors out of the field (at least as long as the government permitted it).

Industrial research promoted corporate growth. Large companies that became more secure in their primary markets and that derived new commercial opportunities from their laboratories naturally expanded. A large portion of GE's business after 1910 came from opportunities supplied by research. The same would have undoubtedly been true for Bell except for its regulated-utility status, which provided the company's greatest security, but also the ultimate block to its expansion. Industrial research significantly spurred productivity growth through the rationalization of procedures, the development of more efficient, cost-effective production methods, and high-level trouble-shooting to ameliorate production or service difficulties – activities and accomplishments that came to characterize Bell's national network and, to a lesser extent, GE's operations.[4]

Research in industry

When GE established its laboratory in 1900, it helped to create a new type of research environment in the United States. Industrial research differed in most cases from research pursued in academia because corporations expected to see business-related results issue with some consistency from their laboratories. This strongly influenced industrial researchers' methods and goals. Even in an institution as open to new ideas and approaches as the GE Research Laboratory after 1913, Whitney made certain that most work tied in with company needs. The researchers knew that they were being judged on their contributions to a laboratory which was itself judged on how well it met corporate needs. Team research methods at AT&T brought physicists, chemists, mathematicians, and engineers together in pursuit of corporate technology. It is not surprising that the way in which these people approached science and technology differed both from that of academia and from that of most other types of industrial employment, such as chemical analysis or engineering design.

As I have shown, the relationship between science and technology in the industrial research environment was complex, and the ability – indeed, the necessity – to transcend the usual scientific and engineering disciplines gave these industrial efforts their greatest power. Willis Whitney discovered through his experience in failed electrochemical analysis of arc-light electrodes that adopting the theoretical constructs and research programs of the scientific disciplines made little sense in an industrial research environment. To be effective, industrial scientists and engineers had to develop their own ways of knowing, whether by experiment, observation, and deduction, or by the creation of mathematically based technological theories and design methodologies. The system of developing technological theories was a major step in bringing science and technology so close together that it became impossible in many instances to distinguish between them. Here we find much of the essence of the modern scientific enterprise.[5]

The industrial researchers' methods could be quite sophisticated. Whereas it has often been assumed, even by philosophers of science and technology, that the pursuit of science was somehow "deeper" than that of technology,[6] this analysis of research at GE and Bell has shown that the depth of knowledge involved in the development of corporate technology by people like Coolidge, Langmuir, Arnold, and van der Bijl was often just as great as for those involved in any other kind of work.

The industrial research experience, with its unique system of motivations and rewards, changed the way scientists looked at science, causing them to emphasize the combined development of theory and practice. Within the industrial research environment, the drive to understand and concomitantly develop technologies of corporate concern often became overwhelming. In some cases, researchers lost interest in the larger issues of the scientific disciplines, even though they had come to industry with a "pure science" perspective.[7] Industrial research offered the opportunity to undertake long-term projects on complex "real-world" problems, and many researchers ultimately found this to be more satisfying than the usual disciplinary approaches, which tended to segregate scientific from technical components.

It is important to realize that even though most new industrial researchers undertook their jobs with the ethos of science assimilated in graduate study, they became corporate employees, working at least in part for the same types of job-related satisfaction, recognition, and remuneration as managers and other employees. Like most professionals employed by industry (e.g., attorneys, psychologists, accountants), scientists and research engineers had to balance their professional identities with their corporate roles. The values that they developed were necessarily compromises between the independent, self-directed ones associated with science (and professionalism generally) and the directed loyalty common to business. The often antithetical cultures of business and science thus had to accommodate each other in order to achieve the industrial research synthesis.[8]

Between 1900 and 1920 the number of scientists working in American industry increased dramatically, largely due to the establishment of industrial research.[9] Counting only the eighteen companies with the greatest number of scientists on their staffs in 1920, industrial employment of Ph.D.s rose from 4 in 1900 to 28 in 1910 and to 172 in 1920. In 1900 only about one-tenth of the new physics Ph.D.s trained in America chose an industrial position, whereas by 1920 that proportion had grown to one-fifth of a considerably larger pool. Between 1913 and 1920, the membership of industrial research physicists in the American Physical Society rose from approximately 10% to 25% as the society's membership doubled.[10]

Of course, not all scientists and research engineers fit into the industrial environment. To be successful at industrial research, one had to have a cooperative manner, for the highly individualistic approach that characterized much of the larger scientific community was ineffective and ultimately intolerable in the industrial laboratory. Moreover, while knowledge of the latest developments in science was quite valuable, research directors like Whitney and Jewett soon found that the most important attributes for a good industrial researcher were thorough grounding in the basics of chemistry, physics, and mathematics; strong interest in the interactions of science and technology; and a decided experimental bent.

With such attributes and with the facilities provided by industrial laboratories, ambitious researchers could both make important contributions to their employers' welfare and establish reputations for themselves in science and engineering. Upon the achievement of security for the labs at GE, Bell, and elsewhere, industrial researchers were often encouraged to publish. Many responded by writing articles for professional journals. Whereas in 1910 only 2% of the papers in America's leading journal of physics research, *Physical Review*, had come from industrial laboratories, by 1915 that figure had increased dramatically to 14%, and it climbed to 22% in 1920. In this way, the areas of research interesting to industry came forcefully to the attention of the larger scientific and technical communities, causing researchers outside the industrial labs to consider some of the issues raised within them. The development of concern with the electron physics of vacuum-tube operations is an excellent case in point. By the early 1920s there was, as one physicist noted, a "fever of commercialized science" sweeping the American scientific community – involving not only those in industry, but their colleagues in government laboratories and in universities as well. The larger scientific community soon considered industrial research to be so important that 131 of the scientists "starred" as outstanding in their fields in the 1938 edition of *American Men of Science* had done their research in industrial labs. Thirteen of these worked for AT&T, twelve for GE.[11]

GE, Bell, and the growth of American industrial research

GE and Bell were not alone in undertaking major research efforts in the period between 1900 and World War I. Changes in science, technology, and business during the 19th century led a number of large, technology-based corporations to support ongoing research efforts, though in most cases little is known about their organization and administration. For example, the Rockefeller-run Standard Oil Company of Indiana established a chemical laboratory during the 1880s in an attempt to develop refining techniques for heavily sulfurated supplies of crude oil. By 1902 the laboratory had been transformed into what one historian calls "the acknowledged center of research in petroleum chemistry . . . in the United States." Under the direction of Ph.D. chemist William Burton, the hydrogen-molecular "cracking" process for refining crude oil to yield greater proportions of gasoline emerged from this laboratory in 1913.[12] For a number of years, control of the new process enabled Standard Oil to dominate the industry, bringing it substantial licensing revenues. After this success, research at Standard expanded and diversified.

At DuPont, America's premier manufacturer of high explosives before the First World War, a research laboratory was established in 1902 under Ph.D. chemist Charles Reese. As the first research organization at DuPont with no direct production responsibilities, this "Eastern Laboratory" worked to standardize procedures throughout the company, to utilize waste acids and solvents, and to improve chemical yields. Although the lab's staff did develop several new products, it put most of its effort into solving general production problems and rationalizing chemical processes. In 1911, as DuPont moved toward a corporate strategy of diversification,[13] the Eastern Lab was consolidated with other chemical and engineering groups to form the Chemical Department. It had a staff of 120 and an annual budget over of $300,000 by 1912. The Chemical Department's activities were circumscribed, however, by short-term company needs because DuPont found itself in difficult commercial circumstances as a result of its attempt to enter a number of new market areas. Only after the company's reorganization and diversification in the 1920s would more broad-ranging research activity be encouraged.[14]

Many other companies established research between the turn of the century and 1920. A study conducted by the newly formed National Research Council (NRC) of the National Academy of Sciences found that in the latter year about 300 companies claimed to have industrial research laboratories. By 1921 the count had already risen to over 500.[15] Even though most of these labs would certainly not meet the criteria of the industrial research definition used here, these figures indicate that a considerable number of American companies were conducting some kind of scientific–technical research by the early 1920s and that they believed support of "industrial research" – however they defined it – was in their own best interests.

Arthur D. Little, the Boston consulting chemist who had offered Willis Whitney a job before he accepted the position at GE, was in part responsible for this phenomenon. Little's seminal research-consulting business, begun in 1886, provided scientific services for hundreds of industrial clients, including such major corporations as the United Shoe Machinery Company, General Motors, and International Paper. Little wrote and lectured extensively on the value of industrial research in an attempt to alert businessmen to what he saw as "The Handwriting on the Wall" – that is, the coming domination of industrial markets by science-based products and processes.[16] Little helped alert American industry to changes in technology that required companies to become involved in research if they wanted to remain internationally competitive.

The First World War also helped make this point. Wartime suspension of German imports like rubber, optical instruments, pharmaceuticals, and strategic chemicals forcefully demonstrated

American dependence on foreign suppliers. It became quite clear that for both military and economic reasons, American industry had to develop and control these technologies on its own. The NRC had been formed by American scientists in 1916 to help coordinate military-related research for possible American war involvement. It came out of the war determined to promote and coordinate peacetime research, both in academia and in industry. The NRC's Industrial Research Division made use of well-known, highly regarded industrialists and research directors to proselytize for scientific–industrial research. Through after-dinner speeches, articles in popular and professional journals, and more directly through not-so-subtle forms of peer pressure, the council got its message across to industry and to the general public.[17] Two of the companies frequently held up as examples in this effort were GE and Bell. Willis Whitney, Frank Jewett, and J. J. Carty were among the most active NRC promoters, spreading to the uninitiated their corporate research gospel. This yielded them a number of results, including public recognition and internal corporate support.

The influence of these two laboratories actually predated the World War and the efforts of the NRC. As early as 1910 Whitney had published articles describing and promoting his conceptions of effective industrial research. Records from the GE Research Laboratory files show that a number of companies consulted with Whitney in the process of establishing their own laboratories; some new research directors even came to visit.[18] British chemist C. E. K. Mees, hired by George Eastman in 1912 to organize the Eastman Kodak Research Laboratory, spent a day touring the Schenectady facility. He came away impressed with Whitney's philosophy of research administration and determined to maintain a minimum of formal structure in his incipient operations. Bell's dramatic success in achieving transcontinental telephony in early 1915 brought J. J. Carty into the limelight. Ever the company man, Carty made good use of his newfound celebrity to publicize the value of Bell research by promoting the use of science in industry, pointing to Bell's successful work as an example.[19]

Yet, not every company that took up industrial research succeeded – at least not at first. The lessons that GE, Bell, and other pioneering companies had learned about combining science, technology, and business, and about integrating their laboratories with other company operations might be set forth in articles and speeches; but, for a number of reasons, such lessons were not easily applied. Every industry faced a different set of problems. Each company had its own types of resources, needs, and methods of operation. What worked well for one company might not work at all for another. Indeed, the two case studies discussed here show that at GE and AT&T, companies with overlapping areas of commercial and technical interest, very different types of industrial research methodology worked best.

Just as the GE board of directors appears to have been unconvinced of the efficacy of a permanent research program for some time, the directors and managers of many other companies remained skeptical, or at least unclear, as to how industrial research could contribute to their operations. Furthermore, most companies were run by a diverse set of managers with differing responsibilities, perspectives, and agendas who vied for resources and authority. Personal experience and the needs of the operations they oversaw often circumscribed their understanding of the corporate interest. Industrial research not only threatened their resources but might also undercut their plans for corporate operations, innovation, and growth. Under these circumstances the apparent success of industrial research at companies like GE and Bell could be less than fully convincing. At General Motors, for example, engineers and managers alike initially believed that the General Motors Research Corporation (founded in 1920) would have little impact on the company or on the automobile industry, and they strongly resisted cooperating with it.[20] The general manager of one GM division, at least, thought that the lab's only value would be for corporate public relations. Not surprisingly, the laboratory's first major project, the "copper-cooled" engine, failed because of lack of cooperation from the production divisions. GM's director of research, Charles Kettering, even suspected that production managers were sending saboteurs into the laboratory in attempts to scuttle the project![21]

Indeed, America's adoption of industrial research did not go quite so smoothly as advertised. Each company had to find its own way. The form that its research ultimately took was influenced by a number of factors: needs and opportunities within the company and within the industry of which it was part; structure of its operations; and the way in which contemporary science and technology related to its commercial interests. Few companies seem to have followed exactly the models provided by GE and Bell, and for good reasons. Yet it is also true that GE and Bell served as important stimuli to the industrial research movement that flowered in the decade after the First World War. Their successes – and their promotion of the place of science in industry – helped bring to the attention of an entire generation of corporate managers the value of supporting the complex, integrated activities of industrial research. That few companies chose to follow their leads directly indicates only that GE and Bell were not typical corporations and hence their operations were not appropriate for most companies.

Whatever form it took, research by American industry increased dramatically during the 1920s and 1930s. Large companies more readily became involved than small ones. The number of firms claiming to support industrial research rose from 500 in 1921 to almost 1,000 in 1927, over 1,600 in 1931, and more than 2,200 in 1940. A survey made in 1928 indicated that 52% of the nearly 600 manufacturing concerns queried supported research of some type; 11% of the remainder expected to undertake it soon.[22] However, a relatively small number of large, innovative firms pursued science, technology, and commercial ends together in the sense that I have defined industrial research, and they employed a high percentage of the nation's industrial researchers: the forty-five largest research laboratories in 1938 contained over half; the thirteen largest over a third. This concentration of industrial research resources, mostly in the electrical, chemical, pharmaceutical, automotive, and petroleum industries, led President Franklin D. Roosevelt's Temporary National Economic Committee to report in 1939 that "there is probably no other basic function of general economic activity so dominated by a few enormous concerns." The committee concluded that such a concentration of research and development activities in a limited number of firms had substantial ramifications for control of the economy.[23]

What the establishment of industrial research demonstrates, then, is the emergence of a new, science-based industrial strategy. Using the diverse patents and technical expertise generated in their laboratories, a few innovative corporations acquired the ability to exercise considerable control over the evolution of national markets, from electric lighting and radio to synthetic fabrics, sulfa drugs, and television. Only those companies that were already financially secure and prepared to make major adjustments in managing corporate innovation could compete with them on an equal basis.

But the coming of the Second World War and increasing government involvement in industry changed the competitive environment once again by the 1950s. New government policies for defense-related support of industrial research turned labs directly into profit centers, for government-sponsored research was done on a "cost-plus" basis. This tended to disrupt research laboratories' internal corporate linkages.[24] In addition, compulsory licensing of important patents, based on stricter judicial interpretations of the antitrust laws, prevented powerful companies from establishing market control. This opened the way for smaller firms to make use of results issuing from the large corporations. The early stages of industrial research at GE and Bell were thus artifacts of an era when scientific, technological, and economic conditions encouraged the establishment of laboratories. Government's laissez-faire attitude toward development of technology and regulation of its use made them extremely useful in market control.

In the 1980s conditions have changed once again. Japanese and European competition in the development and control of markets through technological innovation has spurred American companies to invest heavily in research. At the same time, a considerably more business-oriented federal government has shown little concern with antitrust issues while providing strong tax incentives for research. Industrial research is once more being perceived as a driving force behind vital innovation and growth.

Under these circumstances, corporate directors and research managers rightfully ask how to make best use of their research resources. This is a complicated question; industrial research has often been analyzed but rarely comprehended, and finding a formula for success is difficult if not impossible. Perhaps the study presented here can help us to understand the industrial research process a little better and, in particular, to see how its many facets fit together. This book has shown that successful industrial research involves every part of a company's organization and that research has to be tailored to corporate structure and needs. The relationship between research and development, engineering, production, finance, sales, and other company operations is complex and often subtle. No rules can be made, only lessons learned – here through history.

Industrial research has transformed science, technology, and a host of economic relationships. It helped create and maintain the modern American corporate state at the same time that it brought major advances in consumer technology. Managed imaginatively, it should continue to perform these functions in the years to come.

Notes

Preface

1 Philip Boffey, "Industry Takes Dominant Science Role," *New York Times*, 17 July 1984, pp. C1/C9; *Business Week*, "A Deepening Commitment to R&D," 9 July 1984, p. 64.

2 Quoted in Richard Rosenbloom and Alan Kantrow, "The Nurturing of Corporate Research," *Harvard Business Review*, January–February 1982, pp. 118–19; see also Robert Hayes and William Abernathy, "Managing Our Way to Economic Decline," *Harvard Business Review*, July–August 1980, p. 67.

Chapter 1

1 According to historian John Beer, industrial research laboratories appeared in Germany during the 1870s and 1880s because of that country's "ample supply of academically trained scientists, [its] national tradition of painstaking work, and [its] pressing need to convert the few raw materials which [it] possessed into valuable products. . . ." Beer, "Coal Tar Dye Manufacture and the Origins of the Modern Industrial Research Laboratory," *ISIS*, 49 (1958):124.

2 These figures are based on surveys by the National Academy of Sciences–National Research Council. See George Perazich and Philip Field, *Industrial Research and Changing Technology*, Report no. M-4 (Philadelphia: WPA, National Research Project, 1940); Louis Galambos, "The American Economy and the Reorganization of the Sources of Knowledge," in Alexandra Oleson and John Voss, eds., *The Organization of Knowledge in Modern America, 1860–1920* (Baltimore, 1979), pp. 278,282(n. 45).

3 See Kendall Birr, "Industrial Laboratories," in Nathan Reingold, ed., *The Sciences in the American Context: New Perspectives* (Washington, D.C., 1979), p. 20.

4 The period of the rise of American industrial research was marked by a dramatic increase in the percentage of patents that were, upon application, assigned to corporations – a very strong indication that the inventors were corporate employees. Corporate-assigned pat-

ents jumped from 18% in 1900 to 58% in 1936. John Jewkes, *et al.*, *The Sources of Invention* (New York, 1959), p. 88.

5 The "Rule of Reason" for dealing with restraint of trade, which was enunciated by the Supreme Court in 1911, argued that certain economic arrangements were "reasonable" because they promoted industrial activity. Thus, some trusts could be "good" (in the public interest) and others "bad" (contrary to it). Support of research sometimes helped make the distinction.

6 Louis Galambos has argued persuasively that a stable corporate structure was the *sine qua non* for the establishment of industrial research. See "The American Economy and the Reorganization of the Sources of Knowledge," pp. 274–8.

7 An important distinction used throughout this book is that between *invention* and *innovation*. The latter indicates carrying through with an invention, or with any development, to actually put it into service on a commercial basis.

8 See George Wise, "A New Role for Professional Scientists in Industry: Industrial Research at General Electric, 1900–1916," *Technology and Culture*, 21 (1980):408–29.

9 See Leonard S. Reich, "Irving Langmuir and the Pursuit of Science and Technology in the Corporate Environment," *Technology and Culture*, 24 (April 1983).

10 On this issue see David Dickson, *Alternative Technology and the Politics of Technical Change* (Glasgow, 1974), especially pp. 15–40.

Chapter 2

1 I do not mean to suggest here that before the late 19th century the advance of technology never required input from science. The interaction of the chemical industry and chemistry is a conspicuous counterexample.

2 Louis Galambos, for example, has written of an emerging historical perspective in which "the primary process of change involved organization building, both public and private, and the creation of new and elaborate networks of formal, hierarchical structures of authority that gradually came to dominate our economy, polity, and culture." Galambos, "Technology, Political Economy, and Professionalization: Central Themes of the Organizational Synthesis," *Business History Review*, 57 (1983):471.

3 Brooke Hindle, *The Pursuit of Science in Revolutionary America* (Chapel Hill, N.C., 1956), p. 69; Ralph S. Bates, *Scientific Societies in the United States* (Cambridge, Mass., 1965), p. 10. "Philosophical" at the time included the study of nature. The term "arts" as used by the American Academy was more akin to what the 20th century calls "industrial arts" than to pursuit of literature, painting, etc.

4 Oliver Evans, *Abortion of the Young Steam Engineer's Guide* (Philadelphia, 1805), p. 22. It is important to realize that when Evans spoke of "scientific works" he was using the terminology in a broad sense, including such material as writings on the technical aspects of design. Evans published the results of his own research on boilers to aid others and, he hoped, ensure safety. See Greville Bathe and Dorothy Bathe, *Oliver Evans* (Philadelphia, 1935), pp. 151,253.

5 Bruce Sinclair, *Philadelphia's Philosopher Mechanics: A History of the Franklin Institute, 1824–1865* (Baltimore, 1974), pp. 2–3. For reasons based in social and political ideology, Americans tended to think of their science as "useful knowledge" – as opposed to what they perceived as the idle speculations of upper-class Europeans.

6 Arthur Molella and Nathan Reingold, "Theorists and Ingenious Mechanics: Joseph Henry Defines Science," *Science Studies*, 3 (1973):330–7. Early in his career Henry taught at the Albany Academy and Princeton University, then became first secretary of the Smithsonian Institution.

7 Sinclair notes: "In terms of a serious desire to elevate technical practice, [scientific] lectures had their limitations, and the Institute was left with an unsettled tension between objectives and implementation." *Philosopher Mechanics*, p. 120.

8 By the 1820s science was an avocation for many upper-middle- and upper-class citizens. A number of local scientific societies and "Lyceums of Natural History" had been established in the previous decade, and the *American Journal of Science*, founded in 1818 by Benjamin Silliman, published articles and spread news of the growing community. George Daniels, *American Science in the Age of Jackson* (New York, 1968), pp. 14–17.

9 Parliament sent a team of industrialists and engineers to report on American industry and invention following the Americans' exemplary showing at the British "Crystal Palace" industrial exhibition in 1851. Quote from Frank Fox, "The Genesis of American Technology, 1790–1860," *American Studies*, 17 (Fall 1976):38.

10 Concerning Morse's reliance on Joseph Henry for scientific input in his work on the telegraph, see Arthur Molella, "The Electric Motor, the Telegraph, and Joseph Henry's Theory of Technological Progress," *Proceedings of the IEEE*, 64 (1976):1276–8.

11 Many antebellum American colleges emphasized religious and classical studies. Although the science taught there could be substantial in quantity, it was generally intended to illuminate religious doctrine and to produce well-educated leaders who could provide moral direction for the community. See Stanley Guralnick, "The American Scientist in Higher Education, 1820–1910," in Nathan Reingold, ed., *The Sciences in the American Context: New Perspectives* (Washington, D.C., 1979), pp. 99–113,128.

12 From the MIT Act of Incorporation, in William B. Rogers, *Life and Letters of William Barton Rogers* (New York, 1896), Vol. 2, p. 223. One president of MIT commented that at the time of its founding no real demand yet existed for people with such training. MIT and similar institutions helped to create that demand by the demonstrated capabilities of their graduates. Francis Walker, "The Place of Schools of Technology in American Education," *Educational Review*, 2 (1891):211.

13 Quoted in Frederick Rudolph, *The American College and University: A History* (New York, 1962), p. 252; Charles R. Mann, "The American Spirit in Education," *U.S. Bureau of Education Bulletin*, No. 30 (1919), p. 6. A movement similar to American university-level technical education was taking place in Germany at about the same time with the founding of the *technische Hochschulen*, beginning in 1851.

14 John Rae, "The Application of Science to Industry," in Alexandra Oleson and John Voss, eds., *The Organization of the Sources of Knowledge in America, 1860–1920* (Baltimore, 1979), p. 252. On the tension between "shop" and "school" cultures in engineering see Monte Calvert, *The Mechanical Engineer in America* (Baltimore, 1967).

15 Daniel Kevles, "The Physics, Mathematics, and Chemistry Communities: A Comparative Analysis," in Oleson and Voss, eds., *The Organization of Knowledge in Modern America*, pp. 139–40. The head of the Coast Survey reported to a congressional committee in 1886: "We are not fomenting science. We are doing practical work for practical purposes." Only practical work impressed congressmen. *Ibid.*, p. 145.

16 See Owen Hannaway, "The German Model of Chemical Education in America: Ira Remsen at Johns Hopkins, 1876–1913," *Ambix*, 23 (1976):145–64.

17 Self-dubbed the "Scientific Lazzaroni," this group included professors of science at Harvard and Yale, and the heads of the Smithsonian and the U.S. Coast Survey. See A. Hunter Dupree, *Science in the Federal Government* (Cambridge, Mass., 1957), pp. 118–19,135–41.

18 Henry Rowland, "A Plea for Pure Science," in *The Physical Papers of Henry A. Rowland* (Baltimore, 1901), p. 594.

19 Most American scientists of the late 19th and early 20th centuries concentrated their efforts on gathering facts, measuring physical constants, and analyzing materials and chemical compounds. Even Rowland achieved fame largely through his contribution to the techniques of spectroscopy. There were, of course, exceptions. J. Willard Gibbs at Yale made major conceptual and analytical advances to thermodynamics and statistical mechanics – but he had few students and little following in America.

20 Diagnosed as a diabetic and resigned to an early death, Rowland worked on this advanced telegraph system in an attempt to provide his family with financial security.

21 W. Carson Ryan, *Studies in Early Graduate Education* (New York, 1939), p. 23.

22 *Science*, Vol. 1, No. 1 (Feb. 9, 1883), p. 3. One suspects that this was a response to the "pure science" ideology expressed in Rowland's "Plea for Pure Science," presented to the AAAS that same year.

23 Robert Rosenberg, "American Physics and the Origins of Electrical Engineering," *Physics Today*, 36 (October 1983):48–54.

24 Philip A. Lang, quoted in Harriet Sprague, *Frank J. Sprague and the Edison Myth* (New York, 1947), p. 12.

25 See H. P. Hammond, "Promotion of Engineering Education in the Past Forty Years," *Proceedings of the Society for the Promotion of Engineering Education*, 41 (1933):47; and F. C. Pratt, "The Relation of Engineering Education to Industry," *Proceedings of the Society for the Promotion of Engineering Education*, 33 (1925):137.

26 Michael Pupin, *From Immigrant to Inventor* (New York, 1923), p. 289. Herman von Helmholtz, with whom Rowland studied and worked briefly in Germany, was one of the outstanding physicists of his generation. Significantly, Rowland gave the keynote address at the National Conference of Electricians, called in 1884 to establish the American Institute of Electrical Engineers. See *The Operator* (1884):170–1 for the text of his speech.

27 Edwin Layton, "Scientific Technology, 1845–1900: The Hydraulic Turbine and the Origins of American Industrial Research," *Technology and Culture*, 20 (1979):65.

28 Sinclair, *Philosopher Mechanics*, pp. 145–6. Research on waterwheel design had previously been done in Britain, but it employed models. Scale differences often made the results difficult or even impossible to apply in practice.

29 Layton, "Scientific Technology," pp. 64–89.

30 Edwin Layton, in "Mirror-Image Twins: The Communities of Science and Technology in 19th Century America," *Technology and Culture*, 12 (1971):562–80, suggests that disciplines of "engineering science" developed during the course of the century in those areas where the usefulness and intelligibility of science made clear its relationship to engineering practice.

31 Otto Mayr, "Yankee Practice and Engineering Theory: Charles T. Porter and the Dynamics of the High-Speed Steam Engine," *Technology and Culture*, 16 (October 1975):570–602.

32 Jeffrey Sturchio, *Chemists and Industry in Modern America* (Ph.D. dissertation, University of Pennsylvania, 1981), p. 77. One student of Booth's, Joseph Wharton, used his analytical skills to develop a new process for malleable nickel, leading him to profits of over a

million dollars. Wharton later made another fortune in iron and steel. Steven Sass, *The Pragmatic Imagination: A History of the Wharton School* (Philadelphia, 1982), pp. 8–23.

33 Howard Bartlett, "The Development of Industrial Research in the United States," in National Research Council, *Research – A National Resource* (Washington, D.C., 1941), Vol. 2, p. 25.

34 *Ibid.*, pp. 25–8.

35 A patent conferred the legal right to control an invention's use. Based on congressional acts of 1836 and 1870, the U.S. Patent Office granted patents for terms of seventeen years when an inventor demonstrated the originality of a useful idea that had been "reduced" to practice.

36 Quoted in *The Autobiography of Andrew Carnegie* (Boston, 1920), p. 182. Also, see Harold Livesay, *Andrew Carnegie and the Rise of Big Business* (Baltimore, 1975), pp. 109–30.

37 In his study of the American electrical industry, Harold Passer defines the engineer–entrepreneur as "the person with technical training who can see commercial possibilities in the application of scientific principles and who labors to perfect useable products and techniques." Passer, *The Electrical Manufacturers, 1875–1900* (Cambridge, Mass., 1953), p. 1.

38 See, Passer, *The Electrical Manufacturers*, for descriptions of these men and their work.

39 See Carroll Pursell, *Early Stationary Steam Engines in America* (Washington, D.C., 1969).

40 In 1800 there were no American cities approaching 100,000 inhabitants, whereas by 1870, 10% of the population lived in fourteen cities of that size; by 1900 the proportion had reached 20% and the number of cities with over 100,000 inhabitants climbed toward forty. National population rose from 4 million in 1790 to 13 million in 1830, 40 million in 1870, and 76 million in 1900.

41 Alfred D. Chandler, Jr., *The Visible Hand: The Managerial Revolution in American Business* (Cambridge, Mass., 1977), pp. 109–20.

42 Along with such competition came attempts at product differentiation and a dramatic increase in advertising – from about $50 million in 1867 to $500 million in 1900. See Daniel Boorstin, *The Americans: The Democratic Experience* (New York, 1973), pp. 89–164.

43 This happened with products as disparate as cigarettes, sewing machines, cameras, steel, and condensed milk.

44 Adam Smith's *Inquiry Into the Nature and Causes of the Wealth of Nations* (London, 1776) has been called the Capitalist Manifesto. Its paean to the marketplace's ability to allocate resources efficiently has influenced every generation of economists and businessmen since it was written. Alfred Chandler argues persuasively in *The Visible Hand* that during the late 19th century a number of large

corporations, unwilling to accept uncertainties from the "invisible hand," began to control several important functions previously left to the market mechanism.

45 See Glenn Porter, *The Rise of Big Business, 1860–1910* (Arlington Heights, Ill., 1973), pp. 16–20.

46 *Ibid.*, pp. 85–101.

47 Robert Wiebe, *The Search for Order, 1897–1920* (New York, 1967), especially pp. 111–95.

48 In 1899 alone, over 950 firms were involved in mergers valued at a total of more than $2 billion. During the decade after 1895 the largest 100 American corporations increased their size by an average of four times, gaining control of about 40% of all industrial capital.

49 On the Taylor system and the cult of efficiency see Samuel Haber, *Efficiency and Uplift: Scientific Management in the Progressive Era, 1890–1920* (Chicago, 1964).

50 *Science*, 18 (17 August 1903):68.

51 GE's William Coolidge, who came of age during the Progressive era, expressed this attitude when he noted that the industrial researcher found "satisfaction in seeing his scientific discoveries promptly and effectively applied, not only for advancing the industry, but also truly serving the public." Coolidge, "Organized Industrial Research," *Science*, 79 (9 February 1934):130.

52 For example, Frank Jewett, a Ph.D. physicist who received his degree from the University of Chicago in 1902, remarked that his graduate advisor, Professor Albert A. Michelson, "thought that when I entered industrial life, which was a field where patents were a part, I was prostituting my training and my ideals." Quoted in George Folk, *Patents and Industrial Progress* (New York, 1942), p. 153.

53 Victor Clark, *History of Manufactures in the United States* (New York, 1929), Vol. 3, p. 170.

54 Quoted in John Broderick, *Willis Rodney Whitney* (Albany, N.Y., 1945), p. 188.

55 In "The Physics, Mathematics, and Chemistry Communities" (pp. 152, 163), Daniel Kevles calculates that in the twenty-five years after 1890 American universities granted 300 doctorates in physics and 500 in chemistry – almost ten times as many as they had in the twenty-five years before.

56 Daniel Kevles, *The Physicists: The History of a Scientific Community in Modern America* (New York, 1978), pp. 75–90.

57 For example, the innovative products of the German electrical firm Siemens and Halske rested on Siemens's accomplishments as a physicist. Siemens and Halske was a strong competitor to GE in America during the 1890s. See David Cahan, "Werner Siemens and the Origin of the *Physikalische-Technische Reichsanstalt*, 1872–1887," *Historical Studies in the Physical Sciences*, 12 (1982):268.

58 Louis Galambos, "The American Economy and the Reorganization

of the Sources of Knowledge," in Oleson and Voss, eds., *The Organization of Knowledge in Modern America*, pp. 274–8.

59 John Rae documents the high proportion of industrial managers who were engineers. See his "Engineering Education as Preparation for Management," *Business History Review*, 29 (1955):64–74.

60 John Beer, "Coal Tar Dye Manufacture and the Origins of the Modern Industrial Research Laboratory," *ISIS*, 49 (1958):123–31.

61 See Joseph Schumpeter, *Capitalism, Socialism, and Democracy* (New York, 3d edition, 1962), especially pp. 81–6.

Chapter 3

1 With the arc, electricity jumped a gap between two carbon electrodes, creating a light which was, unfortunately, inappropriate for interior use because of its brilliance and the exhaust gases it produced.

2 A multiplex telegraph sent several messages over one wire at the same time. A duplex sent two; a quadruplex sent four, half in each direction. The automatic sent recorded messages faster than operators could transmit and receive by hand.

3 Quoted in Matthew Josephson, *Edison: A Biography* (New York, 1959), pp. 133–4.

4 Information on these and many other inventions can be gleaned from material in the archives of the Edison National Historic Site, in West Orange, N.J., and from Thomas E. Jeffrey, *et al.*, eds., *The Thomas A. Edison Papers, A Selected Microfilm Edition*, Part I (1847–78) (Frederick, Md., 1985 [other parts forthcoming]). Forthcoming volumes of Reese V. Jenkins, Leonard S. Reich, *et al.*, eds., *The Thomas A. Edison Papers* (Baltimore: The Johns Hopkins University Press) will contain selected documents and references.

5 Josephson, *Edison*, pp. 188, 234, 250, 264.

6 Thomas P. Hughes, "Edison's Method," *American Patent Law Association Bulletin*, (July–August 1977):440. Of course, Edison's perceptions of the possibilities were often in advance of those of his contemporaries.

7 *Boston Herald*, January 28, 1883, quoted in Josephson, *Edison*, p. 263.

8 Quoted in *ibid.*, pp. 269–70.

9 Terry Reynolds and Theodore Bernstein, "The Damnable Alternating Current," *IEEE Proceedings*, 64 (September 1976):1339.

10 With $E = \text{Voltage}$, $I = \text{Current}$, and $R = \text{Resistance}$; given $E = I \times R$ (Ohm's Law) and $\text{Power} = E \times I$, then $\text{Power Loss} = I^2 \times R$. From these equations it is evident that for transmission of a given amount of power, high voltage permitted low current, and power lost in transmission depended only on the amounts of current and resistance. Since resistance was a function of wire diameter, employing

high voltage for long-distance transmission meant that a smaller, cheaper wire could be used.

11 See Reynolds and Bernstein, The Damnable Alternating Current," for an account of the campaign.

12 "General Electric Company: Origins and Early Development," Harvard Business School Case No. BH139 (1966), p. 10.

13 Alfred D. Chandler, *The Visible Hand: The Managerial Revolution in American Business* (Cambridge, Mass., 1977), pp. 428–30; Harold Passer, "Development of Large Scale Organization: Electrical Manufacturing Around 1900," *Journal of Economic History*, 12 (1952):379–84.

14 Chandler, *The Visible Hand*, pp. 430, 432.

15 In the year before the merger, each of the two companies had sales between $10 and $11 million, with profits of about $2 million for EGE and $3 million for T–H. However, in the eight months after its formation, General Electric reported $12 million in sales and $3 million in profits, yielding annual sales and profit rates of $18 million and $4.5 million, respectively. Harold Passer, *The Electrical Manufacturers, 1875–1900* (Cambridge, Mass., 1953), p. 328.

16 *Ibid.*; "Second Annual Report of the General Electric Company," 31 January 1894; "Fourth Annual Report of the General Electric Company," 31 January 1896.

17 John T. Broderick, *Forty Years With General Electric* (Albany, N.Y., 1929), p. 32; Passer, *The Electrical Manufacturers*, pp. 349–65.

18 The patent expired at this early date because, according to contemporary law, a U.S. patent ran out coincidently with the earliest termination of a foreign patent on the device. Edison's Canadian patent expired in 1894.

19 Passer, *The Electrical Manufacturers*, pp. 161–2. Because the agreement was based on the use of patent rights – rather than simply on an assignment of market shares – its standing under antitrust law was unclear.

20 Passer, *The Electrical Manufacturers*, pp. 331–3.

21 Quoted in *ibid.*, p. 304.

22 John W. Hammond, *Men and Volts*, (New York, 1941), p. 211. On the introduction of electric power in American industry, see Richard DuBoff, *Electric Power in American Manufacturing, 1889–1958* (New York, 1979).

23 Passer, *The Electrical Manufacturers*, pp. 258–70.

24 *Ibid.*, p. 292.

25 *Ibid.*, p. 310; Hammond, *Men and Volts*, pp. 275–84; DuBoff, *Electric Power in American Manufacturing*, p. 18; Thomas P. Hughes, *Networks of Power: Electrification in Western Society, 1880–1930* (Baltimore, 1983), p. 197.

26 Inside research and development, like Elihu Thomson's work on X-ray apparatus during the late 1890s, often fell victim to the

company's conservative bureaucratic procedures. Information about this incident was communicated to the author by W. Bernard Carlson, who is working on a book about Thomson and GE.

27 William Emmet, *The Autobiography of an Engineer*, (New York, 1940), pp. 135–8. Philip L. Alger, *The Human Side of Engineering* (Schenectady, N.Y., 1972), p. 25. Note the similarity of this project to the Franklin Institute's waterwheel experiments and the Merrimack Manufacturing Company's work on water turbines in the 1830s and 1840s.

28 Communicated to the author by GE historian George Wise, who has seen the records of the Works Lab.

29 John A. Miller, *Workshop of Engineers* (Schenectady, N.Y., 1953), pp. 2–5. In recognition of this function's importance for American industry, Congress established the National Bureau of Standards in 1901. It was modeled in part on the *Physikalische–Technische Reichsanstalt* in Germany and on the National Physical Laboratory in Britain.

30 The method was based on James Clerk Maxwell's differential equations for AC circuits, which Steinmetz translated to a system amenable to graphical analysis. See Ronald Kline, "Science and the Engineer: The Work of C. P. Steinmetz," unpub. MS presented at the 1982 annual meeting of the Society for the History of Technology.

31 Kline, "Steinmetz," p. 5; C. P. Steinmetz, "Theory of the Induction Motor," *AIEE Transactions*, 11 (17 October 1894):754–60.

32 George Wise, *The Corporation's Chemist: A Biography of Willis R. Whitney*, unpub. MS in the author's possession, 1981, pp. 93,97.

33 Hammond, *Men and Volts*, p. 263; Wise, *The Corporation's Chemist*, p. 97.

Chapter 4

1 Arthur A. Bright, *The Electric Lamp Industry* (New York, 1949), pp. 126–7.

2 Quoted in John A. Miller, *Yankee Scientist – William D. Coolidge* (Schenectady, N.Y., 1963), p. 3.

3 At the time of Edison's initial triumph, a reporter had characterized his lamp as giving light like "the mellow sunset of an Italian autumn." Quoted in Matthew Josephson, *Edison: A Biography* (New York, 1959), p. 224.

4 A lumen is the light emitted by one candle. A watt is the amount of power produced by one ampere of current flowing at a pressure of one volt.

5 Bright, *The Electric Lamp Industry*, p. 168; Alex Berman, "Henri

Moissan," in C. C. Gillispie, ed., *Dictionary of Scientific Biography* (New York, 1974), Vol. 9, pp. 450–2.

6 Bright, *The Electric Lamp Industry*, pp. 174–6. Much higher costs for electricity in Europe made the more expensive but more efficient lamp attractive there.

7 *Ibid*., pp. 221–7.

8 Steinmetz never actually received the doctorate. An active socialist, he was forced to flee Germany in 1888 just before the award of his degree.

9 Steinmetz to E. W. Rice, 9 July 1897, Document No. L5791, John H. Hammond File, GE Main Works Library, Schenectady, N.Y. (hereafter Hammond File.) This material was compiled by Hammond in preparation for his book *Men and Volts* (New York, 1941).

10 Steinmetz to Rice, 20 September 1897, Hammond File L5794. In the letter Steinmetz suggested as appropriate types of projects for the lab research on titanium and on the production of nitrogen from the air.

11 In the same letter to Rice, Steinmetz spoke of "*our* proposed establishment of the . . . laboratory." Emphasis added.

12 On Bradley and the Ampere Company see Martha Trescott, *The Rise of the American Electrochemical Industry, 1880–1910* (Westport, Conn., 1981), p. 186.

13 Steinmetz, "Review of Engineering Work During the Year 1898," 5 January 1899, Hammond File L5467. In 1898 Steinmetz had been relieved of his duties with the Calculating Department and made consulting engineer, a position that permitted him to conduct his own research and to give more time to advising the company in matters relating to the development of electrical technology. John A. Miller, *Modern Jupiter* (New York, 1958), pp. 92–3.

14 Davis to the editor, *General Electric Review*, April 1933.

15 Davis to Rice, 21 September 1900, Hammond File L2987.

16 Steinmetz to Rice, 21 September 1900, Elihu Thomson Papers, GE Works, Lynn, Mass., quotes on pp. 3,4 (hereafter Thomson Papers). I thank W. Bernard Carlson for bringing these materials to my attention; "Interview with A. G. Davis," 14 November 1927, Hammond File L2992.

17 Thomson to Steinmetz, 24 September 1900, Hammond File L2987; Thomson to Rice, 24 September 1900, Hammond File L2988.

18 "Interview with A. G. Davis," 14 November 1927, Hammond File L2992.

19 William White, *The Story of Electronics Development at the General Electric Company*, unpub. MS, 1955, Introduction, pp. 2–3. Copy at the Whitney Library, GE R&D Center, Schenectady, NY (hereafter Whitney Library).

20 Thomson to Steinmetz, 24 September 1900, Thomson Papers.

21 Cross to A. G. Davis, 1 October 1900, and Steinmetz to Thomson, 8 October 1900, Thomson Papers.

22 George Wise, "Ionists in Industry: Physical Chemistry at General Electric, 1900–1915," *ISIS*, 74 (1983):11.

23 "Interview with A. G. Davis," 14 November 1927, Hammond File L2992; Kendall Birr, *The General Electric Research Laboratory: A Case Study in the History of Industrial Research* (Ph.D. dissertation, University of Wisconsin, 1951), p. 85.

24 Cross to Davis, 1 October 1900, Thomson Papers.

25 "Interview with A. G. Davis," 14 November 1927, Hammond File L2992; "The Research Laboratory – Its Beginning and Growth. Information Obtained from Dr. W. R. Whitney," 7 January 1926, Hammond File L342. John Broderick, *Forty Years With General Electric* (Albany, N.Y., 1929), p. 93.

26 Whitney to Ida Schultz, 9 March 1901, Schultz Papers. Cited in George Wise, *The Corporation's Chemist: A Biography of Willis R. Whitney*, unpub. MS in the author's possession, 1981, p. 128, note 44.

27 *Ibid.*, p. 131.

28 Whitney to H. S. Pritchett, 6 August 1901, H. S. Pritchett Presidential Papers, MIT Archives, Cambridge, Mass.; Whitney to Agnes Whitney, 21 June 1901, in the possession of Agnes Wendel, quoted in George Wise, *The Corporation's Chemist*, p. 113.

29 Willis Whitney Laboratory Notebook 1, 9–10 July 1901, Building 5 Library, GE Schenectady Works, Schenectady, N.Y. (hereafter Whitney Notebook); Willis Whitney, "Research as a Financial Asset," *General Electric Review*, 14 (1911):326–7.

30 Wise, *The Corporation's Chemist*, pp. 137–43; William Weedon, "A Contribution to the Study of the Electric Arc," *Transactions of the American Electrochemical Society*, 5 (1904):171–87.

31 Whitney Notebook 1, 20 September 1902.

32 "General Electric Annual Report for 1901," 31 January 1902, p. 13.

33 Steinmetz to J. Riddell, 8 February 1901, Hammond File L5697; to E. W. Rice, 19 February 1901, Hammond File L5695; to G. E. Emmons, 27 March 1901, Hammond File L5698. In proposing the lab, Steinmetz had written to Rice, "I shall be very glad to direct such an experimental laboratory, provided that the administration is put in the hands of the chemist." 21 September 1900, Thomson Papers; "Interview with John T. H. Dempster," 1940, in "Laboratory Affairs – 40th Anniversary," Whitney Library.

34 The words are Howell's. Howell to E. W. Rice, 15 September 1903, in "Laboratory Affairs – General," Whitney Library (hereafter LAG); Whitney Notebook 2, 5 October 1903.

35 Whitney Notebook 2, 5 October 1903.

36 References to meetings of the council appear throughout Whitney's

notebooks from 1903 to 1913; see also "Laboratory Advisory Council Meeting," 26 January 1910, copy at the Public Information Office, GE R&D Center (hereafter Public Info. Office). In later years other GE managers and even some consultants sat on the advisory council.

37 On staff numbers see Birr, *The General Electric Research Laboratory*, Appendix III, p. 540; Whitney requested leave in his letter to MIT's President Pritchett, 6 August 1901, MIT Archives.

38 Whitney, "Research as a Financial Asset," p. 327.

39 Bright, *The Electric Lamp Industry*, pp. 145–8; David Loth, *Swope of GE* (New York, 1958), p. 46.

40 A company officer later recalled: "The lamp world was much upset by the announcement of a German lamp the filament of which was a tantalum wire which while taking only two-thirds of the current of the GEM lamp lasted twice as long. If true, and the cost was reasonable, it meant good-bye to the millions of dollars worth of carbon lamp business . . . ." Samuel Ferguson, unpublished speech, n.d.(c. 1925), Hammond File L6441.

41 "General Electric Incandescent Lamp Information," n.d.(c. 1925), Hammond File L3438.

42 Whitney Notebook 2, 2 October 1904 and 29 June 1905; Wise, *The Corporation's Chemist*, p. 155; Birr, *The General Electric Research Laboratory*, Appendix III, p. 540.

43 *Ibid.*, pp. 157–8.

44 Samuel Ferguson, unpublished speech, n.d.(c. 1925), Hammond File L6443; Birr, *The General Electric Research Laboratory*, pp. 97–8.

45 John Howell to John Hammond, 30 April 1929, Hammond File L3842; Wise, *The Corporation's Chemist*, p. 160.

46 William Coolidge, "Ductile Tungsten," *Transactions of the American Institute of Electrical Engineers*, 29 (1910):963; Birr, *The General Electric Research Laboratory*, p. 100.

47 Coolidge letter to his parents, December 1906, quoted in Miller, *Yankee Scientist*, p. 58; "To Accompany Summary of 1906–1910," 1 June 1911, LAG.

48 In his letter to John Hammond, Howell noted that representatives of Westinghouse had already visited the *Auer Gesellschaft* when he and Whitney arrived. 30 April 1929, Hammond File L3842; Wise, *The Corporation's Chemist*, p. 163.

49 Quoted in John Broderick, *Willis Rodney Whitney* (Albany, N.Y., 1945), p. 205; Coolidge to his mother, 26 May 1906, Coolidge Papers, GE R&D Center, quoted in Wise, *The Corporation's Chemist*, p. 162.

50 Coolidge to his mother, 5 March 1906, Coolidge Papers, quoted in Wise, *The Corporation's Chemist*, p. 162.

51 "Value and Quantity of All Lamps Sold by Edison and National

Works of General Electric Company," 3 June 1929, Hammond File L3976.

52 Bright, *The Electric Lamp Industry*, pp. 186, 193; Wise, *The Corporation's Chemist*, p. 165.

53 7 October 1908, C. P. Steinmetz Papers, Schenectady County (N.Y.) Historical Society, pp. 5,6.

54 Whitney to "Dearest Folks," 14 July 1904, in possession of Agnes Wendel, quoted in Wise, *The Corporation's Chemist*, p. 151; Birr, *The General Electric Research Laboratory*, pp. 151–2; "Research Laboratory Report, Schenectady Works," 1907 and 1908, Public Info. Office.

55 Independent Lamp and Wire Co. vs. General Electric, U.S. Court of Appeals for the Third Circuit, No. 2615 (October 1920), Defendant's Record, pp. 175–85; Wise, *The Corporation's Chemist*, pp. 180–1; Coolidge, "Ductile Tungsten," pp. 961–4.

56 William Coolidge, "The Development of Ductile Tungsten," in Cyril Stanley Smith, ed., *The Sorby Centennial Symposium on the History of Metallurgy* (New York, 1965), p. 446.

57 Coolidge, "Ductile Tungsten," p. 965; "Research Laboratory Reports, Schenectady Works," 1907, 1908, and 1911, LAG; Summary of Work Done in the Research Laboratory During 1910," LAG. Bright suggests that research expenses were about one-seventh as great as the amount expended for patent right purchases. *The Electric Lamp Industry*, p. 196.

58 For these reasons ductile tungsten also fostered expanded use of electric lighting in then nonstandard applications such as flashlights and headlamps for the growing automobile industry. Bright, *The Electric Lamp Industry*, p. 197.

59 "Relative Yearly Sales of Different Types of Incandescent Lamps in the United States, 1907–1914," n.d., Hammond File L244; Bright, *The Electric Lamp Industry*, p. 149; Wise, *The Corporation's Chemist*, p. 206; "General Electric Company: The Middle Years," Harvard Business School Case No. BH157 (1969), p. 6.

60 Wise, *The Corporation's Chemist*, pp. 197–8; Kendall Birr, *Pioneering in Industrial Research* (Washington, D.C., 1957), p. 147.

61 James A. Cox, *A Century of Light* (New York, 1979), p. 115.

62 For example, in 1913, when profits on the sale of incandescent lamps were on the order of $10 million, lab expenses totaled less than $250,000. See "Research Laboratory Report, Schenectady Works, 1913," Public Info. Office.

63 Coffin stayed on as chairman of the board, carefully maintaining control of GE's finances. Rice directed day-to-day operations.

64 Whitney to Frank Lovejoy, 24 October 1912, LAG. Kodak was then in the process of setting up its own industrial research laboratory.

65 For background on Langmuir's early life and career, see Leonard Reich, "Irving Langmuir and the Pursuit of Science and Technology in the Corporate Environment," *Technology and Culture*, 24 (April 1983):202–9.

66 Irving Langmuir, "Atomic Hydrogen as an Aid in Industrial Research," *Science*, 67 (24 February 1928):203.

67 Irving Langmuir, "Fundamental Research and Its Human Value," *Scientific Monthly*, 46 (1938):361.

68 Bright, *The Electric Lamp Industry*, p. 323. Arc lights were still used for ultra-high-powered applications, such as searchlights.

69 *Langmuir's Priority Record*, Arnold vs. Langmuir, Interference No. 40,380, in the United States Patent Office, n.d.(c. 1922), pp. 118–19,149. L. A. Hawkins to George Morrison, 19 August 1914, LAG; "Research Laboratory Report, Schenectady Works, 1914," Public Info. Office.

70 Wise, *The Corporation's Chemist*, p. 206. This was one of GE's recurrent strategies: gaining a large portion of a new market area, then lowering costs, both for itself and the consumer. This increased GE's profits and retained its market share while stimulating sales.

71 "Report of the Research Laboratory for the Year 1916," 4, January 1917, LAG.

72 Wise, *The Corporation's Chemist*, p. 206; Bright, *The Electric Lamp Industry*, pp. 250–1, 270; Birr, *Pioneering in Industrial Research*, p. 147.

73 Alexanderson had been able to construct alternators of several kilowatts output at frequencies up to 200,000 cycles per second. However, he could not use the devices for voice communication because he lacked an adquate modulator.

74 White, *The Story of Electronics Development at the General Electric Company*, Chapter 3, pp. 1–4,17.

75 Birr, *The General Electric Research Laboratory*, p. 125; Saul Dushman, "Note on Work on Kenotrons," 1–15 July 1915, pp. 1,4, Whitney Library; Albert Hull, "The Dynatron," *Proceedings of the Institute of Radio Engineers*, 6 (1918):5–35.

76 Birr, *The General Electric Research Laboratory*, p. 128. Irving Langmuir Laboratory Notebook 581, 5 November 1914, Langmuir Papers, Library of Congress Manuscript Collection, p. 207.

77 White, *The Story of Electronics Development in the General Electric Company*, Chapter 3, pp. 26–7. Birr, *The General Electric Research Laboratory*, p. 123; William White, "Report of Work, October and November 1916," Whitney Library.

78 Birr, *The General Electric Research Laboratory*, pp. 133–4.

79 William Coolidge Laboratory Notebook entry, 10 December 1912, quoted in Herman Liebhafsky, *William David Coolidge* (New York, 1974), p. 25.

80 Albert Davis to Ernest Thurnauer, 26 December 1913, Coolidge X-ray Papers, GE R&D Center, quoted in Wise, *The Corporation's*

Chemist, p. 237. The wording is very interesting here, suggesting how the technology should be "exploited" for corporate purposes and that not to do so would be costly to GE, if not directly, then through public relations difficulties.

81 Whitney to Rice, 17 March 1916, in *ibid.*, p. 238; Whitney to G. H. Glowes (Eli Lilly Company), 16 March 1920, LAG.

82 "Information from Willis Whitney," 7 January 1926, Hammond File L344; Lawrence Hawkins, *Adventure Into the Unknown* (New York, 1950), p. 10; Birr, *Pioneering in Industrial Research*, p. 62.

83 "General Electric Annual Report for 1901," 31 January 1902, p. 13.

84 "Lawrence A. Hawkins," Columbia Oral History Collection, Columbia University, p. 8; Wise, *The Corporation's Chemist*, p. 228; Birr, *Pioneering in Industrial Research*, p. 72.

85 Lawrence Hawkins to J. P. Tarbox (Curtis Engineering Corporation), 6 January 1919, LAG; Hawkins to Whitney, 12 December 1922, Willis R. Whitney Papers, Union College Archives, Schenectady, N.Y. (hereafter Whitney Papers).

86 "Research Laboratory Report, Schenectady Works," 1910, 1913, and 1916, Public Info. Office; Birr, *The General Electric Research Laboratory*, pp. 540, 152–3.

87 Lawrence Hawkins, "Industrial Research," *General Electric Review*, 18 (June 1915):420; Whitney to T. H. Skinner, 28 April 1910, LAG; Birr, *The General Electric Research Laboratory*, p. 149.

88 Formed in 1915 by Secretary of the Navy Josephus Daniels and headed by Thomas Edison, the board was intended to help prepare the American military for possible entry into the European conflict by facilitating the use of American inventive skills to provide the army and navy with advanced technologies of war. See Daniel Kevles, *The Physicists: The History of a Scientific Community in Modern America* (New York, 1978), pp. 105–24.

89 Birr, *The General Electric Research Laboratory*, pp. 190–6.

90 27 November 1915, p. 76. Mazda was the name of the ancient Persian god of light.

91 Whitney to Rice, 15 July 1921, LAG.

92 Birr, *Pioneering in Industrial Research*, pp. 156–7; Lawrence Hawkins, "History of the General Electric Research Laboratory," MS basis of 1950 book, 1937, copy at the Whitney Library, p. 56. *The Nation* noted in 1928 that "A sentence which begins 'Science says' will generally be found to settle any argument in a social gathering, or sell any article from toothpaste to a refrigerator." Quoted in Spencer Weart, "The Rise of 'Prostituted' Physics," *Nature*, 262 (July 1976):14.

93 Hawkins to Whitney, 3 April 1923, Whitney Papers; e.g., Saul Dushman, "A New Device for Rectifying High Tension Alternating Currents," *General Electric Review*, 18 (1915):156–67, which promoted Langmuir's claims for the high-vacuum patent over Bell's

H. D. Arnold. In his "Report of Work for 1925," Saul Dushman noted: "A great deal of our time has also been taken up during the past year with investigations on infringing tubes and patent suit problems in general." 12 January 1926, microfilm reel 21, Whitney Library.

94 Birr, *Pioneering in Industrial Research*, pp. 108–11, 115–17. GE set up a subsidiary, The Carboloy Company, to develop the market. The Research Laboratory worked closely with it.

95 One investment counselor advised in 1929: "The modern investor, if he is discrete and cautious in the purchase of securities, not only scrutinizes the Board of Directors, but also extends his investigation to the research department of the corporation whose securities he anticipates buying. . . . The real wealth of the modern corporation and the potentialities for enhancing its earnings are created in the laboratory." Raymond Yates, "Wall Street and the Research Laboratory," *Scientific American*, November 1929, p. 382.

96 Loth, *Swope of GE*, pp. 6, 145–6. Loth quotes Whitney as saying (p. 125): "The only thing [Swope] ever asked me was 'Have you got everything you need?' "

97 Birr, *The General Electric Research Laboratory*, Appendix III, p. 540.

Chapter 5

1 John Beer, "Coal Tar Dye Manufacture and the Origins of the Modern Industrial Research Laboratory," *ISIS*, 49 (1958):123–31; George Meyer-Thurow, "The Industrialization of Invention: A Case Study from the German Chemical Industry," *ISIS*, 73 (1982):363–81.

2 Whitney often invoked Bacon as his guiding light. See, for example, Willis Whitney, "The Organization of Industrial Research," *Journal of the American Chemical Society*, 32 (1910):71–3.

3 The electrochemists saw the operation of an electric arc as analogous to that of a storage battery, with oxidation at one electrode and reduction at the other. The research program that this suggested on electric arcs gave inconsistent – and hence useless – results. George Wise, *The Corporation's Chemist: A Biography of Willis R. Whitney*, unpub. MS in the author's possession, 1981, pp. 137–41.

4 G. R. Fonda, quoted in "Come in Rain or Shine," unpub. internal GE MS, 1958, copy at Public Information Office, GE R&D Center (hereafter Public Info. Office).

5 Saul Dushman, "Statement at the 40th Anniversary Celebration of the Laboratory," in "Laboratory Affairs – 40th Anniversary," 1940, Whitney Library, GE R&D Center, Schenectady, N.Y. (hereafter

Whitney Library); "Oral History: Anthony Nerad," n.d.(c. 1975), p. 12, copy at Public Info. Office.

6 Willis Whitney Laboratory Notebook, 25 April 1908, p. 307, Building 5 Library, Schenectady Works (hereafter Whitney Notebook); Whitney to John Parker, 1 August 1950, copy at Public Info. Office; Kendall Birr, *Pioneering in Industrial Research* (Washington, D.C., 1957), p. 70. Birr incorrectly dates the establishment of the executive engineer's position as 1904.

7 George Wise interview with Harold Mott-Smith, 1 March 1977, p. 11, copy at Public Info. Office.

8 Whitney to F. W. Lovejoy, 24 October 1912, p. 4, "Laboratory Affairs – General," Whitney Library, GE R&D Center (hereafter LAG).

9 Whitney to F. W. Lovejoy, 24 October 1912, LAG; see, e.g., William White, Laboratory Notebook 5, 27 March–1 April 1916, p. 7, GE Main Works Library, which discusses a meeting of the group concerned with "radio matters." In a memorandum to one lab researcher, Whitney began, "Could I create an interest in you in a series of fool stunts which have, I think, the promise in them of some useful results." He then set out a series of experiments on motor generators. Physicist Albert Hull noted that Whitney effectively "peddled his problems" within the lab. John Broderick, *Willis R. Whitney* (Albany, N.Y., 1945), p. 90; Birr, *Pioneering in Industrial Research*, p. 73.

10 Willis Whitney Diary, 27 December 1908, copy at Public Info. Office; quote from Broderick, *Whitney*, p. 46.

11 "Oral History: Louis Navias," n.d.(c. 1975), p. 3, copy at Public Info. Office. Concerned about the methods being used in one project, Whitney asked Langmuir for an opinion. "He's doing what I would do," Langmuir responded, and Whitney was mollified. "Oral History: Anthony Nerad," p. 8.

12 William White, *The Story of Electronics Development at the General Electric Company*, unpub. MS, 1955, Chapter 1, pp. 2–4, copy at the Whitney Library; Whitney, "The Organization of Industrial Research," p. 73.

13 That is, *more interesting* to GE. Albert Hull, "Dr. Albert W. Hull," unpub. autobiographical MS, n.d.(c. 1945), p. 11, copy at Public Info. Office. Emphasis added. Even Langmuir was asked to abandon some projects when his pursuit of science had gone beyond practicality. In 1928 Whitney suggested that he drop his work on hot gases and turn it over to others because, as one of his assistants related, "the lab had to move ahead to engineering." G. Wise interview with H. Mott-Smith, 1 March 1977, p. 8, copy at Public Info. Office.

14 Birr, *The General Electric Research Laboratory: A Case Study in the*

History of Industrial Research (Ph.D. dissertation, University of Wisconsin, 1951), pp. 213–14; see, e.g., Irving Langmuir, "Report of Work for 1924," 16 January 1925, microfilm reel 30, Whitney Library.

15 Birr, *Pioneering in Industrial Research*, p. 73.

16 Hull, "Dr. Albert W. Hull," p. 11.

17 11 July 1903, LAG.

18 See patent letter files, microfilm reel 12.2, Whitney Library. In responding to one man's request for a pay increase, Whitney noted: "Told him to wait 2 weeks to see if I could satisfy myself as to his willingness to attempt to do right about reports." Whitney Notebook, 30 July 1903, p. 30.

19 Whitney Notebook, 29 February 1908, p. 268; quote from George Wise, "A New Role for Professional Scientists in Industry," *Technology and Culture*, 21 (1980):422. In the District Court of the United States, District of New Jersey, General Electric Co. vs. Independent Lamp and Wire Co., In Equity No. 648, October Term 1920, Defendant's Record of Testimony, p. 631.

20 Whitney, "The Organization of Industrial Research," p. 75.

21 "The Research Laboratory – Its Beginning and Growth. Information Obtained from Willis R. Whitney," 7 January 1926, Document No. L343–44, John H. Hammond File, GE Main Works Library, Schenectady, N.Y. (hereafter Hammond File).

22 Hull, "Dr. Albert W. Hull," p. 9.

23 *Ibid*.

24 C. G. Suits and J. M. Lafferty, "Albert W. Hull," *National Academy of Sciences Biographical Memoirs*, 41 (1970):221; Leonard Reich, "Research, Patents, and the Struggle to Control Radio," *Business History Review*, 51 (1977):217.

25 Lawrence Hawkins, "Historical – Laboratories," n.d.(c. 1925), Hammond File L375; Steinmetz to Rice, 7 October 1908, p. 5, Charles P. Steinmetz Papers, Schenectady County Historical Society, Schenectady, N.Y. (hereafter Steinmetz Papers).

26 For example, the Research Lab depended on the Testing Lab at the Schenectady Works for much of its analytical chemistry. Whitney to Raymond Bacon, 11 March 1916, LAG.

27 Steinmetz to Rice, 7 October 1908, pp. 5–6, Steinmetz Papers; Birr, *The General Electric Research Laboratory*, p. 238.

28 Hawkins to Whitney, 15 March 1923, p. 3, Willis R. Whitney Papers, Union College, Schenectady, N.Y. (hereafter Whitney Papers). Hawkins to J. P. Tarbox, 6 January 1919, LAG; William White, "Report of Work, October and November 1916," p. 5, microfilm reel 20, Whitney Library; E. F. W. Alexanderson to J. H. Payne, 27 March 1923, Binder 90, E. F. W. Alexanderson Papers, Union College, Schenectady, N.Y. (hereafter Alexanderson Pa-

pers). G. S. Meikle Laboratory Notebook, 8 November 1914, GE Main Works Library, Schenectady, N.Y.

29 Whitney to G. H. A. Glowes, 16 March 1920, LAG. Whitney mentioned as examples of company technologies being followed by staff members: lamp exhaust, lamp glass, lamp gas purification, transformer steels, and insulating varnishes.

30 "PROGRESS REPORT OF THE RESEARCH LABORATORY. THIS REPORT SHOULD BE CONSIDERED STRICTLY CONFIDENTIAL." Copies of many of these reports, the earliest dated 15 November 1912, are at the Public Info. Office.

31 Birr, *The General Electric Research Laboratory*, pp. 229–30.

32 G. Wise interview with Harold Mott-Smith, 1 March 1977, p. 11, copy at Public Info. Office.

33 G. Wise interview with Vincent Schaeffer, 24 May 1977, p. 7, copy at Public Info. Office.

34 Birr, *The General Electric Research Laboratory*, p. 227. Whitney Notebook, 12 July 1907, p. 196. Whitney noted: "Monthly or oftener our men visit the factories in connection with definite experimental or developmental work. There is great need for this, because every cheapening process of the factory introduces something new, which often makes it possible to improve the quality at the same time." Whitney to Rice, 15 July 1921, LAG; Transcript of Record, Independent Lamp and Wire Co. vs. General Electric Co., Vol. 2, Defendant's Record, 18 September 1920, p. 637.

35 Whitney to G. H. A. Glowes (Eli Lilly Co.), 16 March 1920, LAG.

36 Whitney to Rice, 7 September 1916, LAG; "Research Laboratory Report, Schenectady Works," 1912, 1913, 1914, 1915, and 1916, copies at Public Info. Office. Items sold within GE included such things as special fuses, carbon brushes, and radio equipment. Some services (e.g., lamp testing) received credits as well. Since the lab's manufacturing expenses did not include overhead, the credits cannot strictly be considered as profit.

37 F. C. Pratt to C. E. Patterson, 11 July 1914, quoted in Birr, *The General Electric Research Laboratory*, pp. 217–18.

38 *Ibid.*, p. 215; S. Ferguson to E. W. Rice, 31 March 1911, LAG; "Value for 1911 of Apparatus and Materials Originating in the Research Laboratory," LAG.

39 Whitney had the reputation of fostering "pure" research among his staff. For example, Coolidge later noted in an interview: "It's because Dr. Whitney is there that Langmuir and I can play around. He stands between us and the demands that we do something practical." Quoted in Maurice Holland and Henry Pringle, *Industrial Explorers* (New York, 1928), pp. 29–30. But of course Langmuir, and especially Coolidge, almost always *did* do "something practical."

40 John A. Miller, *Yankee Scientist: William David Coolidge* (Schenectady, N.Y., 1963), p. 50; Wise, *The Corporation's Chemist*, pp. 136–37.

41 George Wise, "A New Role for Professional Scientists in Industry," p. 418; Miller, *Yankee Scientist*, p. 5; Leonard Reich, "Irving Langmuir and the Pursuit of Science and Technology in the Corporate Environment," *Technology and Culture*, 24 (April 1983):209. Whitney to G. H. A. Glowes, 29 March 1920, LAG.

42 Whitney Laboratory Notebook, 29 February 1908, p. 267.

43 Birr, *The General Electric Research Laboratory*, pp. 228–9; Whitney, "The Organization of Industrial Research," p. 78; G. R. Fonda, "Come in Rain or Shine."

44 Whitney, "The Organization of Industrial Research," p. 78.

45 Willis Whitney, "Discussion," *Transactions of the American Electrochemical Society*, 16 (1909):224–5; Irving Langmuir, Laboratory Notebook 458, 24 July 1913, p. 231, Langmuir Papers, Library of Congress Manuscript Collection (hereafter Langmuir Papers); L. Hawkins to Whitney, 22 December 1922, p. 3, Whitney Papers.

46 Wise, *The Corporation's Chemist*, p. 195. Wise calculates the GE Research Lab's output between 1900 and 1910 as about one-third that of the average for U.S. academic physics laboratories.

47 Whitney Laboratory Notebook, 20 January 1904, p. 92. When he unveiled ductile tungsten in Europe, Coolidge noted that the response he got "left no question in my mind as to whether our secret had, until then, been well kept from the entire European tungsten lamp industry." William Coolidge, "The Development of Ductile Tungsten," in Cyril Stanley Smith, ed., *The Sorby Centennial Symposium on the History of Metallurgy* (New York, 1965), p. 447.

48 Coolidge lamented that most of his research would probably end up on "the scrap heap," which was "a poor place to look for memorial tablets." He preferred a project where he "could publish [his] results." Coolidge to his mother, 15 December 1907, quoted in Wise, *The Corporation's Chemist*, p. 180; "Oral History: Anthony Nerad," p. 3.

49 Quoted in Suits and Lafferty, "Albert Wallace Hull," p. 217.

50 Reich, "Irving Langmuir," pp. 206, 219–21.

51 Whitney Laboratory Notebook, 25 June 1908, p. 60. Saul Dushman, "An Album of Memories," unpub. MS, n.d.(c. 1948), p. 3, copy at Public Info. Office.

52 Colin Fink, "Ductile Tungsten and Molybdenum – Discussion," *Transactions of the American Electrochemical Society*, 17 (1910):233–4.

53 Birr, *The General Electric Research Laboratory*, pp. 227–8. Many of those who left for research management positions helped spread Whitney's and GE's research philosophy.

54 Wise, *The Corporation's Chemist*, pp. 157–8. Wiedemann himself was considered an expert in experimental technique.

55 Cyril Stanley Smith, *Metallurgy as a Human Experience* (New York, 1977), pp. 3,30–1; Eda Fowlks, "The Other Revolution," unpub. MS in the author's possession, n.d.(c. 1980), p. 6. General Electric Co. vs. Independent Lamp and Wire Co., District Court of the U.S., District of New Jersey, In Equity 648, Defendant's Record of Testimony, pp. 71–2; *ibid*., Brief for Plaintiff on Final Hearing, pp. 9–42.

56 Coolidge, "Ductile Tungsten," *Transactions of the American Institute of Electrical Engineers*, 29 (1910):962–3; John Howell and Henry Schroeder, *History of the Incandescent Lamp* (Schenectady, N.Y., 1927), p. 102.

57 Howell and Schroeder, *History of the Incandescent Lamp*, p. 116. At or above their annealing temperatures, most metals experience a shifting and reorientation of their internal structure that reduces stress and decreases brittleness.

58 Howell and Schroeder, *History of the Incandescent Lamp*, pp. 103–4; Coolidge, "Development of Ductile Tungsten," pp. 448–9.

59 Howell and Schroeder, *History of the Incandescent Lamp*, pp. 107–9; Coolidge Laboratory Notebook, 12 August 1909, quoted in Herman Liebhafsky, *William David Coolidge* (New York, 1974), p. 38.

60 Howell and Schroeder, *History of the Incandescent Lamp*, pp. 109–10; Fowlks, "The Other Revolution," p. 6.

61 Howell and Schroeder, *History of the Incandescent Lamp*, pp. 111–12; Wise, *The Corporation's Chemist*, p. 182.

62 "The Drawn Tungsten Filament for Incandescent Lamps," n.d.(c. 1925), Hammond File L250 – L252; Howell and Schroeder, *History of the Incandescent Lamp*, pp. 112–13.

63 Coolidge, "Development of Ductile Tungsten," p. 447.

64 *Ibid*., p. 448; Wise, *The Corporation's Chemist*, p. 184.

65 See, e.g., Coolidge, "Ductile Tungsten," pp. 961–5; Colin Fink, "Ductile Tungsten and Molybdenum," *Transactions of the American Electrochemical Society*, 17 (1910): 229–34; W. E. Ruder, "Solubility of Wrought Tungsten and Molybdenum," *Journal of the American Chemical Society*, 34 (1910):387–9.

66 General Electric Co. vs. Independent Lamp and Wire Co., District Court of the U.S., District of New Jersey, In Equity 648, October Term 1920, Brief for Plaintiff on Final Hearing, p. 43.

67 On Langmuir's drive for reputation and income, see Reich, "Langmuir," pp. 205–9.

68 Percy Bridgman, "Some of the Physical Aspects of the Work of Langmuir," in C. G. Suits, ed., *The Collected Works of Irving Langmuir* (New York, 1962), Vol. 1, p. xxxiii. Langmuir's apparatus consisted of a light bulb connected to a vacuum system, a pressure

gauge, a meter to measure energy consumption (thus indicating filament temperature), and a means to analyze gases.

69 See, e.g., "The Characteristics of Tungsten Filaments as Functions of Temperature," *Physical Review*, 7 (1916):302; and "Tungsten Lamps of High Efficiency," *Proceedings of the American Institute of Electrical Engineers*, 32 (1913):1894. Quoted in Albert Rosenfeld, *The Quintessence of Irving Langmuir* (New York, 1966), p. 129. Langmuir may have had Coolidge in mind when he referred to a "direct and logical attack."

70 Langmuir Laboratory Notebook No. 458, 21 May 1913, Langmuir Papers, pp. 144–51; Bridgman, "Physical Aspects," p. xxxvi; Langmuir, "The Effect of Space Charge and Residual Gases on Thermionic Currents in High Vacuum," *Physical Review*, 2 (1913):450–86; George Wise, "Ionists in Industry: The Beginnings of Physical Chemistry Research at General Electric, 1900–1915," unpub. MS read at the annual meeting of the Society for the History of Technology, 1981.

71 Irving Langmuir, "The Condensation Pump," *Journal of the Franklin Institute*, 182 (1916):719–43; White, *Electronics Development at General Electric*, p. III-3, on the oven; Langmuir U.S. Patents 1237210 (tungsten "getter") and 1126233 (molecular gauge).

72 Quoted in Rosenfeld, *Langmuir*, p. 119.

73 Langmuir to his mother, 9 February 1910, Box 2, Langmuir Papers.

74 "Convection and Conduction of Heat in Gases," *Physical Review*, 34 (1912):401; "Convection and Radiation of Heat," *Transactions of the American Electrochemical Society*, 23 (1913):299; "Laws of Heat Transmission in Electrical Machinery," *Proceedings of the American Institute of Electrical Engineers*, 32 (1913):391.

75 Robert Kohler, "Irving Langmuir and the 'Octet' Theory of Valence," *Historical Studies in the Physical Sciences*, 4 (1974):45.

76 The papers appeared in the *Journal of the American Chemical Society*, 38 (1916):2221–95 and 39 (1917):1848–1906; Kohler, " 'Octet' Theory," p. 47.

77 C. G. Suits and M. J. Martin, "Irving Langmuir," *National Academy of Sciences Biographical Memoirs*, 45 (1974):223; Kenneth Kingdon, "From Submarines to A-Bombs," *G.E. Research Laboratory Bulletin* (1959):12.

78 Langmuir, "Summary of Work for 1924," 16 January 1925, pp. 8–9, microfilm reel 30, Whitney Library.

79 Vincent Schaeffer, interviewed by George Wise, 24 May 1977, p. 3, copy at Public Info. Office; Irving Langmuir, "Address to the American Chemical Society," (1920), in Lawrence Hawkins, *Adventure Into the Unknown* (New York, 1950), pp. 35–6. See, e.g., Irving Langmuir (with H. A. Jones), "The Characteristics of Tungsten Filaments as Functions of Temperature," *General Electric Review*, 30 (1927):310–15, 354–61, 408–12.

80 H. Mott-Smith, interview by George Wise, 1 March 1977, pp. 6–7.

81 Kingdon, "From Submarines to A-Bombs," p. 13.

82 Suits and Martin, "Irving Langmuir," p. 222.

Chapter 6

1 A harmonic telegraph transmitted several musical tones upon which signals were impressed. Resonant detectors at the receiver responded to each note and separated the signals. The duplex and quadruplex telegraphs sent two and four messages respectively, half in each direction.

2 For much greater detail as well as an understanding of the excitement in Bell's work, see Robert V. Bruce, *Bell: Alexander Graham Bell and the Conquest of Solitude* (London, 1973), pp. 120–76. Allegations were made that a dishonest patent examiner gave Bell information about Gray's invention, and that Bell amended his application accordingly. See *ibid.*, pp. 172–3,277–8.

3 To put this value in perspective, $100,000 in 1876 would be worth well over $1,000,000 at the time of this writing.

4 Gerald Brock, *The Telecommunications Industry* (Cambridge, Mass., 1981), p. 93.

5 Quoted in W. H. Doherty, "Early Corporate History," in M. D. Fagan, ed., *A History of Engineering and Science in the Bell System: The Early Years (1875–1925)* (Bell Telephone Laboratories, 1975), p. 26.

6 John Brooks, *Telephone: The First Hundred Years* (New York, 1975), pp. 65–6.

7 Bruce, *Bell*, p. 258. After working as a telegraph operator, Vail joined the Postal Service in 1868, where he soon made major improvements to operations and routing. In 1876, at age thirty, he became head of the Railway Mail Service Commission. During his tenure as Bell general manager, Vail showed his technical orientation by taking out a dozen telephone-related patents. John Paine, *In One Man's Life: The Personal and Business Career of Theodore N. Vail* (New York, 1921), p. 159.

8 Alvin Harlow, *Old Wires and New Waves* (New York, 1936), p. 382; Brock, *The Telecommunications Industry*, pp. 94–5; Alfred D. Chandler, Jr., *The Visible Hand* (Cambridge, Mass., 1977), p. 201.

9 Bell himself called Forbes "a wealthy man of great influence who has a reputation of thorough integrity." Arthur Pier, *Forbes – Telephone Pioneer* (New York, 1953), p. 80.

10 Brooks, *Telephone*, pp. 83–4; Brock, *the Telecommunications Industry*, p. 106.

11 This information on administrative structure was provided to the

author by Dr. Robert Garnet, historian at AT&T. See Robert Garnet, *The Telephone Enterprise: The Evolution of the Bell System's Horizontal Structure, 1876–1909* (Ph.D. Dissertation, The Johns Hopkins University, 1984), esp. pp. 103–39.

12 Brooks, *Telephone*, pp. 81–2; Brock, *The Telecommunications Industry*, pp. 107–8. James J. Storrow to John E. Hudson, 17 November 1891, quoted in U.S. Federal Communications Commission, *Investigation Pursuant to Public Resolution No. 8*, 74th Congress, Exhibit 1989, p. 10. Copy at FCC Library, Washington, D.C. (hereafter FCC Investigation).

13 Herbert Casson, *The History of the Telephone* (Chicago, 1911), p. 79; N. R. Danielian, *AT&T: The Story of Industrial Conquest* (New York, 1939), p. 94.

14 Each year, Edison received $6,000 compensation and up to $4,000 for expenses. Between 1884 and 1886 he assigned a number of telephone-related patents to Bell. In 1886 the agreement was changed so that, for the same consideration, Edison made himself available to the company as a consultant. "Agreement Between American Bell Telephone Company and Thomas A. Edison," October 1884 (no day), Document File, Edison Archives, West Orange, N.J.; "Agreement Between American Bell Telephone Company and Thomas A. Edison," 16 February 1886, Box 1221, AT&T Archives and Historical Library, New York (hereafter AT&T Archives).

15 Testimony of T. N. Vail, Western Union Telegraph Company, et al. vs. The American Bell Telephone Company (1907), in FCC Investigation, Exhibit 2112, p. 20.

16 Quoted in *ibid.*, p. 12.

17 Horace Coon, *American Telephone and Telegraph: The Story of a Great Monopoly* (New York, 1939), p. 91.

18 Brock, *The Telecommunications Industry*, p. 107; U.S. Federal Communications Commission, *Investigation of the Telephone Industry*, (Washington, D.C., 1939), p. 353.

19 Brock, *The Telecommunications Industry*, p. 107; Brooks, *Telephone*, p. 108. Bell's long-distance lines accounted for some of the discrepancy in assets. It should be noted that the parent company did not have full control over the prices charged by the licensees, nor was it always able to make them conform to its technical standards (accounting for some service inconsistencies).

20 Brooks, *Telephone*, p. 121.

21 Coon, *AT&T*, p. 100.

22 Berliner had already applied for a patent on a resistance-type telephone transmitter when Watson recommended that he be hired. Anders had also proven himself as a telephone inventor before he joined the staff, with a system that permitted two telephones on the same line to be rung independently. Quotes from Vail to Thomas

Lockwood (Bell patent attorney), 5 February 1881, FCC Investigation, Exhibit 1951A, Appendix C.

23 "Improvements in Efficiencies of Transmitters," 25 June, 1907, Boston Files, Folder 445, Bell Telephone Laboratories Archives, Short Hills, N.J. (hereafter BTLA).

24 "American Bell Telephone Company Annual Report for 1880," p. 6.

25 W. H. Doherty, "Early Corporate History," p. 38; Lillian Hoddeson, "The Emergence of Basic Research in the Bell Telephone System, 1875–1915," *Technology and Culture*, 22 (1981):521.

26 "Annual Report of the American Telephone and Telegraph Company for 1902," p. 7; "Annual Report of the American Telephone and Telegraph Company for 1906," p. 7.

27 Hoddeson, "Emergence of Basic Research," p. 522; Hayes to John Hudson (member of the board of directors and soon to be president), 26 October 1887, FCC Investigation, Exhibit 1951A, p. 44.

28 Hayes to Hudson, 7 March 1892, FCC Investigation, Exhibit 1951A, p. 47.

29 Quoted in FCC Investigation, Exhibit 1951A, p. 74.

30 Neil Wasserman, "The Path from Invention to Innovation: The Case of Long-Distance Telephone Transmission at the Turn of the Century," unpub. MS provided by the author, 1982, pp. 60–1; Doherty, "Early Corporate History," p. 41.

31 Wasserman, "The Path from Invention to Innovation," pp. 49–55. See George H. Clark, *The Life of John Stone Stone* (San Diego, 1946).

32 Hayes to Hudson, 30 March 1896 and 12 January 1899, AT&T Archives. I thank Michal McMahon for bringing this incident and these source to my attention.

33 For an explanation of Campbell's work, see James E. Brittain, "The Introduction of the Loading Coil: George A. Campbell and Michael I. Pupin," *Technology and Culture*, 11 (January 1970):36–57. Had Alexander Graham Bell been so hesitant, the controlling patents on the telephone would most certainly have gone to Elisha Gray and Western Union!

34 George Campbell, "Notes on Legal Work Upon the Case," 22 November 1911, p. 1, J. J. Carty Executive Files, Folder 17, BTLA; Wasserman, "The Path from Invention to Innovation," pp. 32–8, 108–9, 131–4.

35 Hoddeson, "The Emergence of Basic Research," p. 524.

36 Jewett said that Michelson thought he was "prostituting my training and ideals" by going to work for Bell. Testimony before the Temporary National Economic Committee, quoted in George Folk, *Patents and Industrial Progress* (New York, 1942), p. 153. Jewett's engineering alma mater, Throop, later became the California Institute of Technology.

37 Doherty, "Early Corporate History," pp. 42–3. Campbell to Lloyd Espenschied, 4 May 1950, Box 32, Lloyd Espenschied Papers, Division of Electricity, Smithsonian Institution.
38 "Engineering Department Annual Report for 1906," pp. 4–5. In this report Hayes set out his frustrations, both in dealing with uncooperative operating company engineers and in being forced to take on complex technical problems without adequate background research.
39 Hoddeson, "The Emergence of Basic Research," p. 528.

Chapter 7

1 Morgan to Vail, 9 May 1907, quoted in Federal Communications Commission, *Investigation Pursuant to Public Resolution No. 8*, 74th Congress, Exhibit 2096F, Appendix 13, sheet 1 (hereafter FCC Investigation).
2 W. S. Gifford, "The Place of the Bell Telephone Laboratories in the Bell System," *Bell Telephone Quarterly*, 4 (1925):89–93; F. B. Jewett, "R&D in the Bell System," 9 March 1926, pp. 3–4, Frank B. Jewett Collection, Folder 111, Bell Telephone Laboratories Archives, Short Hills, N.J. (hereafter BTLA).
3 J. J. Carty to E. J. Hall (AT&T vice-president), 17 July 1907, p. 3, Box 2045, AT&T Archives and Historical Library, New York (hereafter AT&T Archives); Neil Wasserman, "The Path from Invention to Innovation: The Case of Long-Distance Telephone Transmission at the Turn of the Century," unpub. MS provided by the author, 1982, pp. 134–6, 152.
4 Horace Coon, *AT&T: The Story of a Great Monopoly* (New York, 1939), p. 105; John Brooks, *Telephone: The First One Hundred Years* (New York, 1975), pp. 129–30; R. W. Devonshire to Thomas Edison, 30 September 1907 and Edison to Devonshire, 1 October 1907, Box 1221, AT&T Archives. I thank Paul Israel for bringing these documents to my attention.
5 Alfred D. Chandler, *The Visible Hand* (Cambridge, Mass., 1977), p. 202; Robert Garnet, "Organizational Changes Within the Bell System, 1909–1974," unpub. MS, provided by the author, 1984, pp. 8–9.
6 "American Telephone and Telegraph Company Annual Report for 1914," pp. 36–42. Between 1910 and 1920, AT&T holdings, both direct and indirect, accounted for 81% to 88% of the associated companies' equity. Robert Garnet, *The Telephone Enterprise: The Evolution of the Bell System's Horizontal Structure, 1876–1909* (Ph.D. Dissertation, The Johns Hopkins University, 1984), p. 232. Garnet

provides an excellent analysis of Vail's reorganization of the Bell System. See pp. 222–41.

7 Quoted from "American Telephone and Telegraph Company Annual Report for 1907," p. 18.

8 Morgan helped by seeing to it that any independents who showed signs of financial difficulties had their credit cut off. The Panic of 1907 had weakened many of them badly.

9 See Hugh Aitken, *Syntony and Spark: The Origins of Radio* (New York, 1976) for a discussion of early work on the commercialization of radio.

10 Hayes to Frederick Fish, 2 April 1907, quoted in W. Rupert Maclaurin, *Invention and Innovation in the Radio Industry* (New York, 1949), p. 65.

11 Lockwood to Vail, 8 July 1907, quoted in Maclaurin, *Invention and Innovation*, p. 66.

12 Leonard Reich, "Industrial Research and the Pursuit of Corporate Security: The Early Years of Bell Labs," *Business History Review*, 54 (1980):511.

13 De Forest and his partners made substantial profits through the sale of heavily "watered" stock in the stations. Their activities also resulted in a court injunction and a fine because of de Forest's repeated infringement of a Fessenden patent. I thank Susan Douglas for bringing these points to my attention.

14 Maclaurin, *Invention and Innovation*, pp. 80–1. De Forest had earned a Ph.D. in physics from Yale, but he invented largely by an imaginative cut-and-try method.

15 Georgette Carneal, *A Conquerer of Space* (New York, 1930), p. 198; *New York Times*, 1 April 1908, p. 4.

16 17 April 1909, p. 1.

17 *New York Tribune*, 1 November 1908, quoted in "For Period up to Time of Vacuum Tube Radiotelephone, 1914," in notebook titled "Rate Cases," AT&T Archives.

18 Quoted in "For Period up to Time of Vacuum Tube Radiotelephone, 1914." Carty replied to the operating company president that radio remained unreliable and the company was in the process of gathering information. "Fear on the Part of the Public of Radio Competition with Telephone Wires – Examples of Letters from AT&T Stockholders," in *ibid.*

19 I. B. Crandall to C. E. Scribner, 30 March 1914, Case File 320036, Vol. T-2, BTLA. As late as 1914 AT&T used an electromechanical repeater on the New York to Washington, D.C., line.

20 "Additional Force Required – Engineer," 8 April 1909, quoted in Federal Communications Commission, *Investigation of the Telephone Industry* (Washington, D.C., 1939), pp. 189–90.

21 FCC Investigation, Exhibit 1951A, p. 133.

22 Frank Jewett, "General Repeater Study," quoted in Thomas Shaw, "The Conquest of Distance by Wire Telephone," *Bell System Technical Journal*, 23 (1944):372; Oliver Buckley, "Frank B. Jewett," *National Academy of Sciences Biographical Memoirs*, 27 (1952):246. Note Jewett's use of "skilled physicists" to impress upon his special audience the practical, engineering possibilities of science.

23 "Western Electric Engineering Department Annual Report for 1911," p. 23, BTLA (hereafter WEEDAR).

24 H. D. Arnold, U.S. Patents 1118172 (applied for 1912, granted 1914) [hereafter (1912/14)]; 1118173 (1912/14); 1118174 (1912/14); 1118175 (1912/14); J. W. Emling, "Telephone Transmission – The Wire Plant," in M. D. Fagan, ed., *History of Engineering and Science in the Bell System: The Early Years (1875–1925)* (Bell Telephone Laboratories, 1975), p. 258; WEEDAR for 1911, pp. 24–5; quote from WEEDAR for 1912, pp. 3 (quote), 5.

25 WEEDAR for 1911, p. 26.

26 E. H. Colpitts, "Disclosure of John Stone Stone and Lee De Forest October 30 and 31, 1912," 26 November 1912, Case File 320036, Vol. T-1, p. 1, BTLA; General Electric Co. vs. De Forest Radio Co., District Court of the U.S., District of Delaware, In Equity 589598, Printed Record of Final Hearing (1926), Vol. 1, p. 557.

27 Lloyd Espenschied, "Some Early Bell Labs Milestones in the Development of the Vacuum Tube" unpub. MS, 1945, Box 5, Lloyd Espenschied Collection, Division of Electricity, Smithsonian Institution (hereafter Espenschied Collection); quotes from E. H. Colpitts, "Report on the Development of the Cathode Beam Detector and Repeater," 25 November 1912, Case File 320036, Vol. T-1, BTLA, and from E. H. Colpitts, "Disclosure of John Stone Stone and Lee De Forest," p. 9.

28 Jewett to Lockwood, 27 December 1912, Case File 320036, Vol. T-1, BTLA; Lockwood to Carty, 17 February 1913, and Arnold's comments on same, dated 26 February 1913, quoted in Lloyd Espenschied, "Progress in Understanding the Audion," unpub. MS, 1948, p. 3, Box 5, Espenschied Collection; Gleason Archer, *History of Radio to 1926* (New York, 1938), pp. 107–9.

29 E. H. Colpitts, "Use of Gaseous Valve as Telephone Repeater," 26 November 1912, Case File 320036, Vol. T-1, pp. 3–4, BTLA; Gerald Tyne, *The Saga of the Vacuum Tube* (Indianapolis, Ind., 1977), pp. 86–7.

30 E. H. Colpitts, "1915 Radio Telephone Tests Over Transoceanic Distances," unpub. MS, 1939, Notebook C3, pp. 3–4, AT&T Archives; R. A. Heising, "1915 Arlington Radio Experiments," unpub. MS, n.d. (c. 1937), p. 1, Paul Watson Collection, Box 5, Division of Electricity, Smithsonian Institution.

31 The molecules combined with metal evaporating from the filament

at high temperature, forming a solid precipitate. In Equity 589598, Vol. 2, p. 714; L. M. Whyte, "The Young Man and the Tube," *WE* (Western Electric corporate journal), 25, No. 7 (1973):31–3; In Equity 589598, Vol. 1, p. 591; Vol. 2, p. 714; Espenschied, "Progress in Understanding the Audion," p. 3.

32 In Equity 589598, Vol. 1, p. 614; Tyne, *Saga of the Vacuum Tube*, p. 90.

33 H. J. van der Bijl, who supervised the work, reported on the apparatus used: "In this bulb the distance between plate, filament and grid could be changed electromagnetically from without. Four grids of different mesh were mounted on a stem which could be rotated electromagnetically so as to bring any one of the four grids into position." Van der Bijl Laboratory Notebook 41, 18 April 1914, BTLA.

34 Espenschied, "Progress in Understanding the Audion," p. 4; van der Bijl Laboratory Notebook 41, 18 April 1914; O. E. Dunlap, *Radio's 100 Men of Science* (New York, 1944), p. 228.

35 Leonard Reich, *Radio Electronics and the Development of Industrial Research in the Bell System* (Ph.D. dissertation, The Johns Hopkins University, 1977), pp. 57–60.

36 Quoted in Frank Jewett, "John J. Carty: Telephone Engineer," *Bell Telephone Quarterly*, 16 (1937):170.

37 Frederick Rhoades, *John J. Carty* (New York, 1932), pp. 79–80; WEEDAR for 1916, p. 7.

38 Brooks, *Telephone*, p. 130. One researcher spoke of "the almost military conduct attitude which began with J. J. Carty and ran down through the organization. . . . The 'boss' was promised what he wanted and heaven and earth were torn up to give it to him"; Carl Englund, "1915 Radio Transmissions," unpub. MS, n.d.(c. 1935), p. 10, AT&T Archives.

39 Quoted in Rhoades, *Carty*, p. 82.

40 Heising, "1915 Arlington Radio Experiments," p. 18; John Mills to Carty, "Definition of Terms Used in the Literature of Wireless Transmission," 3 February 1916, J. J. Carty File, Book 50, Vol. 1, BTLA. Espenschied claimed that George Campbell served as "a scientific 'wet nurse' " to Carty, quoted in Lloyd Espenschied, "G. A. Campbell, His Inventive Contributions: The Wave Filter," unpub. MS, 1954, p. 1, Box 14, Espenschied Collection.

41 W. H. Doherty, "Early Corporate History," in Fagan, ed., *History of Engineering and Science in the Bell System*, pp. 50–1; Frank Jewett, "The Engineering Department of the Western Electric Co.," *Western Electric News*, 3 (June 1914):2.

42 Lloyd Espenschied, "The Telephone Company's Early Record," unpub. MS, 1962, pp. 4–5, Box 8, Espenschied Collection. Another researcher who questioned Jewett's technical capabilities com-

mented: "He went up the line so fast that his mistakes never caught up with him." John Mills, quoted in Espenschied to Herman Affel, 11 April 1958, Box 18, Espenschied Collection.

43 R. V. L. Hartley, Laboratory Notebook 202, 9 May 1919, BTLA; Heising, "1915 Arlington Radio Experiments," p. 1. Jewett's position was primarily that of an administrator of science, rather than a practitioner. In the modern era of organized research and development, this new role – like that of the politician of science – became vital to maintaining support and direction for some of the most important research institutions.

44 Englund, "1915 Radio Transmissions," p. 5.

45 WEEDAR for 1914, page D. See also pp. 20–2.

46 "Wireless Wafts Voice 4,600 Miles: Future of Wireless Phone," 1 October 1915, Box 1144, AT&T Archives. For technical reasons, transatlantic wired telephony was not possible for several more decades. Problems included inherently high attenuation and distortion in cables of this length and the infeasibility of placing vacuum-tube repeaters on the ocean floor.

47 Colpitts to Jewett, "Wireless Telephony," 19 January 1914, p. 1, Case File 320036, Vol. A, BTLA; E. M. Miller to B. Gherardi, 15 April 1913, Joint File O&E and D&R 212, BTLA.

48 R. H. Wilson to Colpitts, 11 November 1922, FCC Investigation, Exhibit 243, Appendix 7, p. 1; Colpitts to Jewett, "Wireless Telephony," 19 January 1914, p. 12, Case File 320036, Vol. A, BTLA; Lloyd Espenschied, "The Budding and Blossoming of Multiplex, Wide-Band, Electronic Communications," unpub. MS, n.d., Box 18, Espenschied Collection.

49 Espenschied to E. L. Bowles, 2 July 1952, p. 11, Box 17, Espenschied Collection; Heising, "1915 Arlington Radio Experiments," p. 8.

50 Lloyd Espenschied, "Biography of John Carson," unpub. MS, 1956, p. 1, Box 7, Espenschied Collection; E. B. Craft and E. H. Colpitts, "Radio Telephony," *American Institute of Electrical Engineers Transactions*, 38 (1919):311; Heising, "1915 Arlington Radio Experiments," p. 8.

51 Heising, "1915 Arlington Radio Experiments," p. 1; Arnold, U.S. Patents 1129942 (1914/15), 1403475 (1915/22), 1129943 (1914/15); R. V. L. Hartley Laboratory Notebook 37, 7 May 1915, BTLA; Reich, *Radio Electronics and the Development of Industrial Research in the Bell System*, pp. 64–6.

52 Espenschied, "The Budding and Blossoming of Multiplex, Wide-Band, Electronic Communications," p. 6. The combination was actually patented jointly in the names of Arnold and Colpitts, U.S. Patent 1388450 (1915/21).

53 Heising, "1915 Arlington Radio Experiments," pp. 9–10.

54 See, for example, E. H. Armstrong's classic article, "Some Recent

Developments in the Audion Receiver," *Institute of Radio Engineers Proceedings*, 3 (1915):215–38; E. H. Colpitts to H. W. Nichols, 25 January 1915, Joint Files O&E and D&R 2523, Vol. 1, BTLA; H. D. Arnold, U.S. Patents 1200796 (1915/16), 1504537 (1915/24), 1367224 (1916/21).

55 William Wilson, "A New Type of High Power Vacuum Tube," *Bell System Technical Journal*, 1 (1922):5; Heising, "1915 Arlington Radio Experiments," pp. 9–10, 16–17.

56 To officially demonstrate New York-to-California wired/wireless communication, Vail spoke the "first words" to Carty. Bell researcher John Mills later recalled: "Word came that Mr. Vail was ready to talk and we cut the New York line through to the transmitter. I was monitoring in and heard a voice say 'Hello, hello,' and then Mr. Carty's reply, 'Hello, Mr. Vail, I recognized your voice instantly.' Just then the operator told me that Mr. Vail was not yet on so I flashed a profane message to [California] to that effect. A few seconds later Vail's voice was heard, and Carty replied exactly as before." Quoted in "Personal Recollections of Arlington Radio," p. 9, Box 1114, AT&T Archives; Heising, "1915 Arlington Radio Experiments," pp. 10–15, 26.

57 Quoted in *Electrical World*, 9 October 1915, p. 790.

58 H. W. Nichols, U.S. Patent 1325574 (1915/19); J. Carson, U.S. Patent 1309459 (1915/19); Lloyd Espenschied, "Advent of Electronic Telephony," unpub. MS, n.d., Box 8, Espenschied Collection.

59 WEEDAR for 1914, p. E; WEEDAR for 1915, pp. 4,24; WEEDAR for 1916, pp. 3,42.

60 T. N. Vail, quoted in FCC Investigation, Exhibit 2112, p. 20.

61 Reese Jenkins, *Images and Enterprise: Technology and the American Photographic Industry, 1839–1925* (Baltimore, 1975), see especially p. 5.

62 J. P. Morgan's recent death may also have removed some of the impetus toward monopolization. Brooks, *Telephone*, pp. 132–7.

63 Jewett, "J. J. Carty: Telephone Engineer," p. 80; Heising, "1915 Arlington Radio Experiments," p. 5.

64 Reich, *Radio Electronics and the Development of Industrial Research in the Bell System*, pp. 70–85; Tyne, *Saga of the Vacuum Tube*, p. 146.

65 Thayer to Jewett, 29 May 1919, Joint File O&E and D&R 2523, Vol. 2, BTLA; Lloyd Espenschied, "High Speed Transoceanic Radio Telegraphy," 21 April 1919, *ibid.*

66 17 May 1919, Joint File O&E and D&R 2523, Vol. 2, BTLA.

67 "Discussion of the Development Expense on Radio Incurred by the Bell System," Notebook C3, Section 1, Chart labeled "Grand Summary," AT&T Archives. By comparison, the entire budget for the GE Research Laboratory was $553,000 in 1916 (the last year for which figures are available), and over $300,000 of that came

from in-house manufacture and services. "Research Laboratory Report, Schenectady Works, 1916," Public Information Office, GE R&D Center, Schenectady, N.Y.

68 Reich, *Radio Electronics and the Development of Industrial Research in the Bell System*, Appendix B, pp. 196–212.

69 Harry Thayer, "The Development of Development and Research," *Bell Telephone Quarterly*, 4 (1925):5–6; WEEDAR for 1919, pp. 78–89; WEEDAR for 1922, Appendix 1. At the end of 1921 total employment in the Engineering Department stood at almost 2,900. *Ibid.*, Appendix 3.2.

70 WEEDAR for 1922, pp. 59–72. Much of this research was conducted in conjunction with the Development and Transmission Branches.

71 "Notes on Research and Development Policy," 1924, Box 53, AT&T Archives.

72 W. H. Doherty, "Early Corporate History," in M. D. Fagan, ed., *A History of Engineering and Science in the Bell System: The Early Years (1875–1925)* (Bell Telephone Laboratories, 1975), pp. 52–3; FCC Investigation, Exhibit 50, p. 64.

Chapter 8

1 See the tree-structure diagram of the administration of the department in 1915: W. H. Doherty, "Early Corporate History," in M. D. Fagan, ed., *A History of Engineering and Science in the Bell System* (Bell Telephone Laboratories, 1975), pp. 50–1.

2 R. A. Heising, "1915 Arlington Radio Experiments," unpub. MS, n.d. (c. 1937), Vol. 5, Paul Watson Collection, Division of Electricity, Smithsonian Institution; Carl Englund, "The 1915 Radio Transmission," unpub. MS, n.d. (c. 1935), pp. 28–9, Box 1114, AT&T Archives and Historical Library, New York (hereafter AT&T Archives).

3 B. B. Webb, "Arlington Radio Demonstration," unpub. MS, n.d. (c. 1935), p. 2, Box 1114, AT&T Archives.

4 John Mills, "Personal Recollections of Arlington Radio," unpub. MS, n.d. (c. 1935), p. 7, Box 1114, AT&T Archives.

5 Heising, "1915 Arlington Radio Experiments," p. 5.

6 Jewett to E. B. Craft, 4 June 1914, Case File 320036, Vol. A, AT&T Bell Telephone Laboratories Archives, Short Hills, N.J. (hereafter BTLA).

7 Of all the researchers at work on vacuum tubes and radio during this period, only one appears to have left and gone on to aid the competition. A. M. Nicolson resigned from the company to become a private consultant and independent inventor in 1923. See, for example, Nicolson, U.S. Patent 1636921, applied for 1926;

granted 1927 (hereafter [1926/27]), assigned to the Wired Radio Company. Note that, unlike GE, Bell did not at this time have a general colloquium for the purpose of sharing research results.

8 Lloyd Espenschied, "Progress in Understanding the Audion," 1948, p. 5, Box 5, Espenschied Collection, Division of Electricity, Smithsonian Institution (hereafter Espenschied Collection). Notation handwritten and dated 26 June 1970. Van der Bijl returned to his native South Africa to head a new industrial organization.

9 Lloyd Espenschied, "Bell System Sources of Vacuum Tube Historical Information," unpub. MS, 1944, p. 2, Box 5, Espenschied Collection. These papers were written under the heading "Memorandum for File." See, e.g., I. B. Crandall, "Energy and Current Regulation in Vacuum Tubes," 5 July 1915, 5 pp., Case File 320036, Vol. T-2, BTLA.

10 Jewett to Carty, 3 July 1914, Case File 320036, Vol. T-2, BTLA.

11 Jewett to Millikan, 18 June 1914, Case File 320036, Vol. T-2, BTLA; Jewett to *Physical Review*, 9 July 1914, *ibid.*; J.W. Woodrow, "Experiments on the Production and Measurement of High Vacua," *Physical Review*, 4 (1914):491–7. See Jewett to Carty, 10 November 1916, J.J. Carty File, Book 50, Vol. 2, BTLA.

12 Unsigned, August 1963, p. 542. Armstrong's paper was titled "Some Recent Developments in the Audion Receiver," *Institute of Radio Engineers Proceedings*, 3 (1915):215–38. For an account of Armstrong's life and work see Lawrence Lessing, *Man of High Fidelity* (New York, 1969).

13 Espenschied, "Progress in Understanding the Audion," pp. 4–5; Paul Pierce Laboratory Notebook, 11 February 1913, quoted in Lloyd Espenschied, "Some Early Bell Labs Milestones in the Development of the Vacuum Tube," unpub. MS, 1945, p. 5, Box 5, Espenschied Collection.

14 Lloyd Espenschied, "Genesis of Electronic Carrier and Radio, 1912–1916, Case 37014," unpub. MS, 1954, pp. 8–9, Box 14, Espenschied Collection; Heising, "1915 Arlington Radio Experiments," p. 13.

15 Campbell to Espenschied, 4 May 1950, Box 32, Espenschied Collection.

16 Quoted in Federal Communications Commission, *Investigation Pursuant to Public Resolution No. 8*, 74th Congress, Exhibit 2112, p. 2 (hereinafter FCC Investigation).

17 R. A. Heising, "Modulation in Radiotelephony," *Institute of Radio Engineers Proceedings*, 9 (1921):316. Lloyd Espenschied called these minor variations "paper patents." See Espenschied, "John Mills Patents on Radio and Carrier," unpub. MS, 1945, Espenschied Papers, BTLA.

18 R. A. Heising to L. Espenschied, 29 November 1962, Box 7, Espenschied Collection. Emphasis added.

19 "Western Electric Engineering Department Annual Report for 1916," p. 34 (hereinafter WEEDAR).
20 H. W. Nichols, "Alexanderson High Frequency Alternator," 17 May 1915, Case File 200670, Vol. 2–A, BTLA; Arnold, U.S. Patent 1375481 (1915/21); Van der Bijl, U.S. Patent 1301525 (1915/19); Heising, U.S. Patents 1341211 (1915/20) and 1383807 (1915/21).
21 J. J. Carty, "Science and Business," *National Research Council Reprint*, 55 (1924):4.
22 H. D. Arnold, "So-Called 'Ionization' Pressure of the Corona Discharge," paper presented to the October 1916 meeting of the American Physical Society. Abstract in *Physical Review*, 9 (1917):93.
23 During his early years at Bell, Jewett actually hoped to return to academia through an appointment to the University of Chicago faculty. *The Autobiography of Robert A. Millikan* (New York, 1950), pp. 52–3; Frank Jewett, "Industrial Research with Some Notes Concerning Its Scope in the Bell System," *American Institute of Electrical Engineers Transactions*, 36 (1917):854; WEEDAR for 1919, p. 58. Western Electric also began to sell home appliances at this time. They were manufactured by outside suppliers to Engineering Department specifications and sold under the Western Electric name. See *ibid.*, p. 70.
24 J. G. Roberts (attorney in the AT&T Patent Department) to Jewett, 24 June 1919, Case File 320036, Vol. T-3, BTLA; see, e.g., R. V. L. Hartley, "Vacuum Tube Amplifiers in Parallel," *Institute of Radio Engineers Proceedings*, 9 (1921):250–4; T. C. Fry, "The Thermionic Current Between Parallel Plane Electrodes," *Physical Review*, 17 (1921):441–52.
25 Jewett to Carty, 10 November 1916, J. J. Carty File, Book 50, Vol. 2, BTLA. See, e.g., W. Wilson, "The Loss of Energy of Wehnelt Cathodes by Electron Emission," *National Academy of Sciences Proceedings*, 3 (1917):426–7; George Southworth, *Forty Years of Radio Research* (New York, 1962), pp. 59–60.
26 WEEDAR for 1922, p. 75.
27 Jewett, "Industrial Research with Some Notes Concerning Its Scope in the Bell System," p. 850.
28 Robert Kargon, "The New Era: Science and American Individualism in the 1920s," in Robert Kargon, ed., *The Maturing of American Science* (Washington, D.C., 1974), p. 13. See Chapter 10 *infra*.
29 WEEDAR for 1914, p. 36; WEEDAR for 1915, p. 20; WEEDAR for 1916, p. 35. By way of comparison, the GE Research Laboratory's library had 1,400 volumes and 64 journals in 1915.
30 I. B. Crandall, "A History of the Colloquium," *Bell Laboratories Record*, 1 (1925):120.
31 Heising, "1915 Arlington Radio Experiments," p. 2; W. H. Doherty, "The Spirit of Research," in Fagan, ed., *A History of Engi-*

neering and Science in the Bell System, p. 986. The physicist was Karl Darrow, who earned his Ph.D. under Millikan at Chicago.

32 R. V. L. Hartley Laboratory Notebook 202, 32 December 1918, p. 146, BTLA; Heising, "1915 Arlington Radio Experiments," p. 6; see R. Bown, C. Englund, and H. Friis, "Radio Transmission Measurements," *Institute of Radio Engineers Proceedings*, 11 (1923):115–52; R. Bown, D. Martin, and R. Potter, "Studies in Radio Broadcasting Transmission," *Institute of Radio Engineers Proceedings*, 14 (1926):57–131.

33 Davisson to O.W. Richardson, 3 October 1922, quoted in Richard Gherenbeck, *Davisson, Germer and the Discovery of Electron Diffraction* (Ph.D. dissertation, University of Minnesota, 1973), p. 29.

34 Irving Langmuir, "The Effect of Space Charge and Residual Gases on Thermionic Currents in High Vacuum," *Physical Review*, 2 (1913):450,483–4; Gherenbeck, *Davisson, Germer and the Discovery of Electron Diffraction*, p. 31. Langmuir claimed that Arnold could not have achieved high-vacuum operation because Wehnelt filaments required the presence of gas to emit electrons. Arnold asserted that they did not. He claimed priority and later argued that the use of high vacuum was not a patentable invention.

35 H. D. Arnold, "Phenomena in Oxide-Coated Filament Electron Tubes," *Physical Review*, 16 (1920):81. Recall that, for patent defense purposes, the GE attorneys cited Langmuir's scientific publications and Coolidge's medal from the American Academy of Arts and Sciences to emphasize the original nature of their work. See Chapter 5, *supra*.

36 Interference No. 40,380. Arnold vs. Langmuir, District of Columbia Court of Appeals, *Transcript of Record*, 1916, pp. 22–6; WEEDAR for 1916, p. 34; G. E. Folk to E. H. Colpitts, 5 February 1917, Case File 320036, Vol. T-3, BTLA.

37 A. M. Nicolson to Colpitts, 14 December 1914, 26 pp.; C. E. Scribner to D. C. Tanner, 28 December 1914; Tanner to Scribner, 8 February 1915, all in Case File 320036, Vol. T-2, BTLA.

38 Jewett to D. C. Tanner, 8 March 1917, Case File 320036, Vol. T-3, BTLA.

39 C. E. Scribner to D. C. Tanner, 7 May 1914; Colpitts to Arnold, 15 June 1916; Scribner to Tanner, 7 November 1914, all in Case File 320036, Vol. T-2, BTLA.

40 H. B. Thayer to Carty, 13 October 1915, Carty File, Book 50, Vol. 2, BTLA.

41 WEEDAR for 1916, p. 32; quoted in WEEDAR for 1918, pp. 10–11.

42 In his final annual report, Carty's predecessor, Hammond Hayes, noted: "The general relation of the Engineering Department to the telephone interests at large is unsatisfactory. Our organization in

[Bell] is irregular and tends to prevent the improvement of the plant and operating which should be expected from so large and efficient a corps of engineers." "Annual Report – Engineering Department," 31 December 1906, p. 2, BTLA.

43 WEEDAR for 1914, pp. C–D.

44 M. J. Kelly, "The Bell Telephone Laboratories: An Example of an Institute of Creative Technology," *Proceedings of the Royal Society*, 203, Series A (1950):290–7.

45 *The Autobiography of Robert A. Millikan*, p. 118. Van der Bijl had taken his degree at Leipzig and came to do postdoctoral work with Millikan. Mills had been a graduate fellow under Millikan but never received the Ph.D.

46 For references to all of these papers, see Leonard Reich, *Radio Electronics and the Development of Industrial Research in the Bell System* (Ph.D. dissertation, The Johns Hopkins University, 1977), p. 111.

47 According to Jewett, Carty saw the research laboratory as "a sort of collective mind which, made up of experts in many fields who collaborated continually with one another, could arrive quickly at the solutions of [intricate] problems . . ." Quoted in Frank Jewett, "J. J. Carty, Telephone Engineer," *Bell Telephone Quarterly*, 16 (1937):163–4.

48 Quoted in Saul Dushman, "Educating Physicists for Industry," *Journal of Applied Physics*, 8 (1937):64.

49 Testimony before the Temporary National Economic Committee. TNEC *Final Report* (Washington, D.C., 1941), pp. 951–2.

50 Davisson to O. W. Richardson, 29 November 1914, quoted in Gherenbeck, *Davisson, Germer and the Discovery of Electron Diffraction*, pp. 40–1.

51 Englund, "The 1915 Radio Transmission," p. 23; R. A. Heising, "History of Airplane Radio," unpub. MS, n.d., p. 1, AT&T Archives. Germer was an exception, going on to become a scientist in his own right.

52 Southworth, *Forty Years of Radio Research*, p. 64; Jewett, "Industrial Research with Some Notes Concerning Its Scope in the Bell System," p. 848. Only P. I. Wold, who joined the lab with a Cornell Ph.D. in 1915, left during this period to take an academic position.

53 FCC Investigation, Exhibit 1951A, p. 142. Emphasis added.

54 Although not immediately obvious, it is reasonable to consider design methodologies as technologies because they are codified knowledge used to help alter the material world.

55 For an informative discussion of this issue, see Otto Mayr, "The Science–Technology Relationship as an Historiographic Problem," *Technology and Culture*, 17 (1976):663–73.

56 Southworth, *Forty Years of Radio Research*, p. 73.

57 Colpitts's report to Jewett, 6 December 1912, quoted in Espenschied, "Some Early Bell Labs Milestones in the Development for

the Vacuum Tube," p. 4; General Electric Co. vs. De Forest Radio Co., Equity Suit 589,598, District Court of the United States for Delaware, *Printed Record of Final Hearing*, 1926, Vol. 1, pp. 506–7, 589–91, 601–2; Vol. 2, p. 714.

58 C. D. Child, "Discharge From Hot CaO," *Physical Review*, 32 (1911):491–511.

59 Van der Bijl, Lab Notebook 41, 18 April 1914, p. 58, BTLA; unsigned memorandum, quoted in Espenschied, "Some Early Bell Labs Milestones in the Development of the Vacuum Tube," p. 4.

60 Colpitts to Arnold, 15 December 1915, p. 3, Case File 320036, Vol. T-2, BTLA.

61 Colpitts to Millikan, 19 January 1914, Case File 320036, Vol. T-1, BTLA; Espenschied, "Progress in Understanding the Audion," p. 4.

62 H. J. van der Bijl, "Theory of the Thermionic Amplifier," *Physical Review*, 12 (1918):171–98; *idem, The Thermionic Vacuum Tube* (New York, 1920), see especially pp. 44–6.

63 WEEDAR for 1916, p. 36. Papers published by laboratory researchers usually displayed extensive bibliographies to show that the authors had made themselves familiar with all pertinent literature.

64 Doherty, "The Spirit of Research," pp. 975–6. Davisson and Germer actually made a correction to O. W. Richardson's well-known emission equation as a result of their work: W. Housekeeper, "The Art of Sealing Base Metals Through Glass," *American Institute of Electrical Engineers Journal*, 42 (1923):956.

65 Doherty, "The Spirit of Research," p. 977.

66 *Ibid.*, p. 974.

67 R. A. Heising, "The Audion Oscillator," *Physical Review*, 16 (1920):216–37; *idem*, "The Audion Oscillator," *American Institute of Electrical Engineers Journal*, 39 (1920):365.

68 R. A. Heising, "Modulation in Radio Telephony," *Institute of Radio Engineers Proceedings*, 9 (1921):305–52; Carson, U.S. Patent 1448702 (1920/23). Impedance is the combined effect of resistance, inductance, and capacitance in an alternating current circuit.

69 Van der Bijl, *The Thermionic Vacuum Tube*, pp. 151–2; H. W. Nichols, "The Audion as a Circuit Element," *Physical Review*, 13 (1919):414; van der Bijl, *The Thermionic Vacuum Tube*, p. 10; C. J. Davisson to O. W. Richardson, 5 June 1917, RP10, R-346, Archives for the History of Quantum Physics, University of California, Berkeley.

70 Van der Bijl, *The Thermionic Vacuum Tube*, p. 10.

71 Heising, "1915 Arlington Radio Experiments," p. 3. A highly competent mathematician like T.C. Fry might go so far as to use Bessel's function and Fourier's series in his circuit work. See Fry, "Mathematical Methods of Investigation Resulting from the Application of Fourier's Integral," *Physical Review*, 14 (1919):115–36.

72 See, e.g., H. D. Arnold, U.S. Patent 1398665 (1920/21); R. Mathes, U.S. Patent 1442439 (1916/23); R. Hartley, U.S. Patent 1494905 (1919/24); J. Carson, U.S. Patent 1672056 (1924/28).
73 The patent was granted: G. Campbell, U.S. Patent 1227113 (1915/17).
74 Heising, "1915 Arlington Radio Experiments," pp. 3–4.
75 J. McKeen Cattell, ed., *American Men of Science* (3d edition, 1921). Included in the group with bachelor's degrees in engineering were R. Bown, J. Carson, H. W. Nichols, E. Wente, and P. I. Wold.
76 L. A. Hawkins to Whitney, 26 February 1923, p. 2, Willis Whitney Papers, Shaffer Library, Union College, Schenectady, N.Y.
77 3 July 1944, Box 32, Espenschied Collection.
78 Lloyd Espenschied, "Bell System Inventing," unpub. MS, 1940, p. 1, Box 18, Espenschied Collection.
79 Frank Jewett, "Utilizing the Results of Fundamental Research in the Communications Field," *Bell Telephone Quarterly*, 11 (1932):161.

Chapter 9

1 In an interference proceeding, the Patent Office – and the courts when there is an appeal – attempt to determine which of two or more applicants should be awarded priority for an invention.
2 Lloyd Espenschied, "The Origin and Development of Radiotelephony," *Institute of Radio Engineers Proceedings*, 25 (1937):1109.
3 W. Rupert Maclaurin, *Invention and Innovation in the Radio Industry* (New York, 1949), p. 85.
4 "License Agreement, General Electric Company and American Telephone and Telegraph Company, July 1, 1920," Article V, Paragraph 4, Section d,3, in Federal Trade Commission, *The Radio Industry* (Washington, D.C., 1923), p. 134.
5 Gerald Brock, *The Telecommunications Industry* (Cambridge, Mass., 1981), p. 167.
6 Federal Communications Commission, *Investigation Pursuant to Public Resolution No. 8*, 74th Congress, Exhibit 2112, pp. 27–8 (hereafter FCC Investigation).
7 This case is certainly clear for GE. Westinghouse began industrial research considerably later; with its lab not yet fully established during this period, Westinghouse was reacting to GE's exploitation of the newfound radio market. By comparison, most companies that had not yet recognized the need to undertake industrial research, like U.S. Steel, showed little interest in this type of product and market development.
8 "License Agreement, July 1, 1920," Article V, Paragraph 4, Section e,1.
9 Federal Communications Commission, *Investigation of the Tele-*

phone Industry in the United States (Washington, D.C., 1939), p. 209. This is a one-volume summation of the results of the full-scale investigation.

10 Gleason L. Archer, *Big Business and Radio* (New York, 1939), p. 245.

11 *Electrical World*, 79 (1922):419. The least expensive vacuum-tube receiver in 1922 was a single-tube set manufactured by Westinghouse and marketed by RCA for $79.50. GE receivers employed three tubes and sold for $250. Even at these prices for simple sets, it was a year before suppliers caught up with orders on hand. Donald McNicol, *Radio's Conquest of Space* (New York, 1946), pp. 341–2.

12 "License Agreement, July 1, 1920," Article V, Paragraph 4, Section 2.

13 FCC Investigation, Exhibit 289, p. 78. Telegraph company lines could sometimes be used in place of telephone lines, but the quality of transmission was generally poor.

14 William Banning, *Commercial Broadcasting Pioneer: The WEAF Experiment, 1922–1926* (Cambridge, Mass., 1946), p. 55; "Radio Telephone Broadcasting," internal company memorandum quoted in *ibid.*, p. 74.

15 Quoted in Archer, *Big Business and Radio*, p. 54.

16 Gleason L. Archer, *History of Radio to 1926* (New York, 1938), p. 276.

17 FCC, *Investigation of the Telephone Industry*, p. 388. These "broadcast associations" would operate much like the associated companies of the Bell Telephone System.

18 Quoted in *ibid.*, p. 389. At Bell, radio had always been considered as "wireless telephony," and any kind of telephony was clearly a "telephone job."

19 For example, see *Radio Dealer*, 1 (April 1922):30; quoted in Maclaurin, *Invention and Innovation in the Radio Industry*, p. 114.

20 Banning, *Commercial Broadcasting Pioneer*, p. 136.

21 Although profit figures are not available, it is known that sales were large and increasing. RCA reported receiving-set sales figures of $1.5 million in 1921, $11.3 million in 1922, and $22.5 million in 1923. Archer, *Big Business and Radio*, p. 139. Total sales of radio receivers reached $388 million in 1928 and almost $600 million in 1929. T. T. Eoyany, *An Economic Study of the Radio Industry* (Ph.D. dissertation, Columbia University, 1936), p. 75.

22 In his article "Technological Momentum in History: Hydrogenation in Germany, 1898–1933," *Past and Present*, 44 (1969):106–32, Thomas P. Hughes discusses how the development of technology by teams of scientists and engineers can acquire a kind of momentum as the researchers establish personal and professional interests in its continued advance. Hughes applies this concept further in his book *Networks of Power* (Baltimore, 1983), pp. 140–74.

23 "Western Electric Engineering Department Annual Report for 1922," p. 44, BTLA. On the set in the White House, see letters from D. Sarnoff to F. P. Guthrie, 30 April 1924, and Sarnoff to J. G. Harbord, 19 May 1924, quoted in Archer, *Big Business and Radio*, pp. 143–5; RCA memo quoted in *ibid.*, p. 78.

24 *Ibid.*, p. 25; William White, *The Story of Electronics Development at the General Electric Company*, unpub. MS, 1955, p. X-C-2, copy at the Whitney Library, GE R&D Center, Schenectady, N.Y.

25 Maclaurin, *Invention and Innovation in the Radio Industry*, p. 129; FCC Investigation, Exhibit 2112, p. 57; Maclaurin, *Invention and Innovation in the Radio Industry*, p. 136.

26 "License Agreement, July 1, 1920," Article XIII.

27 Archer, *Big Business and Radio*, pp. 207–8.

28 De Forest Radio Co. vs. General Electric Co., U.S. Court of Appeals for the Third Circuit, 44F (2nd) 921 (1925). This point seems to have been missed by Archer and by those who (like Maclaurin) used him as a source. The Supreme Court ruled in 1931 that high vacuum was not a patentable invention and that therefore all patents relating to it were invalid. De Forest Radio Co. vs. General Electric Co., 283 U.S. 664. This had been Bell's contention for some time, so the decision represented a (belated) victory.

29 FCC investigation, Exhibit 2112, p. 30. Bell System revenues for this service amounted to over $28 million between 1926 and 1935.

30 Brock, *The Telecommunications Industry*, pp. 170–2.

31 Quoted in N. R. Danielian, *AT&T: The Story of Industrial Conquest* (New York, 1939), p. 127.

32 Quoted in FCC, *Investigation of the Telephone Industry*, p. 232.

33 Maclaurin, *Invention and Innovation in the Radio Industry*, p. 155. The license agreement had a further advantage for RCA: it assured that the licensees recognized the validity of RCA patents. GE used its strong patent position in the same way when it required ductile-tungsten licensees to make available to it all lamp-related patents they might acquire.

34 Quoted in FCC Investigation, Exhibit 1946, pp. 15–16.

35 Quoted in FCC Investigation, Exhibit 2110, p. 99.

36 Quoted in FCC, *Investigation of the Telephone Industry*, p. 210. The author was John E. Otterson, president of AT&T subsidiary Electric Research Products, Inc., which was established in 1926 to take over commercial development of Bell Labs inventions.

37 See, e.g., Kendall Birr, *Pioneering in Industrial Research* (Washington, D.C., 1957). I do not mean to suggest that research directed at improved products and new markets was not important. It contributed to the advancement of particular companies and the economy as a whole. Whether broad-based or highly focused, research made real contributions on both the micro- and macro-levels of economic development.

38 This did in fact happen to GE in markets for electric traction (street railways), glyptal resins, phenolic plastics, permanent magnetic materials, sodium-vapor lamps, nuclear power, small appliances, and numerous other commercial technologies that, at one time, made important contributions to corporate profitability.

39 Quoted in John Broderick, *Willis Rodney Whitney* (Albany, N.Y., 1945), p. 188.

Chapter 10

1 Jack A. Morton, *Organizing for Innovation* (New York, 1971), pp. 58–62.

2 Of course, specific requests came to the laboratory from other parts of the company and resulted in directed research projects. This happened with the development of metal-cased vacuum tubes and sodium-vapor lamps during the 1930s.

3 Sending stockholders materials that demonstrated "the money value of research" and its "aid to directing growth" helped assure their support for research and their continued confidence. R. W. King and G. C. Southworth, "The Meaning of Research to the Telephone Investor," *Bell Telephone Quarterly*, 3 (1924):65,68,72. For a critique of Bell management policy, see N. R. Danielien, *AT&T: The Story of Industrial Conquest* (New York, 1939), p. 106. Danielien worked on the FCC investigation and wrote his own synopsis because he decided that the FCC's was not critical enough.

4 Statistical data from the period 1948–1966 show that corporate rates of productivity growth have correlated closely with support for long-range research and development activities of the type associated with industrial research. Edwin Mansfield, "How Economists See R&D," in Harvard Business Review, *The Management of Technological Innovation* (Cambridge, Mass., 1982), p. 49.

5 Of course those outside industrial research sometimes worked in similar ways. Edwin Layton has described the evolution of what he calls "engineering science," in which people concerned with finding "real-world" solutions to technical problems had to forego many of the simplifying assumptions of theoretical science, yet used the methods and often the results of the sciences in their work. See Layton, "American Ideologies of Science and Engineering," *Technology and Culture*, 17 (1976):688–701. My findings and Layton's are in many ways complementary.

6 See, e.g., Mario Bunge, "Technology as Applied Science," *Technology and Culture*, 7 (1966):333.

7 C. E. K. Mees, director of research at Eastman Kodak, expressed this concern. The use of the term "pure science" is his. Mees believed there was danger that industrial researchers would become

so absorbed in their work that they would lose touch with outside scientific research. Mees, "The Organization of Industrial Scientific Research," *Science*, 43 (1916):771.

8 According to Robert Merton, the ethos of modern science is made up of four parts: universalism, disinterestedness, organized skepticism, and communism. Merton, *The Sociology of Science* (Chicago, 1973), pp. 268–78. Historian George Wise notes that, by contrast, industrial corporations and the people who manage them are more concerned with particularism, interestedness, organized loyalty, and capitalism. Wise, "The Science–Technology Spiral," unpub. MS in the author's possession, 1977, p. 2.

9 The great majority of new industrial researchers came not from the professoriate but either directly from graduate school or from other industrial positions. Thus the advent of industrial research proved to be a boon to academic science: by providing employment for scientists, it spurred interest in scientific and engineering graduate education, leading to expanded programs and increased numbers of faculty positions.

10 Coming from the listings in *American Men of Science* (3d edition, 1921), these are minimum counts because not everyone was reported. Leonard Reich, *Radio Electronics and Industrial Research in the Bell System* (Ph.D. dissertation, The Johns Hopkins University, 1977), Appendix A, pp. 185–6; Spencer Weart, "The Rise of 'Prostituted' Physics," *Nature*, 262 (1 July, 1976):15,14.

11 W. F. Meggers to F. Hartman, 28 January 1924, quoted in *ibid.*, p. 14; Frank Kottke, *Electrical Technology and the Public Interest* (Washington, D.C., 1944), p. 19.

12 Quote from R. W. Hidy and M. E. Hidy, *Pioneering in Big Business* (New York, 1953), p. 441. John Enos, *Petroleum Progress and Profits* (Cambridge, Mass., 1962), pp. 56–7, 233. The growing market for gasoline because of the large-scale use of automobiles had created a shortage of crude oil, given the small proportion of gasoline that resulted from standard refining practices. The Burton process dramatically increased gasoline yield.

13 DuPont's domination of the market in explosives was then coming under attack by the government. Antitrust litigation soon forced the company to divest itself of the powder works which became the Hercules and Atlas chemical companies. In order to grow, the company thus had to move into new markets.

14 Jeffrey Sturchio, *Chemists and Industry in Modern America* (Ph.D. dissertation, University of Pennsylvania, 1981), pp. 133–6; Alfred D. Chandler, *Strategy and Structure* (Cambridge, Mass., 1962), pp. 78–113. When DuPont research director Charles Stine requested $20,000 in his 1927 budget to undertake scientific work in areas germane to company interests, he invoked GE's success in support of the value of such research to the company. Sturchio, *Chemists and Industry in Modern America*, pp. 140–1.

15 J. W. Williamson, "Industrial Research Laboratories," *Nature*, 121 (1928):409.

16 Arthur D. Little, *The Handwriting on the Wall* (Cambridge, Mass., 1925).

17 Robert Kargon, "The New Era: Science and American Individualism in the 1920s," in Robert Kargon, ed., *The Maturing of American Science* (Washington, D.C., 1974), p. 10; David Noble, *America By Design: Science, Technology, and the Rise of Corporate Capitalism* (New York, 1977), pp. 161–2.

18 E.g., Willis Whitney, "The Organization of Industrial Research," *Journal of the American Chemical Society*, 32 (1910):71–8; Willis Whitney, "Research as a Financial Asset," *Scientific American Supplement*, 21 (3 June 1911):347; see, e.g., Whitney to F. W. Lovejoy (Eastman Kodak), 24 October 1912; Whitney to G. H. A. Glowes (Eli Lilly Co.), 16 March 1920; Whitney to P. B. Liebermann (Hyatt Roller Bearing Co.), 18 July 1916; Hawkins to J. P. Tarbox (Curtis Engineering Corp.), 6 January 1919, all in "Laboratory Affairs – General," Whitney Library, GE R&D Center, Schenectady, N.Y.

19 Reese Jenkins, *Images and Enterprise* (Baltimore, 1975), p. 310; see, e.g., J. J. Carty, "The Relation of Pure Science to Industrial Research," *Smithsonian Institution Annual Report for 1916* (Washington, D.C., 1917), p. 525.

20 Part of the problem was an early lack of concern by corporate management or by the research directors with integrating the laboratory into company operations.

21 Stuart W. Leslie, *Boss Kettering* (New York, 1983), pp. 120,133.

22 George Perazich and Philip Field, *Industrial Research and Changing Technology*, Report no.M-4 (Philadelphia: WPA National Research Project, 1940), p. 65; Noble, *American By Design*, p. 111.

23 The TNEC was formed by President Roosevelt in 1938 to investigate the country's economic problems, especially as they related to monopoly control and the concentration of economic power. Perazich and Field, *Industrial Research and Changing Technology*, pp. 11,68; Noble, *America By Design*, pp. 120–1. Subsequent experience suggests that, given vigorous enforcement of antitrust laws, industrial research has contributed more to diversification than to concentration in the economy – more to the extended life and continued prosperity of corporations than to one company's control over any single market over a long period of time.

24 For a provocative discussion of how and why government became involved in promoting industrial research as well as the influences this had on the laboratories and their intracompany relationships, see Margaret B. W. Graham, "Industrial Research in the Era of Big Science: Servant or Master?" unpub. MS in author's possession, 1983.

Index

Printed in the United States
By Bookmasters